TIME CAPSULE/1942

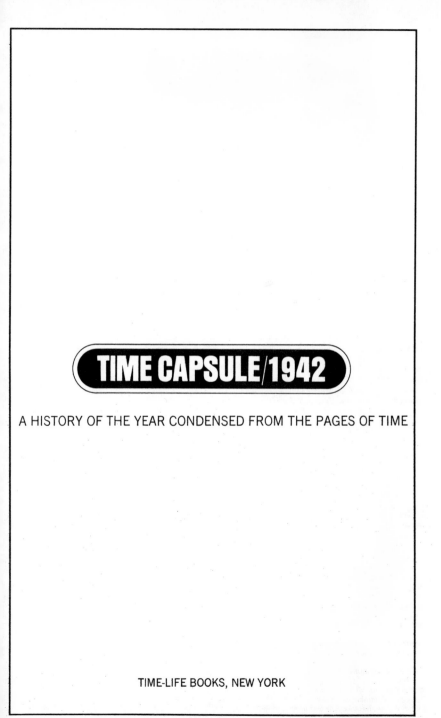

TIME CAPSULE/1942

A HISTORY OF THE YEAR CONDENSED FROM THE PAGES OF TIME

TIME-LIFE BOOKS, NEW YORK

TIME/**1942**

EDITOR *Henry R. Luce*
MANAGING EDITOR *Manfred Gottfried*
EXECUTIVE EDITOR *T. S. Matthews*
SENIOR EDITORS *John K. Jessup, Sidney Olson,*
J. Dana Tasker, Charles Wertenbaker
ASSOCIATE EDITORS *Roy Alexander,*
Robert Cantwell, Whittaker Chambers,
John Davenport, Robert Fitzgerald, John Hersey,
Wilder Hobson, John Osborne, Leon Svirsky

EDITOR *Maitland A. Edey*
EXECUTIVE EDITOR *Jerry Korn*
TEXT DIRECTOR *Martin Mann*
ART DIRECTOR *Sheldon Cotler*
CHIEF OF RESEARCH *Beatrice T. Dobie*

SERIES EDITOR *John Dille*
ASSISTANT *Lee Greene*
RESEARCHER *Lea Guyer*
DESIGNER *Arnold Holeywell*
ASSISTANT DESIGNER *John Woods*
COPYREADER *Rosemarie Conefrey*

PUBLISHER *Rhett Austell*

EVENTS OF THE YEAR

U.S. troops invade North Africa
18

484 die in Boston's great Cocoanut Grove fire
32

Jimmy Doolittle bombs Tokyo
39

The rescue at sea of Eddie Rickenbacker
41

MacArthur leaves the Philippines
64, 70

The fall of Corregidor
66

The battle of Midway
72

Montgomery *v.* Rommel at El Alamein
104

The death of John Barrymore
160

John Steinbeck's "The Moon Is Down"
213

Editors' Note

During the twelve months following Pearl Harbor, the nation buckled down to the immense task of arming itself to combat aggression around the world. There was nothing but bad news at first as the Philippines fell to the Japanese onslaught and General MacArthur was forced to flee to Australia. But then the growing power of the U.S. armed forces began to make itself felt. American bombers raided Tokyo for the first time, the U.S. Navy won a remarkable victory at Midway and G.I.s went ashore in North Africa for their first engagement with German troops.

In this volume, some of these events are first announced in the U.S. at War section starting on page 9. More complete details of the fighting are contained in the World Battlefronts section starting on page 60. And further references to the war occur throughout the book; it overshadows most of the Foreign News section and even permeates the worlds of Sport, Radio, Science, Business and other normally peaceful activities on the home front.

■

Time Capsule/1942 is one of a series of volumes, each adapted and condensed from a year's contents of Time, the Weekly Newsmagazine. The words, except for a few connecting passages, are those of the magazine itself, and therefore reflect the flavor, the attitudes and the state of knowledge of the day—sometimes innocent, sometimes opinionated, sometimes prescient. The book is divided, like the magazine, into departments, and is organized so that each department forms a chronological chapter for the entire year. The dates in the margin are the issue dates of the magazine.

U.S. AT WAR

The Presidency

The U.S. was still recovering from the shock of Pearl Harbor as the year began. All during the first months of 1942 the military situation grew worse as the Japanese swarmed over the Philippines, captured Singapore and Burma. President Roosevelt's immediate tasks were to hasten the nation's military and economic preparations for war and to discuss joint military action with British Prime Minister Winston Churchill, who had flown to Washington for that purpose.

JAN. 5 **ASKING GOD'S HELP:** "The new year of 1942 calls for the courage and the resolution of old and young to help win a world struggle in order that we may preserve all we hold dear. We are confident in our devotion to our country, in our love of freedom, in our inheritance of courage. But our strength, as the strength of all men everywhere, is of greater avail as God upholds us.

"Therefore I, Franklin D. Roosevelt, President of the United States of America, do hereby appoint the first day of the year 1942 as a day of prayer, of asking forgiveness for our shortcomings of the past, of consecration to the tasks of the present, of asking God's help in days to come."

So last week, in an hour of national crisis, the President set aside Jan. 1 as a national day of prayer.

CHRISTMAS WITH CHURCHILL: For the first time since Belleau Wood a U.S. Army was fighting with its back to the wall—in the far-off Philippines. Only a little more than a fortnight after the U.S. had gone to war, the democracies were faced with a possible defeat as serious as the fall of France—the loss of the entire Far East.

For Franklin Roosevelt and Winston Churchill to meet in Washington face to face at this juncture was an elementary step that filled their nations with satisfaction. Never before had a wartime Prime Minister of Great Britain visited the U.S.

Cloaked in censorship, Churchill dropped out of the sky with breathtaking suddenness. Day after his arrival, Winston Churchill sat beside Franklin Roosevelt behind the broad desk of the oval office, waiting with the poker-faced calm of a veteran political speaker while 200-odd U.S. and foreign newsmen gathered for a press conference unique in White House history.

Those who crowded up front saw a pudgy man with cheeks like apple dumplings, blue eyes beneath crooked restless eyebrows, the merest foam-flecking of sandy grey hair on his bald pink pate, a long black cigar clenched at a belligerent angle above his bulldog jaw. From the sleeves of his blue sack coat extended long cuffs, half hiding the small hands folded placidly across his middle.

Franklin Roosevelt, less jaunty than usual, his style a little cramped by appearing as one of a duet, introduced his guest. There were shouts from the rear by newsmen who couldn't see. Churchill stood up, grinned, climbed on his chair, waved his hand. The applause and cheers rattled the windows.

On Christmas Eve Winston Churchill stood bareheaded while Franklin Roosevelt, on the south portico of the White House, went through the annual ceremony of turning on the outdoor Christmas tree's lights. Then he joined the President in broadcasting Christmas greetings to the nation. Said the Prime Minister: "I spend this anniversary and festival far from my family, and yet I cannot truthfully say that I feel far from home. In God's mercy, a happy Christmas to you all."

The real Churchill eloquence came later, at a joint session of Congress. Congressmen who had gone home for the Christmas holiday scurried back to Washington for the historic occasion. There were tears in Winnie Churchill's eyes at the ovation which greeted him, from isolationist and interventionist alike. He shoved his thick, horn-rimmed glasses over his nose, blinked, balanced himself like an old sailor. Then he let go: the growling, galling scorn for his enemies, the passages of noble purple for his friends: "I avow my

Prime Minister Winston Churchill addresses the U.S. Congress. He has tears in his eyes, scorn for his foes, purple prose for his friends.

hope and faith, sure and inviolate, that in the days to come the British and American people will for their own safety and for the good of all walk together in majesty, in justice and in peace."

When Churchill had finished, white-haired, sedate Chaplain Ze Barney Phillips leaned over and whispered: "Mr. Prime Minister, you are the most perfect master of the English language in all the world."

JAN. 12   **CHURCHILL'S NEW YEAR:** On New Year's eve, Prime Minister Winston Churchill was on a special train enroute to Washington after a four-day visit to Canada. A few minutes before midnight, footsteps clumped swiftly down the corridors, compartment doors were rapped in staccato, a voice called: "Everybody up in the diner. The Prime Minister wants to see you." In five minutes a half hundred reporters, photographers, British military and naval attachés filled the diner. At 11:58 Winston Churchill waddled in, waved. His left hand clutched a tall whiskey-&-soda. Toward the stroke of twelve, Churchill raised his glass high and steady, spoke clearly in his soft growl; pausing an instant between each phrase: "Here's to 1942. Here's to a year of toil,—a year of struggle and peril,—and a long step forward to victory."

Everyone drank, shouted: "And a happy New Year to

you sir!" Churchill set his drink on a table, crossed his arms, reached for the hands of those nearest him, and struck up, in his flat, heavy baritone: *"Should auld acquaintance be forgot . . ."* There were more cheers at the end. "God bless you all," said Churchill. He raised his glass for a final toast: "May we all come through safe and with honor."

The Englishmen broke into *For He's a Jolly Good Fellow,* and the Americans joined in. The Prime Minister turned, flipped up his V-for-Victory salute, and left as he had entered, with an odd combination of dignity and familiarity.

THE PEOPLE WIN: The heat was on the White House. First JAN. 26 came Missouri's grey little Harry Truman, chairman of the Senate committee investigating the war program. Senator Truman told Mr. Roosevelt that he was going to rip the whole defense organization up the middle, disclose an awesome mess. Second caller was the G.O.P.'s big bear, Wendell Willkie, who had demanded a single director for the war effort 87 times in the 1940 campaign and 37 times since. Now he told the President he was going to make his 125th such demand in a speech that night.

The burden of the patriotic dissertation by Messrs. Truman and Willkie was the same as that written in heart's blood on countless memos on the President's toy-cluttered desk: give the war effort a single director, give that director total powers. It was the chant of industry, the roar of the press. It was what the people had wanted since June 1940.

That afternoon, in the session of the Supply, Priorities & Allocations Board, smoke curled lazily. A door opened and a girl handed a message to Donald Marr Nelson, SPAB's executive director. He read it, glanced at his watch, whispered to Vice President Henry Wallace. The two left hurriedly for the White House. When Donald Nelson came out, he had been appointed boss of the world's greatest armament effort.

A locomotive engineer's son from Hannibal, Mo., who became, as the $70,000-a-year manager of Sears, Roebuck & Co., the country's No. 1 mass-buyer, Nelson will head the War Production Board with authority greater than any U.S. citizen except the President himself.

FEB. 9   **BIRTHDAY NO. 60:** "Today, Jan. 30, the anniversary of your birth, smoke-begrimed men, covered with the marks of battle, rise from the fox holes of Bataan and the batteries of Corregidor to pray reverently that God may bless immeasurably the President of the United States." So cabled General Douglas MacArthur, who, like Winston Churchill, can turn a dramatic phrase.

MARCH 2   **ATTACK ON THE U.S.:** "Enemy ships could swoop in and shell New York; enemy planes could drop bombs on war plants in Detroit; enemy troops could attack Alaska."

The man who said these things could be done was Franklin Roosevelt, at a press conference. Asked a newsman: Aren't the Navy & Air Force strong enough to deal with anything like that? Said the President: "Certainly not."

The words scarcely had a chance to sink into the awareness of the U.S. public when the West Coast, on guard and tense along 3,250 miles of shore, received the first attack on continental U.S. soil. A submarine emerged from the sea about seven miles north of Santa Barbara, Calif., and for 20 minutes lobbed shells at an oil refinery. First reports: little damage; no one was injured; no fires were started; most of the 25 shells exploded in a field, frightening horses; one went over Highway 101, burst in the foothills.

APRIL 20   **CITIZEN ROOSEVELT:** Wartime living had hit the White House in many ways. Citizen Roosevelt had to go easy on sugar. Sugary desserts had given way to fresh fruits. Except at parties—now small and infrequent—the rule was: no dessert at all if a salad was on the table.

White Housekeepers patched up the linen, cut down old tablecloths into tray cloths and napkins. Leftovers from the White House table reappeared disguised as stew, ragout and hash. Scraps that could not be salvaged went to feed the pigs at a cooperative farm. White House trash had gone to the metals-salvage campaign, and a Treasury truck stopped weekly to collect old paper.

JUNE 22   **THE ROOSEVELT RUBBER LECTURE:** "I want to talk to you about rubber—about rubber and the war—about rubber and the American people." Last week Squire Roosevelt assumed one of his favorite roles, that of patient lecturer to the tenants of his constituency. He spoke over the radio and made very clear the "why" of the rubber shortage.

Rubber was a problem, said Mr. Roosevelt, because 92% of our normal supply had been cut off by the Japanese. The shortage would be even more serious if we had not built up a "huge stockpile" and if we were not building up a great new synthetic-rubber industry.

"There is one unknown factor in this problem," said Mr. Roosevelt cheerfully. The unknown was rubber scrap. How much rubber scrap is there in the country? The President, with the help of 400,000 filling-station operators, proposed to find out. He designated a two-week period in which to get all the old rubber in "where it can stand up and be counted." For all rubber that citizens salvaged from cellars and attics, gas-station operators would pay 1¢ per pound. The Government will pay them back. Then, said Mr. Roosevelt, "We are going to see to it that there is enough rubber to build the planes to bomb Tokyo and Berlin—enough rubber to build the tanks to crush the enemy wherever we may find him—enough rubber to win the war."

TOWARD A UNITED COMMAND: The fact that the Constitution JULY 27 places the command of the U.S. Armed Forces in the White House was no deterrent: U.S. citizens still clamored for a unified command of Army & Navy, demanded that there should be a military man at the top. This week Franklin D. Roosevelt (who had joked that such an appointment would "do myself out of a job") entered formal recognition of an obvious need. He appointed a Chief of Staff to take some of the burden of high command off his hands.

He did not choose the man suggested by the U.S.'s First Citizen Without Portfolio, Wendell Willkie. Willkie's choice was Douglas MacArthur. The President preferred to let the General stay in Australia. His choice was a famed Navy man: grizzled, 67-year-old Admiral William Daniel Leahy, who had resigned only two days before as the U.S. Ambassador to Vichy.

Admiral Leahy, lean and still as sharp of mind and tongue as when he walked the quarterdeck, is a thoroughgoing professional at warfare. As a naval officer he had spent

22 of his 46 years of service at sea, had commanded the battle force of the U.S. Fleet, worked in the top ranks of its high command and finally became Chief of Naval Operations.

FILL-IN FROM AUSTRALIA: Over a long breakfast of scrambled eggs, toast and coffee, President Roosevelt got a firsthand account of warfare in the Pacific from his young, trusted friend, Congressman Lyndon Baines Johnson of Texas. Tall Lyndon Johnson, a Navy lieutant commander, had sought active duty one hour after voting for war against Japan. He had ranged as far as Perth, Melbourne, Sydney, Darwin and Port Moresby. Now he returned to Washington 28 lb. lighter (from a pneumonia attack) but much wiser in the ways of war.

President FDR: Happy birthday from smoke-begrimed warriors. Page 13.   *Lyndon Johnson on the war: "One thing they're not short on is guts."*

In their four-hour talk over the coffee cups, he must have told "the Boss" plenty. But outside the White House, Representative Johnson had only one comment: "There is one thing they are not short on out there, and that is courage and guts and fighting spirit. They've got plenty of that."

AUG. 24 **SERVICE STARS:** In the great debating days before Pearl Harbor, isolationist critics of President Roosevelt liked to declaim: "How would you like your own sons to go to war?" Last week all four Roosevelt sons were deep in the war on many fronts.

¶ Major James, 34, the Marine Corps disclosed last week, had been bombed and strafed on an inspection trip to the Middle East last May, was under fire again in the Battle of Midway.

¶ Lieut. Colonel Elliott, 31, of the Air Corps, had a close brush with the *Luftwaffe* in Africa last spring when his unarmed observation plane was chased by Nazi fighters. He returned to the U.S. for a minor operation, took charge of an aerial-photography unit in Colorado.

¶ Lieut. (j.g.) Franklin, Jr., 28, served aboard a destroyer with the North Atlantic Patrol on convoy duty.

¶ Ensign John, 26, was last heard from on the West Coast, where he was serving as a Navy disbursing officer.

SALISBURY ENTERTAINS: Whites in Salisbury, N.C. (pop. 4,000 Negroes, 14,000 whites) had not wanted Eleanor Roosevelt to come there to address a convention of the African Methodist Episcopal Zion Church of America. But last week Eleanor came just the same—her face aglow, her thoughts confused, her intentions motherly.

The President's wife had her picture taken with Negro leaders. She reviewed a parade of Negro soldiers led by white officers. In the evening, Mrs. Roosevelt gave the address that the Negroes had been anxious to hear, that the whites had feared would put kerosene on Salisbury's coals. Said Mrs. Roosevelt:

"We must have patience and we must try with all our might to bring about recognition of the fact that man must have equal opportunity to get any job he is capable of filling. Minority groups in the United States have taken work bringing small incomes, and therefore set the whole economic level very low, for no other reason but that they belonged to the minority group."

In the South colored folks began organizing themselves into Eleanor Clubs. One group of domestic servants banded together as "Daughters of Eleanor."

TROPHY: To the White House went Lieut. General Thomas SEPT. 28 Holcomb, Commandant of the Marine Corps, with a 4-by-6 ft. Japanese flag which once flew over Makin Island. The flag was captured by U.S. Marines in the raid of Aug. 17 (with the President's Son James as second in command). The President looked at his gift with distaste. Said he: "You can take it back and put it in the historical archives of the Marine Corps. But I don't want to touch it."

OCT. 12 **THE STORY OF A TRIP:** For Franklin Roosevelt it was a special treat—not merely his first chance since Pearl Harbor to put the administrative labyrinths of Washington far behind him, but a trip with all the kind of drama and secrecy that he loves best. For a fortnight he could chuckle at the amazement on the faces of those who saw him touring [all news of the President's travels and whereabouts was banned by tight rules of wartime censorship].

The President's train sped north, then west. Morning brought Detroit. At the Chrysler Tank Arsenal, 300 soldiers swiftly took their posts. FBI agents blocked the doors. Out of the Presidential train rolled the White House phaeton, its top down, the bulletproof windows up. Franklin Roosevelt rode between two giant assembly lines, waving as he went, to 5,000 astounded workmen, who lined up in a solid wall to greet him. On the testing ground, he watched 50 tanks roar through mud and dust. One tank drove straight at him, ground to a stop ten feet away. The young driver stuck his dirty face from the turret and grinned. "A good drive!" shouted the President.

At Willow Run he rode with Henry and Edsel Ford down the half-mile assembly line. It was unbearably hot under the miles of mercury-vapor tubes that light the huge plant; the radiator of his car began to boil.

In Milwaukee, he watched steam turbines and propeller shafts spring to life at the Allis-Chalmers plant. In Seattle, he went through the bustling Boeing aircraft plant.

In Henry Kaiser's Portland shipyards, the President watched the launching of the *Joseph N. Teal*—first ship in the world ever to hit the water ten days after keel laying. The 14,000 workers who watched the ceremony cried "Speech!" Someone pressed a portable microphone into the President's hands. Said he: "You know, I'm not supposed to be here." There were loud cheers. "So you are possessors of a secret—a secret that even the newspapers of the United States don't know. I hope you will keep it." (The newspapers knew it very well, but didn't tell.)

RETURN VISIT: Eleanor Roosevelt could wait no longer: she NOV. 2 had to see for herself. Besides, there was a standing invitation on royal stationery. Last week she flew to England with the regulation 44 lb. of baggage.

The King, in the powder blue uniform of an air marshal, and the Queen, in mourning for the Duke of Kent, were there to greet her. As Mrs. Roosevelt stepped off the train, she smiled broadly, walked straight to the Queen, over whom she towered by a full head & shoulders. Said Mrs. Roosevelt: "How nice to see you again."

Then began a heavy schedule such as only Eleanor Roosevelt can take. After tea at the palace, a chat with the two young Princesses, a state dinner with the Churchills and the Mountbattens, she stayed up until 2 a.m., talking with second son Lieut. Colonel Elliott Roosevelt, now assigned to London.

With the King and Queen she toured London's bomb-gutted East End. In a cavernous bomb shelter (8,000 capacity) she was particularly interested in the children's toothbrush rack. When she got to the Red Cross' Washington Club, the American doughboys greeted her with shouts of "Hi, Eleanor." In a short speech in the cafeteria she made a motherly promise to the troops: warmer socks and faster mail.

THE FIRST BIG PUSH: It was 7 o'clock Saturday night. The NOV. 16 newsmen who cover the White House were at ease, having dinner at home, drinking cocktails at the Press Club. Suddenly the White House switchboard went into action. Out to the scattered newsmen went a warning: stand by at the pressroom for news. Back to the White House the newsmen scurried.

They did not have to wait long. At 9 o'clock—3 a.m. on the coast of Africa where history was in the making—the news was out. The U.S. had invaded North Africa in a vast offensive aimed to control the Mediterranean.

Over the White House hung the confident calm that

comes of effective planning. This time the surprises and the initiative were in American hands. As the action began, Franklin Roosevelt's voice went by short-wave transcription to the people of France and French Africa. In slow, schoolboy French (starting with the inevitable *Mes Amis*) he said: "We come among you to repulse the cruel invaders. Have faith in our words. Help us where you are able. *Vive la France éternelle!*"

After the landing of Allied troops in North Africa, U.S. military leaders sought the help of French Admiral Jean François Darlan in persuading local French officials to halt their resistance. In return, Darlan was recognized by the Allies as Chief of State of French Africa—although he had previously collaborated with the Nazis. The arrangement with Darlan created a major controversy in the U.S.

NOV. 30   **WALKING WITH THE DEVIL:** For five days men of the democracies wondered. The U.S. Government was doing business with one of Hitler's stooges, the opportunist, the Nazi collaborationist, Admiral Jean François Darlan. The invasion of North Africa was the first great political-military venture of the U.S. in World War II. Its tone would set the tone for the others to come. If Norway were invaded, would the U.S. thenceforth move to strengthen the hand of another Hitler stooge, Vidkun Quisling?

To his press conference the President read: "I have accepted General Eisenhower's political arrangements made for the time being in Northern and Western Africa." The word "accepted" clearly meant that General Eisenhower had improvised a solution which had stopped the fighting short of unnecessary bloodshed. The President went on to describe the arrangement with Admiral Darlan as "temporary," and he used the word "temporary" five times. The permanent French Government is to be re-established by the French people themselves "after they have been set free."

Irving Brant of the Chicago *Sun* asked a question that drilled to the nerve of the cavity-like omission in the President's statement: Have you any comment on the position of General de Gaulle? Mr. Roosevelt shook his head, negatively. Some observers were reminded of an old Balkan proverb: "In time of great danger, walk with the devil until you have crossed the bridge." Ahead of the U.S. were many bridges, and many devils.

ELEANOR'S GALLUP POLL: "Mrs. Franklin Roosevelt probably DEC. 21 is the target of more adverse criticism and the object of more praise than any other woman in American history," concluded Pollster George Gallup after sampling national opinion on the First Lady. Some three out of five people questioned approved of something about her: "Her ability and courage to speak out what she believes." About two out of five expressed some disapproval: "Why, the way she acts, you'd think the people elected her President."

One old man in the Midwest had no opinion. "Never heard of her," he answered.

The Nation

BUNDLES FOR A BRITON: When the U.S. people like a man, JAN. 19 they show it, and they like Winston Churchill. They are showing it by sending him letters, telegrams—and presents.

In the halls of the British Embassy the presents piled up: crates of eggs, of oranges, mince pies, pecans, a box of onions, a bag of lima beans, two bottles of Napoleon brandy, 5,000 cigars, a set of corncob pipes, catnip for the Churchill cat, a Shriner's hat, silk scarves, gloves, ties, socks, a sweater, a copy of George Washington's will, a textbook on navigation, a set of Indian arrowheads, a turkey's wishbone (the V-symbol), an autographed picture of Jack Dempsey and a carton of skin lotion, a portrait of Franklin D. Roosevelt done on a typewriter.

END OF A MISSION: Carole Lombard was in a hurry to get JAN. 26 home. For days the movies' best screwball comedienne had been traveling crosscountry patriotically, plugging defense bonds. In Indianapolis she jampacked the city's big Cadle Tabernacle for a rally, in one day raised $2,000,000. Said plain-spoken Miss Lombard: "I'm like the barker at a carnival."

It was after 4 a.m. when she boarded T.W.A.'s flight to Los Angeles. The flight moved on through the night, into a bright Midwestern dawn. At Albuquerque, N. Mex., room had to be found for 15 officers and men of the Army ferry command, returning to their Coast base. Four passengers gave up their seats; one was Violinist Joseph Szigeti. Miss Lombard stayed aboard. In twilight the plane reached Las Vegas, took off again at 7:07 p.m. for the last lap.

At 7:30 miners in Nevada's mountains, some 30 miles southwest of Las Vegas, heard a terrific explosion, saw a vivid flash near the top of Table Rock Mountain. Flames shot up from the lonely peak, then faded. Searching parties started out over snow that bogged horses belly-deep. Men toiled up through some of the most difficult, barren rockland in the U.S. From Los Angeles flew Husband Clark Gable. He reached Las Vegas, sleepless. Breaking away from friends, he tried to scale the mountain, failed, went back to his hotel, haggard, unshaven, weary. Some 14 hours after their start, climbers reached the wreckage. Mangled and burned were Miss Lombard, the other three civilian passengers, the 15 Army flyers, the crew of three. Why the plane had crashed, nobody knew.

Carole Lombard. An explosion in the wilderness ends a bright career.

Clark Gable. An inconsolable star seeks his lost wife.

STANDING ROOM ONLY: No car? No tires? Go by air! No, FEB. 2
said the Government, putting airplane seats under priority
quicker than you could say Donald Nelson. Henceforth a private citizen who wants an air-travel ticket must stand in
line behind Government personnel, the Army, Navy and Marines, businessmen traveling on war business.

Railroad passenger cars, long crowded by defense travel,
have been jammed still tighter since Dec. 7. In 16 days after
the Pearl Harbor attack, 600,000 troops were moved in the
U.S., three-fourths of them in Pullmans, the rest in coaches.
Afoot are plans to take buses off scenic runs, give them to
cities which have no streetcars, rip out seats to make crowded room for standees.

*The "Normandie" lies capsized at the pier. A spark of flame, a puff of
smoke brings disaster to the renamed "Lafayette."*

"NORMANDIE" BURNS: Some 1,500 workers swarmed over the FEB. 16
vast bulk of the famous Atlantic luxury liner, twisting her ele-
gance into a bleak wartime pattern for the Navy. Then one
bright afternoon this week a puff of smoke drifted across
her promenade deck. A few minutes later, the deck was completely ablaze. After two and a half years of idling at a
Manhattan pier, the *Lafayette* (as the U.S. had renamed the
Normandie) was in danger of turning into a fire-blackened
hulk.

Whirled along by a fresh, northwesterly breeze, the flames

licked hungrily along the wooden decks of her broad promenade. Heavy grey smoke roiled up, hiding her great outlines
even from watchers in Manhattan's nearby skyscrapers.

As tons of water poured into the *Lafayette,* she listed 16 de-
grees to port, snapping her hawsers like rubber bands.
Trying to keep her from capsizing, the Navy ordered holes
cut in an empty water tank on the starboard side, to pump
in water for balance. But early next morning, as the tide
came in and lifted her heavy stern from the shallow river bottom, the *Lafayette* toppled, rolled over ignominiously on
her side.

To first suspicions of sabotage, Rear Admiral Adolphus
Andrews, commandant of the Third Naval District, made
blunt reply. Said he:

"The fire started when a civilian worker was using an acety-
lene torch to remove an ornamental lamp from the salon
wall. A spark from his torch apparently leaped into a pile
of life preservers."

FEB. 23 **WORST WEEK:** This was the worst week of the war. The nation took one great triphammer blow after another—vast,
numbing shocks. Such a week had not come to the U.S.
since the blackest days of the Civil War.

As the week began, the *Lafayette,* as important to the
war as any battleship, turned over at her pier. At week's
end, Singapore fell [page 85]. The nation now had only
shreds of hope in the Far East. The Axis had broken
through.

Off the U.S.'s East Coast the sixteenth victim of Nazi submarines, Standard Oil tanker *W. L. Steed,* went down.
Then the Nazi battleships *Gneisenau* and *Scharnhorst,* bottled
up in Brest, suddenly emerged with attendant ships and
planes, cut through the English Channel to home bases in
the North Sea. Nightmarishly the U.S. looked at two new
and fearful words: GERMAN FLEET.

There was some good news. The U.S. hailed General Mac-
Arthur's great-hearted stand in Bataan [page 62], studied
with savage satisfaction the Navy's detailed announcement
of the raid on the Marshall and Gilbert Islands. And the
great U.S. industrial machine hummed ever faster in its war
of production.

UNIDENTIFIED AIRCRAFT: The sirens wailed. An air raid. Los MARCH 9 Angeles citizens crawled out of beds and goggled at the moon. The city had been blacked out. Suddenly, from dozens of Army antiaircraft posts, searchlights lanced the dark. Orange bursts blossomed in the sky. The city shook with the concussion of ack-ack guns. For almost two hours, batteries coughed steadily, spewed 1,430 rounds of ammunition into the night.

Los Angelenos had no doubt that they were being attacked. Said the Los Angeles *Times*: "Roaring out of a brilliant moonlit western sky, foreign aircraft flying both in large formations and single, flew over Southern California. At 5 a.m. the police reported that an airplane had been shot down near 185th St."

There were casualties—but not from bombs. Three citizens had been killed in auto crashes. An air-raid warden had died of a heart attack. Windows had been smashed and several sky-gazers struck by falling shell fragments. One woman was yanked out of bed by police, and hauled off to jail for failing to blackout her house.

But no one found any shot-down plane; no one reported any bombed-out home. In Washington, Navy's Secretary Frank Knox smiled indulgently and cracked: "Just a false alarm." Army's Secretary Henry Stimson challenged him by reading to newsmen a report from Chief of Staff Marshall stating flatly: "As many as 15 planes may have been involved."

One theory was that the planes came from commercial fields, were operated by enemy agents to locate gun positions and to slow up production by causing a blackout. [The Western Defense Command later confirmed that "unfriendly" planes had indeed flown over Los Angeles. It was never explained how they might have gotten there.]

EASTWARD HO: They were U.S. citizens who had spent their MARCH 16 lives on U.S. soil—farmers, fishermen, humble shopkeepers. But they learned last week that, in a nation's hour of peril, having been born a citizen is not enough. So they began to pack their keepsakes, lift their slant-eyed children on their arms, and start on the long migration east across the Sierra Nevadas, to dreary inland country. They were some of the

West Coast's 70,000-odd *Nisei*. Their honorable ancestors were Japanese.

This was martial law, in effect. Lieut. General John Lesesne DeWitt, chief of the Western Defense Command, marked off a strip of land curving some 2,000 miles along the Pacific and along the Mexican border, from Canada to New Mexico. Out of this coastal region all enemy aliens and all *Nisei* must go—even if they have sons in the U.S. Army or Navy.

Some citizens felt the military had good reason to be harsh. In Los Angeles, District Attorney John Dockweiler produced a map showing that Japs (or *Nisei* relatives) hold leases on lands adjoining nearly every strategic spot in Los Angeles County—including highways, railways, power lines, airports, aircraft plants, oil fields, refineries, aqueducts. Japs hold a flat, mile-square tract of semi-desert land near Los Angeles which could be turned into a landing field for bombers in an hour or two. Japanese farmers cultivate most of the foggy shoreline of Palos Verdes (next door to vital San Pedro harbor), where landing parties could sneak in undetected on to a number of good beaches. Other reasons were suggested by the case of Alien George Makamura, in whose seaside home at Santa Cruz FBI men found 69 crates of signal rockets and colored flares.

In Los Angeles, 19-year-old *Nisei* Shigeki (Arthur) Kaihatsu reflected on the problem of his people. A former freshman star on the basketball team at U.C.L.A., young Arthur now works in a vegetable market. Said he: "Most of us *Nisei* are completely loyal. I guess there are some spies among us. I don't know. But the answer seems to be to take the whole bunch of us and dump us in one spot. Then the spies among us can't do any damage, and the rest of us won't be suspected."

That was exactly what General DeWitt thought.

FULL HOUSE: The annual Washington cherry blossom festival, originally set up to lure hundreds of thousands of people to the Capital each spring, was canceled, to keep them away.

MARCH 23 **SLAP:** The story went around the U.S. last week. Everybody who told it swore that it was true. Everybody had got it from a friend of a friend of a friend. It cropped up in Amarillo, Tex. The story:

Riding on a bus, a woman passenger was heard to say: "Well, my husband has a better job than he ever had and he's making more money, so I hope the war lasts a long time."

Another woman got up and slapped her face. "That is for my boy who was killed at Pearl Harbor. And this"—another slap—"is for my boy in the Philippines." At the next stop, the woman who was slapped got off.

ONE LUMP, PLEASE: The U.S. had been warned, and now, MARCH 30 here it came. The Office of Price Administration announced the first wartime rationing. During the week of April 27 no sugar will be sold at all. After that, sugar will be sold only upon presentation of coupons from sugar-rationing books.

One member of every household must go to the nearest local elementary school, register name & address, height, weight, color of eyes and hair, number and relationship of others in the household, the amount of sugar at home (which will be deducted from their quotas). Some 1,500,000 schoolteachers will take the depositions, issue a sugar book for each individual in the family good for 56 weeks' supply.

V FOR VANDYKE: The War Production Board ordered razor APRIL 6 blades cut to one a week for each shaver. Out cropped a lush, thickety growth of feature stories and beard pictures; the Smith Brothers of cough-drop fame sprouted back into the news; radio comics combed their files frantically for beard jokes, from B for beavers, to T for tuft.

MOVING DAY FOR MR. NISEI: Pasadena's Rose Bowl looked like a second-hand auto park. In the chill dawn, 140 battered cars and sagging trucks huddled, piled high with furniture, bundles, gardening tools. At 6:30 a.m. they chuffed and spluttered, wheeled into line, and started rolling. Led by a goggled policeman on a motorcycle, a Jeep and three command cars full of newsmen, they headed for the dark, towering mountains to the east.

Thus, last week, the first compulsory migration in U.S. history set out for Manzanar, in California's desolate Owens

Valley. In the cavalcade were some 300 Japanese aliens and *Nisei*.

At the old Santa Fe station in downtown Los Angeles another group of 500 aliens and *Nisei* boarded a special 13-car Southern Pacific train for Manzanar. At the Army "reception center" the Japs piled out and were greeted by 88 Japanese men and girls who had gone ahead to put the camp in order. In the unfinished, tar-papered dormitories where they will live until the war ends, they made their beds on mattress ticking filled with straw, dined on rice and meat, prunes and coffee.

The emigrants to Manzanar will earn from $50 to $94 a month working on government projects, with $15 deducted for living expenses. All they forfeit is their freedom. They cannot leave the camp without permission.

APRIL 13   **THAT'S ALL THERE IS:** Only a fulltime hoarder, with unlimited bankroll, could keep up with the flood tide of shortages: hair curlers and wigs, lawn mowers and girdles, sugar and quinine, gin and tea, rubber diapers and bronze caskets. Out for the duration went electric toasters, waffle irons, mixers, dishwashers. Out went the nursery's tin soldiers and electric trains.

Flies would be a major menace: swatters could not be made of metal, nor of rubber either. Tire-rationed motorists who had begun to think of buying bicycles woke up one morning to find that bicycles were rationed too.

WHO WEARS THE PANTS?: Filene's in Boston installed three "Slack Bars." Detroit's J. L. Hudson was forced to open a Trouser Shop for Women. In Chicago, Marshall Field's, The Fair and Goldblatt Bros. reported trouser sales from five to ten times greater than last year's. In short, U.S. women, by the million, have renounced skirts in favor of slacks.

MAY 11   **THE GREAT WHITE WAY:** One night last week the greatest concentration of light in all the world blinked out. Suddenly dark were the marquees and façades of Manhattan's Roseland, Lindy's, the Paramount, the Astor; dark were the skyhigh signs. Out went the New York *Times*'s electric bulletins. Broadway's lights probably will not glitter brightly again until the war is over. "Dim-outs" will be the nightly rule, so that no sky-glow can limn ships at sea, betraying them to U-boats.

SUGAR BOOKS: Americans got a good look at each other MAY 18 last week as they all stood in line in the country's school-rooms and firehouses, waiting for their sugar-rationing cards. When it came to filling out the cards, thousands of them did not know their own height. Many were not sure of the color of their eyes (said one white-haired woman: "They are blue ordinarily, but when I fall in love they turn vi-olet"). Some were not even sure of the color of their hair. Many forgot their children's names. Fat ladies shaded their weight a bit. But the U.S. rationers somehow managed to register an estimated 122,604,000 (91%) of the U.S. people for their first ration cards.

The first U.S. experience with regimentation went well. With unlimited chance to cheat, there was little cheating. News of the first week of U.S. rations:

❡ In Milwaukee, a cow called Mooie received an allotment of one pound of sugar a day, the only cure for Mooie's temporary insanity.

❡ A Minneapolis woman brought her neighbor to testify that she had no sugar. "She knows," she explained, "because I always borrow from her."

ATTACK BY SEA: East Coast shipping was paralyzed. From JUNE 1 Portland, Me. to Key West, coastal shipping was for all intents and purposes at a standstill. Axis submarines, operating from Newfoundland to South America, had attacked and sunk an estimated 213 vessels since Pearl Harbor. By week's end at least nine ships had been stricken in the Gulf, some within sight of land. Louisianians gaped at ambulances loading up with survivors.

Censorship thick as a Grand Banks fog hid the facts of the battle. But the sights and sounds which filtered through told the people all they needed to know. The U.S. had been licked all along its Eastern Seaboard.

Plenty of well-informed critics began to rake the U.S. Navy from stem to stern. But three months ago, when isolationist voices yammered for the recall of the fleet to protect U.S. shores, Washington had made its strategy clear.

Said President Roosevelt then: "We must all understand that our job now is to fight at distances which extend all around the globe." The Navy's big and main job was to punch its convoys through to England, Ireland, Russia, Eritrea. The Coasts would have to stand and take attacks.

JUNE 22 **DEATH RATTLE:** A be-rationed Sioux City, Iowa citizen put his views in verse to the chairman of his ration board:

> *And when I die, please bury me*
> *'Neath a ton of sugar, by a rubber tree.*
> *Lay me to rest in an auto machine*
> *And water my grave with gasoline.*

JUNE 29 **OFF AGAIN:** Eugene Talmadge, Georgia's bang-browed cracker Governor, cracked off again last week. The news reached him that 30,000 hale, hearty and draftable Georgians had been rejected by the Army because they were illiterate. Quick as a gallus snap, "furriner"-hating Gene up & said: "New York is the most illiterate state in the Union." He'd been there, and had heard waiters who could hardly talk English. New York City's Mayor LaGuardia snapped back: "When it comes to illiteracy, the distinguished Governor of Georgia speaks for his own class."

JULY 13 **RUBBER HUNT:** Harold Ickes made no bones about it: the Administration's rubber drive was a disappointing failure. Pondering reasons for the drive's widespread flop, Ickes snapped: "We suspect that people are hoarding rubber."

Officialdom had done its best. On Ickes' plea and advice to learn to spit straight, Federal agencies donated office spittoon mats. Uniformed Boy Scouts stood long hours at service stations begging motorists to give up rubber mats from rear compartments; women's clubs formed telephone brigades; appeals were made to crowds at ball games. The White House itself donated 400 lbs. of rubber, including some toys belonging to Fala, the President's scottie. But all this was far from enough. Too many Americans had not bothered to rummage their houses for rubber.

FAIR WARNING: To glamor girls the Office of Price Adminis- AUG. 17
tration addressed a communiqué: "Such long-established
practices as sending up clouds of powder during camouflage
operations, scooping up huge handfuls of cold cream, spray-
ing a cloud of perfume to walk through, must go." There
won't be enough cosmetics to go around unless make-up is
applied with a sparing hand.

CHEESECAKE FOR VICTORY: Buying war bonds was patriotic AUG. 24
but dull. Then the Treasury called in Hollywood and Broadway. As one man the pressagents ordered: "Cheesecake."

The Treasury bond campaign has become one of the liveliest phenomena of the American scene. Breathed no man
alive in the 48 States who was not almost daily exhorted,
begged and bewitched into buying war bonds. Bathing beau-
ties did it. Big, beautiful eyes and slim, wonderful legs did
it. The supreme Empress of Cheesecake, the very Marlene
Dietrich herself, last week was fittingly crowned by the Treasury as the champion bond seller of all. On three crosscountry
trips she upped the pulses and unsnapped the purses of thousands of U.S. males. When worker Edward LaCuoco signed
away 10% of his pay for the duration, Miss Dietrich re-
warded him with a long cinekiss. Mr. LaCuoco said it was
worth it.

ALL-AMERICAN: Americans read the names of the boys who AUG. 31
made the first big U.S. air raid on Europe, the bombing of
Rouen. The list sounded like the roster of an All-American
eleven. There were Edward Czeklauski of Brooklyn, George
Pucilowski of Detroit, Theodore Hakenstad of Bremerton,
Wash. There were Frank Rebbillo of Providence, Zane Gem-
mill of St. Clair, Pa., Frank Christensen of Racine, Wis.,
Abraham Dreiscus of Kansas City. There were also the
older American names like Ray and Thacker, Walsh and
Eaton and Tyler. The war was getting Americanized.

SEX IN THE FACTORY: A very shapely sweater girl wanders in SEPT. 14
to take her place in the swing shift. Low whistles follow her
as she ambles down the aisle between machines. But a few
minutes later a grey-haired factory chaperon catches her in
the ladies' room. The chaperon admires the sweater girl's fig-

ure but says it would be a shame if because of her some man lost a hand under a punch press. Next night the girl comes back in other clothes.

This is only one of a dozen new problems since nearly two million women have gone to work in plane plants and other war industries. Some of the new problems:

¶ Some girls flirt at work. Douglas Aircraft (about 25% of whose employes are now women) had to close its Santa Monica plant's bomb shelter with heavy tar paper (to be broken in case of a real air raid) because swing-shift couples found it too handy for lovemaking during lunch.

¶ Most women now wear slacks, but rebel at keeping their hair covered. Occasionally one gets scalped when the hair gets caught in a machine.

On the plus side, many a factory manager has found that when women are good they are better than men. They are more painstaking as inspectors, are nimbler with their fingers, don't fret or get bored with repetitious work, are generally quicker, are particularly good in assembling small parts.

SEPT. 28 **PRESERVATION OF NATIVE CULTURE:** H. J. Heinz Co. announced that after months of difficult experimentation it had finally succeeded in putting up canned ham & eggs for the breakfasts of the armed forces overseas. Chopped, the ham & eggs needs only to be heated before serving.

NOV. 23 **JOY AND HATE:** The news was magnificent, and it flowed in a full tide. The first flush of elation over U.S. landings in Africa [page 108] had hardly died when the Navy told of smashing the Jap in the Solomons. Never before had the full realization of global war been hammered home so hard in one week—and out of the bitter fighting America had a new pride in itself.

This was it: meeting the enemy face to face, ship for ship, tank for tank, plane for plane—and now, for a change, winning, at least sometimes. But there was a sobering sense of the tasks still to be done—hard and painful and bloody. If anyone did not know this, he was given a jolting reminder by the wiry, keen commander of U.S. Ground Forces. Said Lieut. General Lesley J. McNair in a broadcast to all U.S. troops:

"We must hate with every fiber of our being. We must lust for battle; our object in life must be to kill. There need be no pangs of conscience, for our enemies have lighted the way to faster, surer, crueler killing. They were past masters. We must hurry to catch up with them if we are to survive."

BOSTON'S WORST: Holy Cross had just beaten Boston College DEC. 7 in a football upset; downtown Boston was full of men & women eager to celebrate or console. Many of them wound up at Cocoanut Grove: they stood crowded around the dimly lighted downstairs bar, filled the tables around the dance floor upstairs. With them mingled the usual Saturday night crowd: soldiers & sailors, a wedding party, a few boys being seen off to Army camps. At 10 o'clock Bridegroom John O'Neil, who had planned to take his bride to their new apartment at the stroke of the hour, lingered on a little longer. The floor show was about to start. Through the big revolving door, couples moved in & out.

At the downstairs bar, a 16-year-old busboy stood on a bench to replace a light bulb that a prankish customer had removed. He lit a match. It touched one of the artificial palm trees that gave the Cocoanut Grove its atmosphere; a few flames shot up. A girl named Joyce Spector sauntered toward the checkroom because she was worried about her new fur coat. Before Joyce Spector could reach the cloakroom, the Cocoanut Grove was a screaming shambles. The fire quickly ate away the palm tree, raced along silk draperies, was sucked upstairs through the stairway, leaped along ceiling and wall. The silk hangings, turned to balloons of flame, fell on table and floor.

Men & women fought their way toward the revolving door; the push of bodies jammed it. Nearby was another door; it was locked tight. There were other exits, but few Cocoanut Grove patrons knew about them. The lights went out. There was nothing to see now except flame, smoke and weird moving torches that were men & women with clothing and hair afire.

The 800 Cocoanut Grove patrons pushed and shoved, fell and were trampled. Joyce Spector was knocked under a table, crawled on hands & knees, somehow was pushed through an open doorway into the street. A chorus boy herded a dozen people downstairs into a refrigerator. A few men & women crawled out windows; a few escaped by knocking out a glass brick wall. But most of them, including Bridegroom John O'Neil were trapped.

Firemen broke down the revolving door, found it blocked by bodies of the dead, six deep. They tried to pull a man out through a side window; his legs were held tight by the mass of struggling people behind him. In an hour the fire was out and firemen began untangling the piles of bodies. One hard-bitten fireman went into hysterics when he picked up a body and a foot came off in his hand. They found a girl dead in a telephone booth, a dead bartender still standing behind his bar.

At hospitals and improvised morgues which were turned into charnel houses for the night, 484 dead were counted; it was the most disastrous U.S. fire since 571 people were killed in Chicago's Iroquois Theater holocaust in 1903. One Boston newspaper ran a two-word banner line: BUSBOY BLAMED. But the busboy had not put up the Cocoanut Grove's tinder-box decorations, nor was he responsible for the fact that Boston's laws do not require nightclubs to have fireproof fixtures, sprinkler systems or exit markers.

DEC. 14 **POWER OVER MEN:** To a pleased Paul McNutt, his new authority as Manpower Commissioner looked great & good. Now Franklin Roosevelt, by executive order, had given him something to work with.

¶ Under his control goes the entire Selective Service System. For the first time, McNutt can now tell the 6,400 local U.S. draft boards which men they can have and which they must leave in jobs.

¶ Before the Army & Navy set their draft quotas, they must confer with McNutt, who can carry his case to the President if he thinks the armed forces are raiding the civilian population too heavily.

¶ To stop another leak in the manpower pool, the draft will no longer take men over 38, who are almost invariably more useful in industry.

¶ McNutt can now order an employer to give up a worker who is more needed elsewhere—thus discourage labor hoarding.

CHRISTMAS THAW: "Bona fide Santa Clauses shall be construed to be only such persons as wear a red robe, white whiskers, and other well-recognized accoutrements befitting their station in life, and provided that they had a kindly and jovial disposition and use their high office of juvenile trust to spread the Christmas spirit and shall be exempt from the wage-freezing Executive Order of Oct. 3, 1942."— WLB order of Dec. 4, 1942.

FROZEN MEN: Day before Franklin Roosevelt gave new and DEC. 21 sweeping powers to War Manpower Commissioner Paul McNutt he went over the final draft of the order with a group which included McNutt, War Secretary Henry L. Stimson, Navy Secretary Frank Knox, and WPBoss Donald Nelson. When the President came to the section stopping all enlistments in the armed forces, Secretary Knox is said to have begged:

"Paul, give me just three more months for naval enlistments."

McNutt replied: "Frank, when the President signs that order I won't give you three minutes."

Last week Paul McNutt took his most drastic step to date in ordering some 600,000 workers in 34 categories in the Detroit area "frozen" in their jobs. The order does not

General McNair: "We must hate with every fiber of our being." Page 32.

Manpower Boss McNutt to the Navy: "I won't give you three minutes."

force any person to stay at his present job, does make him provide good & ample reasons for wanting to change. In the works were similar freezings of 110,000 merchant seamen, 1,500,000 West Coast aircraft workers and thousands of Southwestern railroad track workers. These are only samples of what must still come.

The Administration

MAY 4 **TITLE OF THE WEEK:** Biggest order yet of Washington alphabet soup: PWPGSJSISIACWPB. Full name: Pipe, Wire Product & Galvanized Steel Jobbers Subcommittee of the Iron & Steel Industry Advisory Committee of the War Production Board.

JUNE 22 **LET US TO THE TASK!:** Title-of-the-Week: Biscuit, Cracker and Pretzel Subcommittee of the Baking Industry of the Division of Industry Operations of the War Production Board.

MAN OF SENSE: The President had delayed for months before picking a man to head a new superpress bureau: the Office of War Information. Last week he finally summoned sensible, clearheaded radio commentator Elmer Davis to the White House, told him without fuss & feathers that he had been drafted for the biggest new Federal job, to tell the U.S. as much about the war as possible, as fast as possible, with as few contradictions as possible. Calm Mr. Davis, who dislikes fuss & feathers, took the President's order calmly. Two days later he made his last radio news broadcast. Two days after that he went to work in Washington.

The President abolished in one sweeping stroke a galaxy of conflicting agencies: the Office of Facts and Figures (Archibald MacLeish), the Office of Government Reports (Lowell Mellett), the division of information of the Office of Emergency Management (Robert Horton), the Office of the Coordinator of Information ("Wild Bill" Donovan). Donovan's agency was reorganized, its name changed to the Office of Strategic Services, and it was put under the general staffs of the Army & Navy. [Thus began the famed

Elmer Davis. A top newsman who hates fuss and feathers is drafted to tell the U.S. about the war as fast as possible.

secret agency, OSS, which was the precursor of the CIA.]

Long before his low-pitched, easy, flat Midwestern voice became known to the U.S. over CBS, Indiana-born Elmer Davis had earned a reputation as one of the best newsmen in the business. Elmer Davis likes to say that his broadcasts are successful because his voice "sounds like it came from back home."

THE UGLY FACTS: Elder Statesman Bernard M. Baruch, Har- SEPT. 21
vard President James B. Conant and M.I.T. President Karl T. Compton in 37 days had gone to the bottom of the rubber mess to get the ugly facts of wartime life. Seldom had a report to Franklin Roosevelt minced so few words. Said the three wise men: "We find the existing situation to be so dangerous that unless corrective measures are taken immediately this country will face both military and civilian collapse."

To conserve rubber the committee laid down hard and fast rules for all car owners in the U.S., strongly urged that the President put them in effect at once.

¶ Nationwide gas rationing to force a reduction in tire use.

¶ A national speed limit: 35 m.p.h.

And to produce more rubber the committee wants WPB's present slow-moving synthetic program "pushed forward with all possible speed."

The Congress

JAN. 5 **HOT TALK:** Many a Congressman last week got batches of redhot mail asking him why in the blankety-blank he had been so blankety-blank stupid as to vote against fortifying Guam when the Navy asked for it, back in 1939 and 1940. Meantime Congressmen began sounding off with a little hot talk of their own.

¶ Veteran isolationist Senator Pat McCarran of Nevada: "In any peace treaty we should take care of America first. Every other country is looking out for itself and we should look out for ourselves."

¶ Illinois' Senator Scott Lucas: "Japan should be reduced to the point where for 1,000 years she will have no control or force in the family of nations. That goes for Germany and Italy, too."

MARCH 23 **HOT MAIL:** "You can't kill a Jap with your yap."

That was the kind of rude remark the U.S. citizen was writing to his Congressmen last week. Rarely, if ever, had contemporary Congresses seen such mail. The letters were blistering. The average citizen blamed his Congressman for every defeat since Pearl Harbor and told him so in writing that scorched the paper.

John Q. Voter was mad because Congress did not stop strikes, did not stop useless Government expenditures, did not ship aid to MacArthur. Congressmen winced, weaseled, worried. This kind of letter could not be answered with the usual smooth line: "All of the points you raise have been noted."

One Congressman was almost tearful: "Where will we be if public confidence is lost in the Congress?"

Well might Congressmen worry. Some letters and telegrams had ten or 20 signatures. Small-town forums gathered to roast their representatives. Some of the letters criticized the President too: The Public is weary of so much talk from the White House and so little action.

MAY 25 **"TWO-CENT POLITICIANS":** Again a contemptuous laugh went up from the nation. This time it was high-priority gasoline ration cards for Congressmen. The men on Capitol Hill, jealous of their old prerogatives, clinging to their oldtime dignity, were bewildered and sore hurt.

Said Columnist Raymond Clapper: "Congress has remained a collection of two-cent politicians who could serve well enough in simpler days. But the ignorance and provincialism of Congress renders it incapable of meeting the needs of modern government. People don't give a damn what the average Senator or Congressman says. The reason they don't care is that they know what you hear in Congress is 99% tripe, ignorance and demagoguery and not to be relied on."

IF DOLLARS WILL DO IT: If money and equipment were all JULY 6 that is needed to win World War II, the U.S. last week would have had the war wrapped up and salted away. The House unanimously passed a $43 billion Army appropriation bill for 1943, largest appropriation measure on record in any country.

The bill brought a total U.S. military appropriations for World War II to a colossal $205 billion—$51 billion more than the Government spent for all activities (including five other wars) from 1789 to 1940.

Said New York's Republican Representative John Taber, who in other days was wont to stiffen with rage at the idea of even a million-dollar appropriation: "Perhaps it will bankrupt us, but even that is unimportant compared with the necessity."

END OF A THREAT: For a few hours the U.S. Senate chamber re- NOV. 23 flected the feeling and temper of pre-Pearl Harbor times. Three Senators, all onetime die-hard isolationists, rose to lambaste the bill drafting 18- & 19-year-olds. Montana's Burton Wheeler sniffed an Army dictatorship; California's Hiram Johnson was disturbed about the "warlike proclivities" of Secretary of War Henry L. Stimson; North Dakota's Gerald P. Nye shouted that Japan, after five years of war, had not yet taken young men out of schools for its Army.

But other Senators, now that the U.S. was attacking in Africa, were in no mood to listen. After the die-hards had their say, the Senate quickly passed the bill without any strings.

Heroes

JUNE 1 **JIMMY DID IT:** The world found out last week who led the daring, destructive noonday air raid on Japan last month. To the White House, to receive a Congressional Medal of Honor, went pugnacious Brigadier General James Harold Doolittle, 45, speed flyer, engineer, scholar and man of action.

Said the New York *Daily News:* "He should be named Doomuch."

On the day of Pearl Harbor, Jimmy Doolittle, then a major, told friends: "I'm going to get in this thing with both feet. I'm going to Tokyo with a load of bombs." Now, having made good, he told Washington newsmen about his deed of derring-doolittle in formal Army lingo:

"The success of the raid exceeded our most optimistic expectations. It appeared to us that practically every bomb reached the target for which it was intended. About 25 or 30 miles to sea the rear gunners reported seeing columns of smoke rising thousands of feet in the air."

The twin-motored B-25s were flown just over the housetops. It would have been no trick to hit Hirohito's palace, but Doolittle had given specific instructions: don't bomb it. The Doolittle plane was attacked by nine Jap fighters, but he rapidly outdistanced them all. Not an American plane was lost and the 79 volunteers, along with Doolittle, were all nominated for the Distinguished Service Cross. Still undisclosed was the American planes' base.

Unhumorously reporting a heavy Roosevelt jest, the Berlin radio solemnly announced: "Doolittle carried out the attack from the air base at Shangri-La, which was not otherwise described by Roosevelt." [Shangri-La was the name given to a Utopian community in James Hilton's book *Lost Horizon*. The Doolittle raiders had actually taken off from the aircraft carrier *Hornet*; they then flew on toward a planned rendezvous in China, but because of bad weather all 16 bombers either crash-landed or were abandoned in the air by their crews. Of the 80 men involved, three were killed on landing, five landed in Siberia and were interned by the Russians and eight were captured in Japanese-held territory.]

BACK FROM THE WAR: A light drizzle fell all morning. In the JUNE 22 afternoon, people gathered at the funeral home in South St. Louis. There, in a steel casket, the flag draped over, lay the body of Otto J. Weiner Jr., private in the Marines, killed in action on an unnamed Pacific island. The body in the steel casket had come 12,000 miles. On that unnamed island where he was killed, Private Weiner had been a favorite of the native chief. When he died, the natives held a tribal ceremony. They wove a tapestry of bark and sent it along for his parents.

At the cemetery, six bareheaded youths—Private Weiner was only 18—carried the casket to a green hill among the sycamores. Nine solemn-faced Marines fired three volleys into the leaden sky. This was the first burial in home soil of an American killed in action in World War II.

Next morning, again in South St. Louis, the same scene was repeated over the body of Jerome U. Schmitt, 19, private in the Marines, who died of wounds on a Pacific battlefront. There will be no more U.S. funerals of soldiers killed in action abroad. The bodies of Private Schmitt and Private Weiner came all the thousands of miles home through an error. These two that were first will be the last, until the war is done.

A TIME OF GALLANTRY: From a Navy hospital in the South Pa- OCT. 19 cific came a story of the toughness of Marine Private Eugene Moore, 22, onetime checker in a San Francisco grocery, onetime guard on the Huron (S.D.) High School football team, who liked to bake chocolate cakes when he was at home.

Eugene Moore joined the Marines just a year ago; he was one of those landed on Gavutu Island in the Solomons. His tank proceeded up the beach in advance of the infantry, spied a Jap pillbox, stopped to fire. Out of a bomb shelter nearby poured a horde of reckless, howling Japs. They swarmed over the tank, jammed a crowbar in the tank-track.

Said Private Moore from his hospital cot: "One of the Japs stuck his head down inside our turret. I shot him right between the eyes. Suddenly there was a terrific explosion and I felt a burning pain in my neck and realized they must have thrown a grenade down the turret. A few moments later they set fire to the tank. The driver and I figured it was better to get outside and get shot rather than burn to death. The driver poked his head out the front hatch. They shot him. I figured it was better to go out feet first."

From a nearby cot, Private Kenneth Koon (who, shooting from cover, has been credited with 31 of the Japs who swarmed over the tank) told what happened to Gene Moore after he had crawled out: "They kicked him in the face and stomach, they pulled his hair, smashed him with their fists, jabbed him with a pitchfork, knifed him. Then one of them got him by the arms and another by the legs and bounced him off the tank. They finally moved away from the tank and let him lay where he was. I have never seen one man take such a beating."

The Japs left Gene Moore for dead. The Navy so reported him to his family. But the Marines picked him up; Navy doctors saved his life. In San Francisco Gene Moore's father, recalling his son's cake-baking, said: "I used to kid him, tell him he should have been a girl. I don't see how we could have raised such a fellow."

NOV. 2 **CAPTAIN EDDIE:** The Army merely announced that late in the afternoon of Oct. 21 Captain Eddie Rickenbacker's plane radioed from somewhere in the Southwest Pacific that there was only one hour's supply of gasoline left. Nothing was heard after that.

Tough, square-jawed Eddie Rickenbacker, ace of American flying aces in World War I, was on a special mission from Hawaii to a Pacific combat area for the Secretary of War. With him in the big four-motored bomber were seven others. Army & Navy patrol planes soared over the blue waters, looking for the plane's wreckage and for yellow rubber life rafts which might be carrying Rickenbacker, his aides and crew. But in Honolulu, Army GHQ was gloomy.

At 52, Eddie Rickenbacker had, almost better than any other American, spanned the gap from youthful hero to solid citizen, from daring combat flyer to successful businessman. Young Eddie went to work at twelve in Columbus, Ohio: glass works, brewery, steel mill, monument works, shoe factory, bicycle shop. The shop was also an automobile garage. Eddie learned to drive, moved on to an auto factory, studied engineering via the International Correspondence School. It was speed that interested him. At 20, known on all racing tracks as a man "with a heavy foot," he cleaned up $40,000 as a driver.

When World War I came, Eddie enlisted, was assigned a job as chauffeur for Colonel Billy Mitchell of the Army Air Service. Rickenbacker was so impressed by flying that he persuaded Mitchell to help him get a transfer to flying school. He learned quickly and was soon flying in combat. As a flyer Eddie was resourceful, by turns cautious and daring. No U.S. flyer learned so well the corkscrew roll which enabled him to see ahead, behind, above, below and to the side; no flyer topped his bag of 21 German planes and four balloons.

When he came home half a dozen cities claimed Ace Rickenbacker as a native son. He took over as operator of the Indianapolis Speedway. In 1938 he found his real niche as the hard-driving president of Eastern Air Lines. Last week in Manhattan, his handsome, grey-haired wife waited for further news. Said she: "He's not reckless and he knows the air. He always said he was the darling of Lady Luck."

AFTER 24 DAYS: When the big Army bomber which was taking NOV. 23 Captain Edward Vernon ("Eddie") Rickenbacker on a special mission for the Secretary of War ran out of gas in the Southwest Pacific, the U.S. press sadly hauled out Eddie's obituaries. But the Navy's big Catalina flying boats crossed and recrossed the vast area where he might have gone down. After 23 endless days they spotted a raft: on it was the bomber's pilot, Captain William T. Cherry Jr. The Navy searched even harder. Next day the good news came: Rickenbacker and two of his crew were found floating in the vast Pacific some 600 miles north of Samoa. Three other crew members were on a tiny island. One, Sergeant Alexander Kaczmarczyk of Torrington, Conn., had died and been buried at sea.

The Navy merely said that Rickenbacker's condition was good despite a 24-day drift at sea, rushed him and all others to a base hospital.

OF HELL AND PRAYERS: The pain-racked frame, the deep- DEC. 28 lined face, the grave voice were those of a man who had

General Doolittle. He should now be named "Doomuch." Page 39.   *Eddie Rickenbacker. He prays, and a sea gull lands on his head.*

seen the horrors of war and the mysteries of death—and lived to tell the tale. Last week Captain Eddie told newsmen his moving story of 24 torturing days adrift:

Just after midnight on Oct. 21 Captain Eddie, with seven Army officers and enlisted men, climbed into a Flying Fortress, took off on a special mission. By next morning the compass had gone awry, the radio was out of kilter, they were lost. They crash-landed in the ocean, clambered into three rafts.

Captain Eddie talked as if out of a bottomless memory: "We organized little prayer meetings in the evening and morning. Frankly and humbly we prayed for deliverance. Then we prayed for food." The Captain glanced at the newsmen, resumed in a low, slow voice: "If it wasn't for the fact I had seven witnesses, I wouldn't dare tell this story because it seems so fantastic. But within an hour after prayer meeting a sea gull came in and landed on my head." They ate the gull raw, used its innards for bait. They caught two fish, ate them raw, too.

Then Captain Rickenbacker told how death came to a 22-year-old sergeant, the only crew member lost. He swallowed salt water when his raft overturned, drank more later, died of salt-water poisoning and starvation. "For two nights I cuddled him like a mother would hold a child, trying to give him warmth from my body. At 3 a.m. I heard his final gasp." Then came the rescue by a Navy flying boat, the trip home.

Captain Eddie spoke of the ordeal of American boys on the Pacific battlefronts; begged war workers to make superhuman efforts to turn out more goods and pleaded with civilians to sacrifice more, complain less. Said he: "If people only knew that the saving of one old rubber tire makes it possible to produce one of those rafts, they might not worry whether they have their automobiles on weekends."

Espionage

MISSION FROM BERLIN: Under the shroud of fog the four JULY 6
men paddled quietly toward shore. The submarine which had brought them vanished into the Atlantic. The beach where the four men landed was a stretch of sand half-hidden by high grass and the low rolling dunes of Long Island's south shore, near Amagansett. They worked fast, dug a hole, gingerly buried a number of wooden boxes, finally buried the collapsible rubber boat itself, covered everything with sand. Then they headed swiftly for New York.

Four nights later, 1,100 miles south along the Atlantic Coast, a second submarine surfaced. Again four men pushed off in a collapsible boat, paddled into palm-bordered Ponte Vedra Beach near Jacksonville. The second batch of silent men made a cache in the sand, headed north.

Among them, the eight men had almost $170,000 in U.S. currency. They looked like respectable, intelligent mechanics from the corner garage. But in the boxes left buried on the beaches were bombs resembling lumps of coal, delayed-timing instruments, incendiary pistols, explosive pencils, acids. The eight men were trained Nazi saboteurs, exported from Germany. Their list of targets included aluminum plants, railroads, bridges, terminals, canals, power plants, reservoirs, even department stores. Their objectives were to damage U.S. industrial production—especially the light-metal plants which make airplane materials—and to spread death and panic.

They all spoke English and had spent many years in the U.S. They were former waiters, machine-tool workers, painters, chauffeurs, butlers. One was a naturalized U.S. citizen. All had been active in the German-American Bund. In the years 1939-41 they had returned to Germany, aided by German diplomats and Nazi funds. Back in Germany they had volunteered or been drafted into training at a Berlin school for sabotage.

Such was the Hollywood thriller which startled newspaper readers this week. J. Edgar Hoover, Chief of the FBI, solemnly declared that the invaders had buried enough explosives on the beaches to conduct a two-year campaign of destruction. The invaders had not lasted long—nor done any reported damage. Six had been seized within ten days; the other two, four days later in Chicago.

AUG. 17 **DEATH FOR THE SABOTEURS:** A swank, black Packard whispered over the mud-covered asphalt street, drew up at the new south wing of the District of Columbia's ancient red-brick jail. Out in the rain stepped greying Coroner Dr. A. Magruder McDonald. In the dim-lit vestibule a dozen reporters sat on death watch for the eight submarine-borne Nazi saboteurs. The Coroner had nothing to say. But his mere presence told them their vigil would soon be over.

Lights in the jail dimmed, as they always do when an electrocution is about to begin. But no official announcement came. In early afternoon the watch got the word—not from the jail, but from the White House. The electrocutions had begun at noon. Six of the spies, their heads in rubber masks with nose-and-mouth slits, had been executed. Four executioners pulled the switches; in an hour and 20 minutes it was all over.

The military commission which tried the saboteurs had recommended that the other two, George John Dasch and Ernest Peter Burger, get life imprisonment instead of death. They had turned informers, and might be useful at the trials of 14 men and women accused of giving the spies shelter in the U.S.

Thus, two months after the spies had landed on Long Island and Florida beaches, ended the biggest spy case in U.S. history.

Labor

ACCOUPLEMENT?: Out of the blue last week came the biggest JAN. 26
labor news in six years. Without warning, wearing an unbe-
coming dovelike look, tough, gruff John L. Lewis clumped
out of his lair brandishing a proposal for—of all things—
labor peace. In a long, cooing letter to C.I.O. President Philip
Murray and A.F. of L. President William Green, labor's
black storm cloud proposed an end to the violent feud which
has split labor for the last six years. Said Mr. Lewis:

"It is obvious that if accouplement (the $15 word for join-
ing together is in the dictionary) could be achieved the
results would be advantageous and in the public interest."

For years the animosity of Mr. Lewis and Mr. Green was
the chief stumbling block to a reunion of labor. According
to one published plan, the new president of accoupled labor
would be A.F. of L.'s Secretary-Treasurer George Meany;
Mr. Green would be turned out to pasture on a $20,000-a-
year pension; Machiavellian Mr. Lewis would get a vice-
presidency; Mr. Murray, who had good reason to believe
he was in the middle of a squeeze play, would be offered
the secretary-treasurer's job. Snapped angry Mr. Murray: "I
think I can speak for myself and nobody can trade me for
a job. I will not be blitzkrieged."

JOHN L. v. THE STRONG BOY: Peace proposals have raised FEB. 2
rows before, but this one took the cake. There was assuredly
much sweetness in Mr. Lewis' proposal—that A.F. of L.
and C.I.O. reunite, kiss and be friends—but there was a no-
table lack of light. Skeptical searchers soon claimed that
they had flashed some light into a dark corner of the plan:
an understanding between Lewis and the boss of the A.F.
of L.'s carpenters, Big Bill Hutcheson, who is just as hard-
boiled as John Llewellyn Lewis. The reported Lewis-Hutche-
son deal was to retire A.F. of L. President William Green,
outflank C.I.O. President Philip Murray, and seize control
of U.S. labor. But Mr. Lewis had badly miscalculated the
temper of Mr. Murray, his onetime devoted follower.

The President was naturally concerned at the possibility
of Lewis and Hutcheson, both isolationists, both Republicans, getting control of a labor movement of some 10,000,-

000 (claimed) members. Moreover, the President could well understand, as Mr. Murray pointed out, that peace negotiations at this point might absorb a lot of time and energy that labor should be expending on the war effort. Something had to be done, quickly. Mr. Roosevelt sent for Murray.

The President proposed a kind of unity without peace. To make it work, he set up a committee which would consult with him on all questions of labor participation in defense work. To sit on the committee, A.F. of L. promptly picked Mr. Green, Secretary-Treasurer George Meany, the teamsters' boss Uncle Dan Tobin. C.I.O. picked Mr. Murray, the autoworkers' R. J. Thomas. Messrs. Lewis and Hutcheson were conspicuously omitted.

At week's end, a semblance of peace had returned to the house of labor. Murray let John Lewis know that he expected him to take a back seat, as Murray had taken a back seat when Lewis was president. John L. Lewis kept a glowering silence. If he had thought Murray was a pushover, he had been wrong. Said Phil Murray, looking more like a strong boy of labor: "This man Lewis never saw the day when he could lick me."

JUNE 8 **JOHN'S VENGEANCE:** From the walls of the room, 150 framed caricatures of John L. Lewis glowered at the audience.

John L. Lewis. Once he was tearful, but now he is scornful. Page 48.

C.I.O.'s Philip Murray: "Lewis never saw the day when he could lick me."

From a raised platform Angry John in the flesh glowered even more ferociously from under his haystack heap of grey hair. Beside him, in silence, sat his longtime associate Philip Murray.

Lewis was there to oust Murray from the vice-presidency he had held for 20 years in the Mine Workers' Union. The formal basis for the ouster: Murray had accepted other offices. (He is the new president of C.I.O.'s United Steelworkers of America.) Real reason: they had finally parted company over John's political beliefs. This moment was Angry John's vengeance.

Since 1916, the two had fought labor's tough and grimy battles together—Lewis always the Big Noise, Murray always the loyal echo. Lewis became president of the Mine Workers, Murray his vice president. When Lewis walked out of A.F. of L., Murray followed. Year and a half ago, at Lewis' tearful pleading, Murray succeeded Old John as C.I.O. president. But no sentimental memories showed last week in the grey, sullen face of John Lewis.

Scornfully Lewis opened up, referred to Murray as his "former friend." Vindictively, in the hot basement room, he piled maledictions on Murray. For two days Murray sat and took it. When he tried to speak, Lewis stooges yelled: "Sit down!" Choked with anger, Murray lapsed into tight-lipped silence. Even girlish-faced, rotund, hard-boiled daughter Kathryn Lewis took a turn at lashing him. Murray, warning the Lewises that their acts would lead to national disunity, finally walked out.

The next day, Lewis ended his performance, declared that the Mine Workers' office of vice president was vacant. The executive board rubber-stamped the action. For the once-pliant Murray it was the end of a sentimental journey. But he had lost no power in C.I.O., most likely had gained prestige. Locals in Lewis' own mine union are already backing away from Angry John. More than any other man in A.F. of L. or C.I.O., Murray had the backing of a united labor force.

LITTLE CAESAR: James Caesar Petrillo, swarthy son of a ditch-digger, profane boss of the American Federation of Musicians, has been the Mussolini of Music in the U.S. for 20 JULY 20 years. His 130,000 dues-paying union fledglings pay him an annual salary of $46,000-plus, to be "protected" from the competition of amateurs. (Once, when eight Chinese Boy Scouts wanted to hail the arrival of a giant panda in Chicago with a fanfare of bugle blasts, Tsar Petrillo insisted that eight paid union musicians be hired as well.)

Last week Protector Petrillo perpetrated his newest outrage in the name of labor. Twenty-two hours before the National High School Orchestra was to begin its thirteenth season of NBC concerts from Interlochen, Mich., Dictator Petrillo ordered NBC to cancel the broadcasts. The 160 boys & girls in the orchestra are not professional musicians, hence cannot play "in competition" with professionals, ruled Caesar Petrillo.

Next week, or soon after, the U.S. would begin to suffer from another Petrillo edict: henceforth musicians may make no recordings for juke boxes—a move which might well stop the recording of all popular music.

AUG. 24 **TROUBLE IN DETROIT:** From Detroit, symbol and seat of America's industrial genius, had come news that made all citizens anxious. Sitdowns, wildcat strikes, poor planning, material shortages, short tempers and bad attitudes of union workers had cut war production.

The news:

¶ In the Lincoln factory the daily quota was 284 vehicles. The men knocked them out easily one day, finished two hours ahead of time. They started to play: first they threw water, then buckets of water, then the buckets. When the Army security officer asked them to go back to work the reply was: the quota was made, that's all there was to it.

¶ Continental Motors does not give the men regular time off to smoke. The men crowd into lavatories, turn them into smoking rooms. "It's the damnedest thing you ever saw," said one workman. "Often a man will spend 45 minutes in the toilet. Foremen don't dare do anything."

OCT. 19 **JOHN LEWIS ON THE MARCH:** In 1935, John L. Lewis marched his United Mine Workers out of A.F. of L. Last week he marched them out of C.I.O. Henceforth John Lewis and his union walk alone.

Politics

WILLKIE WINS: Wendell Willkie, in & out of the Republican APRIL 27
Party, had hammered long & hard at Isolation. He had
more success out than in: a majority of G.O.P. leaders, un-
shaken by the lessons of World War II, held to the ostrich
faith of their fathers that the U.S. must hold aloof from the
outside world.

This week the Republican National Committee met in Chicago to lay down the Party policy for 1942. Chairman Joe
Martin of Massachusetts, as usual, wanted a do-nothing, say-
nothing policy. Ohio's Senator Robert Taft and Illinois'
Senator C. Wayland ("Curly") Brooks, both rock-hard Isolationists before Pearl Harbor, wanted no mention of post-
war attitudes. Wendell Willkie wanted a clear statement
that the Republican Party realizes and accepts the post-war
responsibility of the U.S. to the rest of the world.

Though some Republicans could not believe their eyes,
the 1940 Presidential candidate won. The G.O.P. adopted
Willkie's policy, and said flatly: "Our nation has an obliga-
tion to assist in the bringing about of an understanding,
comity and cooperation among the nations of the world."

EXIT GENE TALMADGE: The usual election-night whoops & hol- SEPT. 21
lers from the Atlanta headquarters of old vote-gettin' Eugene
Talmadge were strangely absent. Ol' Gene sat glumly by
the radio, staring suspiciously through his horn-rimmed
glasses at the voice which told him his days as Georgia Governor were numbered. A news photographer entered, asked
for a big smile in case the trend changed. Ol' Gene snapped:
"Git yore pictures and hurry up."

The trend did not change. The count gave Talmadge 117,-
731; whiz-bang young Attorney General Ellis G. Arnall, 162,-
889. Despite the Palace Guard he built up during three
terms, despite his rabble-rousing, nigger-hating appeal to
Georgia's "wool-hat" boys, Gene Talmadge had taken a
sound trouncing. Thus ended the reign of the most high-
handed, low-browed local dictator that U.S. politics has
known since the days of the late Huey Long.

Until this year, Ol' Gene never had much trouble getting
re-elected. His wild political rallies, with free fish fries and wa-

termelon, panicked Georgia's rural voters. His traveling stooges yipped encouragement to his glowering, grammar-proof oratory. He showed his red galluses and his love for pore folks.

This year Gene Talmadge had an energetic young opponent who knew a few tricks of his own. He also had, hanging around his neck like a millstone, a major political mistake. In flimsy trials before a hand-picked Board of Regents, he had fired some of Georgia's top educators on charges (denied) that they favored teaching Negroes and whites in the same schools. Result: one scholastic association after another had black-listed the University of Georgia, long the State's pride & joy. Georgia finally had a bellyful of Ol' Gene. He played frantically on his campaign theme of "white supremacy, State rights, local self-government and oldtime religion." He sent a fiery campaign booklet to all farmers: *Do You Want Your Child to Go to School With Negroes?* But his attempt to ride back to office on the race issue was a rank failure.

Foreign Relations

JAN. 19 **THE UNITED NATIONS:** A new phrase, the United Nations, slipped into the world's vocabulary. Editorial writers and military commentators used it glibly. And last week they began to wonder what, exactly, it meant—that pact by which 26 nations bound themselves fortnight ago not to make a separate peace with their Axis enemies.

It would be a long time before the full story of the pact's signing came out. What was known was that Britain's Churchill, Russia's Litvinoff and China's T. V. Soong were called into conference at the White House on New Year's Day. Maxim Litvinoff had won one big point. This limited the pledge of the signers to a promise to make war to the end only on the enemies with whom they were already at war. Russia, Litvinoff pointed out, did not want to pledge war against Japan, with which the U.S. is at war—and, he added astutely, presumably the U.S. did not want to pledge itself to fight Finland, with which Russia is at war. It was after 8 o'clock when the U.S., Britain, Russia and China signed the pact.

The representatives of the other nations were invited to sign next morning. When the Greek Minister wrote his neat, self-controlled *Cimon P. Diamantopoulos,* the consonants reached across the parchment. Said Assistant Secretary of State Adolf Berle to the Polish Ambassador: "My dear Ambassador, your Greek colleague has already taken part of the space reserved for you."

The significance of the pact was slowly being digested. So far the only concrete form that unity had taken was in a common determination of 26 nations to beat the Axis. But for the people of the Axis countries that fact could not be other than sobering: 26 nations—count them—26, all determined that Hitler and his tyranny shall be destroyed.

TRAVELER'S TALE: In Cairo, a transport plane set down Wendell Willkie after the first 11,000-mile lap of his fact-finding trip to Russia and China as a dual representative of both Franklin Roosevelt and America's loyal opposition. His wardrobe was a tourist's sun helmet and a rumpled, dark blue business suit with a torn pocket. SEPT. 14

He looked over U.S. troop installations, spoke to U.S. soldiers with amiable profanity: "I just want to say I'm damned glad to see you. God bless you and give 'em hell." He regretted he could not give U.S. correspondents the latest baseball news.

His most important call was at the Egyptian Palace: young King Farouk, waiving protocol, received his guest on the Moslem holy day. His message to King Farouk was doubtless like the one he hammered home everywhere: the Mideast must get on the Allied side of the fence and stay there because "the glory days of the Nazi regime are ending; their high tide is reached, and shortly we will see it recede."

GULLIVER'S TRAVELER: The big, weary man got through with the Washington airport greetings as fast as he decently could. His stop at the Carlton Hotel did not even give him a chance to straighten his tie or give his pants a badly needed hitch. Under orders from the Commander in Chief to OCT. 26

hurry, he crammed his bulk into a limousine, lumbered off to see the President.

Not for 90 minutes did he emerge. Thirty-one thousand miles of flying (most of it in a big Liberator with "Gulliver" painted on its weathered nose in Chinese, English and Russian), through nearly a score of countries and territories flaming with war, separated Wendell Willkie from his last meeting with Franklin Roosevelt. As the President has yet to do, Willkie had met and talked with Joseph Stalin and Chiang Kai-shek. He had spent $161\frac{1}{2}$ hours in the air, smelled the smells of Cairo and seen American soldiers in many countries. Into his ears had been poured the stupidities & wranglings, the hopes & fears of more than half the world. He was so tired he could only toy with the Scotch & soda to which he had so long looked forward. But when he faced the newsmen they could see, underneath his grey fatigue, a burning urgency they had never seen before, even in urgent Wendell Willkie.

What he learned, Private Citizen Willkie would soon say in a full, frank report to the U.S. people. No one knows what he will say. But Wendell Willkie speaks more freely to newsmen than any other man of his public importance. And from what they had already heard him say, have come vibrant clues:

Russia—"Put aside your thoughts about Communism, godlessness. The progress Russia has made is astounding. Siberia is an inexhaustible storehouse of strategic war materials. In my judgment Germany will never conquer Russia."

China—"There is in China a great reservoir of admiration and affection for the U.S., but the reservoir is leaking fast. We have talked a lot about our production figures, but some of our Allies have seen very little of our actual arms."

The War—"Men need more than arms to fight and win this war. They need enthusiasm for the future."

NOV. 16 **SECRETS WILL OUT:** After the U.S. landing in North Africa [page 108] Cordell Hull wore the happy look of a man who at last can tell a burning secret: for 25 months he had shaped his every act toward Vichyfrance so as to prepare for a successful Mediterranean front. Keeping his mouth shut was hard. People called him an appeaser, demanded his resignation. Now, to tell all, the Secretary of State called newspapermen for an unusual Sunday conference. Soberly, but radiating satisfaction, he read:

"People who have been concerned about the Vichy policy of this Government will now be able to see fully and clearly its entire content. The liberation of French Morocco by American military forces carries forward the various purposes and objectives of this Government."

Now the country knew that its State Department had strung along with Vichy in order 1) to get information about Axis activities; 2) to encourage French opposition to Hitler; 3) to encourage the hope of freedom among the French; 4) to minimize French collaboration with Germany; 5) to prepare for war in the Mediterranean area.

His secret told, Cordell Hull cared little about Vichyfrance reaction, remained stonily indifferent when the Laval Government announced that it was breaking relations with the U.S.

Races

HARLEM'S FIRST: Harlem's 200,000-odd Negroes had their JAN. 12 first representative in the New York City Council this week, and the Rev. Adam Clayton Powell Jr. took another step toward becoming the popular hero of U.S. Negroes. Tall (6 ft. 4 in.), husky (210 lb.), young (33), Adam Powell is handsome, light-skinned, a fluent speaker, a good showman. He went to Colgate University, hurled the javelin on the track team, worked summers as a redcap in Manhattan's Grand Central Terminal.

After a year in theological seminary, he stepped into a ready-made job as assistant pastor of his father's Abyssinian Baptist Church, whose 14,000 members are the largest Protestant congregation in the world.

When his father retired four years ago, Powell took over—against the protest of oldsters who had been shocked by his marriage to radio and nightclub singer Isabel Washington, considered him a little too fancy and convivial for a preacher. His sermons dealt with everyday Harlem problems like high

Rev. Adam Clayton Powell Jr. He is New York's first Negro Councilman.

Tenor Roland Hayes. He is humiliated in the state he loves. Page 58.

rents, jobs, the numbers racket. Afterward he stood in front of his pulpit, kissing the women of his congregation.

Until he ran for Councilman, he had been only a sideline politico. His campaign amazed Manhattan politicians. With no machine support, he ran third among six Councilmen elected in New York City. Helpfully, he mailed 200,000 sample ballots to voters, showing how to mark the complicated proportional representation ballot. In Harlem, which gave him some 50,000 No. 1 votes, there were fewer spoiled ballots than anywhere else in the city. If New York Congressional districts are revised, as seems likely, Councilman Powell may turn up in Washington as Harlem's first U.S. Congressman.

MARCH 2 **WHITE MAN'S WAR?:** In Philadelphia Negro Harry Carpenter was held for treason when he told a Negro Army sergeant: "This is a white man's war, and it's no damn good."

Negroes have fought ably in every U.S. war since the Revolution. In the Civil War, the Union had 170,000 black soldiers under arms. But when the first Negro leader, Frederick Bailey Douglass, asked why they were paid less than white soldiers, President Lincoln temporized. Negroes should be glad they could serve at all, said Mr. Lincoln. They had more to fight for than any white man.

Since World War I, the Negro's status as a U.S. fighting man has gone backward. Of the 1,078,331 Negroes registered for the draft in World War I, some 380,000 Negroes served as soldiers—10% of the whole Army. The 292,000 Negro troops the Army expects to have at the end of 1942 will come to 8% of the U.S. armed forces in World War II.

Some of the best U.S. soldiers in 1917-18 were black troops. The famed 15th Infantry (now the 369th Coast Artillery) from Harlem stayed longer under fire (191 days) than any other regiment, yielded no prisoners, gave up no ground, suffered casualties of 40%. Negro veterans still grin delightedly when they recall the "Battle of Henry Johnson," in which a pint-size onetime redcap from Albany, N.Y. killed, wounded and routed a party of 25 Germans single-handed.

In spite of the shortage of skilled labor, black citizens are unwelcome in many war industries. As the war boom got going last year, President Asa Philip Randolph of the Brotherhood of Sleeping Car Porters planned a protest march of 50,000 Negroes on Washington. When he got wind of the plan, Franklin Roosevelt sent for Randolph, then issued an executive order forbidding color discrimination in defense industries. Negroes thought the President had passed a miracle second only to Lincoln's Emancipation Proclamation. The President followed up his order by setting up a Committee on Fair Employment Practice.

NEGROES & THE WAR: In Manhattan, Wendell Willkie told a MARCH 30 dinner meeting that the Navy's rule excluding Negroes from the service except as messmen is "an injustice which makes a mockery of all our fine words." In Washington, the Office for Emergency Management announced that Local 68 of the A.F. of L.'s International Association of Machinists will now let Negroes work in San Francisco defense industries.

"SECOND-CLASS CITIZEN": In the State penitentiary at Rich- JULY 6 mond, Va., young Odell Waller awaited death this week by electrocution. A Negro sharecropper, guilty of murdering a white man, Waller would have died long since if his case had not become a *cause célèbre*.

The case had a humble beginning. Waller sharecropped a wheat and tobacco farm in Pittsylvania County in southern Virginia. His landlord was Oscar Davis, a white tenant farmer who, no matter how hard he worked and sang hymns in the Methodist church, never got out of debt. Black and white, Waller and Davis were two poor, desperate men at the bottom of the South's economic heap. When the Government curtailed Davis' tobacco allotment, Davis cut Waller's acreage and denied the poverty-stricken Negro his due: one-quarter share of the threshed wheat. The Waller family faced a winter of starvation. Waller put a pistol in his pocket, went to Davis to demand his 50 sacks of wheat. According to Waller: "Mr. Davis said I won't gonna get that damn wheat away from here," and reached into his pocket. "He usually carried a gun. I opened my pistol and commenced to shoot at him." Davis, shot four times, died.

A jury of ten farmers (all employers of sharecroppers), one businessman and a carpenter listened to the case for two days, took 52 minutes to find Waller guilty of murder.

Liberals rushed to his defense. Among them was John F. Finerty, a prominent corporation laywer and civil-libertarian, who maintained that Waller had not been tried by a jury of his peers, argued that destitute "second-class citizens" like Waller were barred from serving on Virginia juries, because they could not afford to pay Virginia's $1.50 a year poll tax.

Finerty's appeals for a new trial were denied by one court after another. The U.S. Supreme Court refused the case twice. Protests grew louder & louder. To Humanitarian Finerty it appeared that "a man must die because of an error of his counsel."

Virginians were vexed over "outsiders sticking their noses into Virginia's affairs." But some were also deeply disturbed over Virginia justice. Governor Colgate W. Darden Jr. granted stay after stay. The Richmond *Times-Dispatch* declared: "Add the fact that we are in a war for survival in which we are depending heavily for victory on the colored races, and the significance of the Waller case becomes clearer."

But, said Chief Justice Stone, turning Finerty down: "The petition presents no question cognizable in a habeas-corpus proceeding in a Federal court."

CHANCES: A 25-year-old Negro sharecropper laboriously, in JULY 13 crabbed script, wrote his last testament:

"Have you thought about some people are allowed a chance over and over again, then there are others allowed little chance some no chance at all," wrote Odell Waller. "I accident[ally] fell and some good people tried to help me. Others did everything they could against me so the governor and the coats dont no the true facts. In my case I worked hard from sunup until sundown trying to make a living for my family and it ended in death for me."

A few minutes later Odell Waller died in the electric chair in the Virginia State Penitentiary for killing his white landlord over 50 sacks of wheat.

THE ROME INCIDENT: Twenty miles northeast of Rome, Ga. JULY 27 on a 600-acre farm where his parents once worked as slaves, lives shy, greying Roland Hayes, 55, who earned as high as $100,000 a year when he was the world's greatest Negro tenor. Among the neighborhood whites he is respected; he gives one charity concert a year in nearby Calhoun.

But in Rome, where he does his weekend shopping, quiet Roland Hayes is less well known. Fortnight ago, his wife and nine-year-old daughter Africa (pronounced Afree-ka) went into Higgins Shoe Store, where they had traded for three years. It was a hot day and they sat in the second of six rows of seats, underneath a fan. There was a new clerk: he asked Mrs. Hayes to take a seat at the rear reserved for Negroes. Mrs. Hayes said she preferred to stay under the fan. The day was hot, tempers short. An argument started. Said usually even-tempered Mrs. Hayes: "This is no time to talk about racial prejudice and segregation. Hitler ought to have you."

Someone called police and told them there was "nigger trouble."

Roland Hayes, who weighs 120 lb., told what happened next: "I went to the store to rectify any trouble that might have been caused, and as I left a policeman caught me in the belt and dragged me back. I protested I had done nothing and I denied my wife had cursed. I told them my wife didn't curse. When I said that, a man not in officers' garb gave me all he had on the jaw. Then I was dragged to the patrol car, handcuffed between two officers. I was struck again by this man not in uniform, who leaned through a window to hit me. My wife and I were put in a cell and our little girl left on the outside."

When Chief of Police Charles I. Harris learned his prisoner's name, he telephoned gallus-snapping Governor Gene Talmadge, who usually seizes any chance to sound off on an inflammatory issue. The Governor told Chief Harris to handle the case himself. Hayes and his wife were released on $50 bail. Next day the bail was sent back. When the case was called in court, no one appeared to prosecute. Rome tried to hush up the incident.

Back at his farm, Roland Hayes, who has never been an agitator for Negro rights, reflected: "I am not bitter toward anyone and the humiliation is on the other side. I am only ashamed that this should happen in my native state. I love Georgia."

OCT. 12 **DAR EATS JIM CROW:** The Daughters of the American Revolution, who once outraged music lovers and democrats by refusing to let Contralto Marian Anderson sing in their Constitution Hall, had a wartime change of heart last week. When her stubborn Manager Sol Hurok again asked for use of the Washington hall, the DARters went him one better, formally invited Miss Anderson to be soloist in one of their war-relief concerts this winter.

MILESTONES

BORN: Douglas MacArthur Brotherson, Douglas MacArthur Bryant, Douglas MacArthur Francis, Douglas MacArthur Miller, Douglas MacArthur Gunner, Douglas MacArthur Salavec, Douglas MacArthur Thompson, and Douglas Harold MacArthur; all in New York City.

DIED: Martin Van Buren, 86, last surviving grandson of the eighth President; in Manhattan. He never married, never worked for a living, once remarked that his only tangible possessions were three suitcases full of clothing—one in England, one in Bar Harbor, one in Manhattan's dowager-like Murray Hill Hotel.

MISCELLANY

FALSE ALARM: In Madisonville, Tex., the fire department finally found a way to get rid of crowds that interfered with their work. At every alarm the assistant chief drove a spare truck in the wrong direction, led all the fire buffs astray.

KIBITZER: In a Los Angeles court, Bernard William Butynski asked permission to change his name to Bernard William de Groot.

(WORLD BATTLEFRONTS)

The Axis powers held the initiative during much of 1942. After their devastating attack on Pearl Harbor in December 1941, the Japanese moved on to attack the Philippines, the Netherlands East Indies, Malaya, Singapore and Burma, the latter being the main Allied supply route into China. In the Atlantic German submarines were doing their best to cut off Allied shipping to Europe. The major Allied undertaking of the year was an invasion of North Africa to slow down Nazi General Erwin Rommel's drive toward the Suez Canal and also to help the Russians by forcing Hitler to divert some of his troops from the Russian front to Africa.

The Philippines

OVERWHELMING IN NUMBERS: A United States Army, most JAN. 5 of it composed of half-trained Filipinos, last week fought the first great U.S. battle of World War II. By slicing the Philippine Islands' supply line from Pearl Harbor, by heavy attacks on Philippine airfields, by plain wear & tear on the islands' limited aircraft equipment, Japan had won the first requisite of victory: command of the air. Overwhelming in numbers, the Jap flailed at the U.S. positions with rifle, machine gun, tank and plane, careless of his losses. Bitterly, savagely and calculatingly, the tall men from the U.S. and the short men from the island fought back. It was a battle of churning movement: swift slashes of armored cars and men in trucks, ceaseless slamming of artillery, swiftly emplaced, swiftly moved with the tide of battle.

But unless the Philippines could get help from the outside —planes, munitions, men, decisive U.S. Naval intervention— they would be lost. There was not a man in the lines who did not know it. General Douglas MacArthur had said that the islands could be held, but only if their supply was continuous and decisive. He had also said: "Any machine-gun nest can be captured if the attacker is willing to pay the price. So can the Philippines be captured if the enemy is willing to write off the losses."

The Jap was writing off his losses. He came in droves, met withering fire, marched stoically up to it and took his medicine with a grunt. There were more where he came from. The Jap was likely to lose the impetus of his first drive as he hit the prepared defense positions. In the end Douglas MacArthur might still win. His position was desperate. It was likely to get worse. But it was not yet hopeless.

JAN. 12 **PORTRAIT OF A JAPANESE**: "We'll defeat the Japanese in the end," said Secretary of War Henry L. Stimson, "but we shouldn't look at the war with them through rose-colored glasses. There have been reports that the Japanese in the Philippines are badly trained troops, ill-equipped. The cold truth is that the Japanese are veterans and they are well-equipped. The Japanese soldier is short, wiry and tough. He is well-disciplined."

In battle dress a Japanese soldier looks like a badly wrapped brown paper package. His legs are too short, his pants are baggy, his leggings droop, his tunic is loose, his kit askew. But the sloppiness is misleading. For his size, this man-weapon carries an extraordinary amount of equipment. His .25-caliber rifle or machine gun is light and accurate to 1,000 yards. He can carry 400 rounds of its little bullets, twice as many as the load of larger bullets the larger U.S. trooper totes. He carries five days' rations of rice and sardines, and tends to his own cooking. From birth he has been taught the glory of dying for the Emperor.

From the top of his shaved head to the bottom of his splay-toed feet he is hard. His buttocks are big with marching. His eyes are generally good. He walks like a duck, runs like a man cut off at the knees. "They didn't charge," said one U.S. officer, describing a Japanese advance, "but crouched forward just a little bit, lifting their knees high in a sort of imitation goosestep. They kept coming forward in pairs, one directly behind the other."

LAST STAND: This was the brackish taste of defeat that American soldiers had not known in a major battle since Appomattox. Before the week's end the Army of the Philippines had withdrawn from Manila and was holed up on a small peninsula named Bataan. Bataan is almost devoid of roads, tough for armored-force operations, ideal for making the Jap pay for what he might eventually get. Separated from Bataan by only two miles of water lies Corregidor, a tadpole-shaped fortress in the mouth of Manila Bay, with its sandy tail pointed toward the city. It was Corregidor that the Jap wanted most. Until its 12-in. guns are silenced, the Jap can never hope to sail his ships into Manila Bay.

THE CORK: Inch by inch, with the glacierlike superiority of FEB. 2 sheer mass, the Jap forced his way south on Bataan Peninsula. Before him the last big core of resistance stood like a granite cliff of valor. The sleepless, bitter, astute defense made by American and Philippine soldiers had long since made Douglas MacArthur one of the great captains of U.S. military history. He had chosen his position well. Only his left flank, on the sea, was exposed. The right lay on Manila Bay, and the guns of Corregidor still kept the bay clear of heavy Jap forces. On his 62nd birthday this week Douglas MacArthur was still chipper, still bucking up his men by visits to his fronts. He said: "The enemy may hold the bottle, but I hold the cork."

"NERTS TO YOU, JOE": U.S. and Philippine scouts last week in- FEB. 16 tercepted a Japanese suicide squadron on mountainous Bataan Peninsula, hounded & harried the sabotage-bent visitors into a dense, brush-covered last-stand some 125 yards square. Behind the dense, protective foliage the little men burrowed into foxholes. Snipers tied themselves in trees. So close were the two forces that the Japs' labored breathing was clearly heard. His arm in a bloody sling, Captain C. A. Crome shouted one last ultimatum: "Surrender, you bastards, we've got you surrounded!" The answer floated back in perfect English: "Nerts to you, Joe."

MACARTHUR'S LEGEND: The men on Bataan kept watching MARCH 2 for him. Once in a while he would come around. Everything about him—the angle of his heavily braided cap, the swing of his brown, curve-handled cane, the uptilt of his long black cigaret holder, the shine on his four stars and brown shoes—everything was always jaunty. The men watched for his smile: they usually got it. Thus, day after dreary day, Douglas MacArthur cheered his tired men. He himself must have been sustained by the growing realization that he was a national hero. All across the land citizens were paying their various tributes:

¶ V. R. Hood, proprietor of a cleaning establishment in San Antonio, Tex.: "All the people I know think God comes first and then MacArthur."

¶ Charles Bray, an insurance man in Topeka, Kans.: "MacArthur is the greatest general since Sergeant York."

MARCH 16 **MACARTHUR STRIKES BACK:** In the steaming woods that crowd the airdrome on Bataan, the monkeys chattered a tuneless obbligato to the bright-plumaged birds. Below them, men in grease-stained coveralls worked over a handful of pursuit planes—the last, bullet-chipped remnant of Douglas MacArthur's Air Force. Now, after days of ingenious patching, the damaged P-40s were ready to fly. In the woods the pilots climbed into their seats, fastened their helmets and parachute straps. Down the concealed alleyways through the trees the lean airplanes teetered to the airdrome. The Jap was close enough to hear the engines when they began to roar. But by then it was too late. The P-40s streaked across the field.

Less than 15 miles north of the front line, over the wrecked naval station at Olongapo on Subic Bay, the P-40s peeled out of formation. Then smoke began to rise, great billowing clouds of it, and tiny specks in the sky grew into the shapes of airplanes as the raiders headed home. They were back within the hour. The planes mumbled back into the trees, grunted and were silent. The raid had been a smashing success. MacArthur's P-40s, doing a job they were never built to do, had sunk 30,000 tons of shipping (three transports). Caught with his finger in his mouth, the Jap had never got a single plane off the ground. More important still, the raiders had caught the transports while they were still loaded. Hundreds, perhaps thousands of Japanese soldiers had gone down with the ships. The men on Bataan could now live a little longer.

MACARTHUR TO AUSTRALIA: The man who knows how to MARCH 23 stop the Japanese took command this week of the last place in the Southwest Pacific to stop them. When Douglas MacArthur reached Australia, the U.S. and all the United Nations breathed a sigh of relief and hope: "By God, they got him out!"

The siege of Bataan was 53 days old when General MacArthur got his orders to leave last February 22. The orders came from President Roosevelt, who had heeded the insistent cry in the U.S. that MacArthur alive to fight and win was worth more than a hero dead.

EXCELLENCY, A FEW NOTES: MacArthur was gone. Japanese MARCH 30 General pot-bellied Tomoyuki Yamashita, conqueror of Malaya, faced a classic U.S. cavalryman: lean, dashing Jonathan Mayhew Wainwright. Against this opponent, Yamashita moved with ponderous ceremony. On U.S. positions, Jap aviators dropped cans, tied with red ribbons, bearing notes addressed "To His Excellency, Major General Jonathan Wainwright:

"We have the honor to address you in accordance with *Bushido* —the code of the Japanese warrior. You have already fought to the best of your ability. What dishonor is there in following the example of the defenders of Hong Kong, Singapore, and The Netherlands East Indies? Your Excellency: Accept our sincere advice and save the lives of those officers and men under your command. International law would be strictly adhered to."

West Pointer Wainwright knows all about *Bushido,* all about the treatment the Jap has already given to his prisoners. He gave the note the answer it deserved: he ignored it.

WHITE FLAG ON BATAAN: Bataan finally fell and taught the APRIL 20 U.S. a thing it had forgotten: pride of arms, pride in what the young men could do when tested. Bataan taught America a humiliating thing, too: that U.S. soldiers could be beaten, could be taught the fullest ignominy of unconditional surrender.

With Bataan went 36,000 or more courageous U.S. soldiers who had stumbled ragged, sleepless and half-starved through the last days of the most humiliating defeat in U.S. history. In no previous battle had so many U.S. fighting men gone down before a foreign enemy.

The end was slow and agonizing. For 15 days the Jap struck at Bataan with everything he had. Dive-bombers blew great craters in forward positions. Artillery roared endlessly day & night; the nervous chatter of Jap machine guns rattled until it rasped men's nerves like a file. The Jap even struck at the hospital, scattered the wounded like straws. And since the middle of January the men on Bataan had gone short of food.

Jonathan Wainwright had seen that the end was near. From the shores of the Bay he withdrew all his forces to Corregidor. He tried to strike one last blow. Against a Jap breakthrough on the Manila Bay side of the peninsula he threw a corps in desperate counterattack. The glassy-eyed soldiers went forward like men in a dream, so exhausted that many of them could hardly lift their feet, and the Jap mowed them down.

The men on Corregidor saw only a little of the ghastly end. The last, pitifully small ammunition dump on Bataan went up in smoke and flame; three ships at the water's edge were dynamited. Finally, from one of the heights on Bataan, a white flag went up. How many of the 36,000 died fighting, only the Japs knew.

Men still swam the shark-infested stretch from Bataan to the fortress still holding out on Corregidor, and in the last few hours boats got across with nurses and a few survivors. But the biggest part of the battle-trained Army was gone. Now from the heights the Jap, with artillery already emplaced, began slamming away at Corregidor itself.

APRIL 27 **NOT JAPS–MOSQUITOES:** The costliest American shortage in the Battle of Bataan was revealed last week: quinine. There was no more medicine to fight malaria, and in the long run malaria put more soldiers out of action than the Jap. Food was running out and men were getting leaner on a diet of carabao (water buffalo), cavalry horses and mules, but they stayed on their feet and fought until the burning fever of malaria laid them out. Thousands of prostrated fighting men jammed the field hospitals. Others, listless, weary and sometimes out of their heads hung on with their outfits where they were more liabilities than assets.

The men needed only two little quinine pills a day—but there weren't two pills apiece to give them. [The shortage of quinine was caused by the Japanese capture of Java, the chief Allied source of the drug. The next best remedy for malaria, a drug called atabrine, was a German product. Allied drug manufacturers eventually solved the problem by developing an imitation of the German atabrine.]

LIVING ON A BULL'S-EYE: "Corregidor can and will be held. There can be no question of surrendering this mighty fortress to the enemy; it will be defended with all the resources at our command."

Thus Lieut. General Jonathan Wainwright spoke last week to the men on The Rock—the Marines, sailormen and Army men salvaged from Bataan. In the States, men took heart. Jonathan Wainwright was no hollow-voiced orator, to fire his people with false hopes. If he said it could be done, maybe it could. Meanwhile, the forts were pounded unmercifully, and the shelling and bombing made life on Corregidor, as a U.S. Army officer said, something like living on a bull's-eye.

GHOSTLY GARRISON: Toward the end there was no sleep on MAY 18 Corregidor. The ammunition was about gone, the food had run out. The wounded, crowded into the catacombs of The Rock, cried out for help that no one could give. Corregidor was through. Five months after the Jap's first attack, the last island of formal resistance in the Philippines was going. An army of more than 10,000 crack troops, wasted by want, feverish with malaria, without hope of relief, was going to its end.

One day when the sun had gone down and there was little light from the waning moon, the Jap set out in assault boats from Bataan. In the great rents made in the barbed wire by the Jap's guns he beached his troops. For 24 incredible, bloody hours, American fighting men grappled for Corregidor. But there were always live Japs where the dead ones came from. They poured across the narrow waters in flood, swarmed over and through the defenders. Dashing Lieut. General Jonathan Mayhew ("Skinny") Wainwright was finally forced to the greatest tragedy in a soldier's life. He surrendered.

In Australia, Douglas MacArthur wrote:

"Corregidor needs no comment from me. But through the bloody haze of its last reverberating shot I shall always seem to see the vision of its grim, gaunt and ghostly men, still unafraid."

JUNE 8 **LAST WORD:** Time: early morning of May 5, 1942. Place: the radio dugout on Corregidor. At his key a haggard radio operator taps out the last broken sentences of the most tragic chapter in U.S. military history:

"They are not near yet. We are waiting for God only knows what. How about a chocolate soda? . . . Lots of heavy fighting going on. We may have to give up by noon. We don't know yet. They are throwing men and shells at us and I feel sick at my stomach. . . . They bring in the wounded every minute. We will be waiting for you guys to help. . . .

"The jig is up. Everyone is bawling like a baby. They are piling dead and wounded in our tunnel. I know now how a mouse feels. Caught in a trap waiting for guys to come along and finish it up. Got a treat. Can pineapple.

"My name Irving Strobing. Get this to my mother, Mrs. Minnie Strobing, 605 Barbey Street, Brooklyn, N.Y. Message: My love to Pa, Joe, Sue, Mac, Garry, Joy and Paul. God bless 'em all. Hope they be there when I come home. God bless and keep you. Love.

"Sign my name and tell my mother how you heard from me."

Battle of the Pacific

JAN. 5 **WAKE'S 378:** It was Christmas week out there under the wide open sky on a sandspit in mid-sea. Back home, stores bustled and parti-colored lights blinked from the trees in a million windows. But for the Marines on Wake Island it was the week when they fought and died in their last, hopeless stand.

For more than three weeks the little band of 378 seasoldiers had been under repeated Jap attack. Frying in the Pacific sun on their desolate four-mile-long atoll they had seen a Jap cruiser and two destroyers standing off the island with the "Surrender" signal flapping gaily from their halyards. Bantam (5 ft. 5 in.) Major James Patrick Sinnott Devereux, the detachment commander, returned a Marine's answer: "Come and get us."

General Wainwright: "Corregidor can and will be held." Page 66.   *Major Devereux to the Japs at Wake Island: "Come and get us."*

Then the Jap got another answer. Somehow, either by bombardment from the four fighter planes still on the island or by fire from his six 5-in. guns, little Jimmie Devereux sank the cruiser and one of the destroyers. He reported it tersely to Honolulu. Later he reported his men had sunk a Nip sub.

The Japs kept coming and at last got a landing party on the beach. Reported Major Devereux with magnificent euphemism: "The issue is in doubt." The rest was silence. From Tokyo next day an announcement came: Wake was taken. [After his return from the war, Devereux served for eight years as a U.S. Representative from Maryland.]

FEB. 2 **"PRAISE THE LORD"**: With release of an official report on Pearl Harbor, a trickle of now-it-can-be-tolds began to flow. Best of the first:

On the fateful Sunday morning, the chaplain of a battleship in Pearl Harbor was busy on the afterdeck with a couple of assistants in preparation for divine service. Their polite murmurs were suddenly interrupted by the roar of the Jap. The chaplain dropped his bunting, ran to an antiaircraft gun and began preaching lead to the Japanese. A few minutes later he was heard to intone: "Praise the Lord and pass the ammunition. I just got one of the sons of bitches."

MARCH 23 **34 DAYS ON A RAFT**: Squalls forced the spluttering Navy bomber down onto the dark seas. When it sank, the three men scrambled into a rubber life raft, 8 ft. by 4 ft. They had only their clothes, a .45 automatic pistol, a pocketknife, pliers and a length of ½-inch Manila line. Thirty-four days later, they had sailed and been blown 1,000 miles by one of the worst South Sea hurricanes in history. The man who pulled them through could shake hands with Captain Bligh of the *Bounty*. Hawk-nosed Bomber Pilot Harold Dixon was a hard guy from Oklahoma, who took charge as soon as his beloved bomber sank from sight.

After three days of drifting, the men had talked themselves out. They knew all about every woman any one of them had so much as kissed. The men could only doze because the life raft, said Dixon, was like "sleeping on a Beautyrest mattress and someone smacking you with a baseball bat twice every three seconds, and someone else throwing buckets of cold water in your face." On the fifth day the first rain came. Dixon made "the lads" take off their underwear, tear it into strips which soaked up the rain and could be squeezed into an oar pocket. The next morning Radioman Gene Aldrich used the pocketknife to spear a fish. That night an albatross landed on the raft. Aldrich killed it with the pistol and Dixon, the only one who could swim, dived overboard and retrieved it. The men ate the organs and the entrails, but put the unplucked flesh away to save. In the night it glowed with phosphorescence and Dixon threw it overboard.

On the seventh day Aldrich slashed out with the pocketknife again, this time gilled a four-foot shark. With their pliers the men ripped the shark open. Dixon remembered reading that sharks stored up vitamins in their liver. The liver was "very tasty," so were two sardines in the shark's stomach which the men said "must have been partly digested because they tasted as if they had been cooked." On the 21st day a floating coconut provided slightly brackish milk and meat. By then, as far as he could tell, Dixon was "somewhere in the vicinity of Ireland."

When a hurricane struck a few days later, the men used their shirts and trousers to bail out the mountainous combers breaking over the raft. One wave flipped the raft completely over. Then the men lost everything, including their clothes. On the 33rd day the raft capsized once more. "For the first time," Dixon said, "I was ready to give up." Then came the 34th day and Aldrich shouted: "Chief, I see a beautiful cornfield." Dixon was sure then that Aldrich "had gone." But ahead of them white rollers were breaking on an island beach and behind that there were rows of palms.

At sundown they grounded on the beach, then found that they could scarcely walk because their legs were so cramped. Dixon's hip refused to straighten out, but even so he forced his crew to march up the beach in military fashion.

"If there were Japs," Dixon explained, "we didn't want to be crawling." But there were no Japs, only a deserted copra hut. In this the men slept. All their adventure now lacked was a shapely native girl to find them the next morning. One did.

A PROMISE TO RETURN: MacArthur on Bataan had fought a MARCH 30 limited battle of position in an area about as big as Los Angeles. In Australia last week he prepared to defend an area as big as the U.S. Still tired by his trip from the Philippines, General MacArthur wrote:

"The President of the United States ordered me to break through the Japanese lines and proceed from Corregidor to Australia for the purpose of organizing the American offensive against Japan. A primary purpose of this is the relief of the Philippines. I came through and I shall return."

THE ESCAPE: It was night on Corregidor when MacArthur left. He stepped aboard a boat. With him were slim, brunette Jean Faircloth MacArthur; their four-year-old son, Arthur, the boy's hovering Chinese nurse, Ah Ju. With them, on this and a second boat, were some of the staff officers who were to accompany General MacArthur to Australia. In a hidden inlet on Bataan, Major General Hugh Casey of the Engineers led the rest of the departing staff aboard two other boats.

The four boats should have met before dawn, then hidden near the shore until the next night. But they had taken a beating since Dec. 7 and their tired engines could not do their rated 39 knots. The two parties had to risk a daylight voyage and did not meet until nearly noon.

At dusk, a Japanese warship appeared on the horizon. Instantly, the small boats' engines were stilled: the four boats lay low. The warship passed MacArthur by. The little boats pitched and shivered in the high swells; the hardiest officers aboard thought that their necks were snapping off. Toward dawn, three hours behind schedule, the little fleet made its intended landfall—on or near the Island of Mindoro, no more than 100 miles from the nearest Japanese lines and Manila. Awaiting General MacArthur were two Flying Fortresses. From the take-off point to northern Australia was an eleven-hour flight for the Fortresses. It was a course straight across Japan's new Pacific barriers, a course Douglas MacArthur expected to retrace some day.

Despite the disaster at Pearl Harbor and the loss of Wake Island, there was a sizable U.S. fleet in the Pacific. In short order it dealt crippling blows to the Japanese Navy in two famous engagements—the Battle of the Coral Sea and the Battle of Midway.

MAY 18　**IN THE CORAL SEA:** It was the greatest battle in the history of the U.S. Pacific Fleet. It was fought below the equator, in the Coral Sea off Australia's northeast coast. For five days, smudged with belching smoke screens and roaring with bomb bursts, a U.S. naval force and Army bombers from land bases took turns tearing into a heavy Jap task force, invasion-bound. The U.S. aircraft had the edge. They burst through the Jap fighters again & again, rained bombs and aerial torpedoes at the surface craft. The battle ended in a nightmare of retreat, with U.S. aircraft hacking at the enemy every step of the way. By conservative U.S. count he had lost 21 ships, sunk or disabled. And he had unquestionably taken a beating—the first serious defeat of his headlong career through the South Pacific.

MIDWAY: For weeks the Army & Navy had known that some- JUNE 15 thing Japanese was up. Pins moved on Intelligence maps when the Japs shifted battleships, carriers and cruisers and part of the Japanese main fleet moved southward toward a rendezvous at Formosa. Aircraft and light naval units suddenly withdrew from Australia's outlying islands.

By last fortnight the Japanese had amassed a great armada that included at least five carriers, three to five battleships, many cruisers, destroyers and submarines, with troop transports. The U.S. command knew that such a force would have assembled only for a major blow. The question was: Where? The admirals had to apply what they call the doctrine of "calculated risk," placing the bulk of what they had where the Jap seemed most likely to strike. They chose Midway. Then they waited.

Midway was worth a Japanese gamble; only Pearl Harbor was more vital to U.S. operations in the Pacific. And, in Japanese hands, Midway could be a steppingstone to Pearl Harbor, Alaska and the U.S. mainland. But the Japanese got a mighty shock. Midway was ready. Marine Corps fighters instantly took the air. On Midway's field were Army bombers, ready to track fleeing Japs to their carriers. Antiaircraft fire blanketed Midway's sky. Jap planes littered the sea. U.S. fighters and bombers, pursuing the rest, found the Japanese main force, closed in for the kill.

Among the great naval battles of the world this one was of a new kind. Communiqués indicated that the greater portion of the two fleets never got within a day's sailing distance of each other. Most of the action was fought by aircraft. But three days after the battle opened, six months after Pearl Harbor, Admiral Chester W. Nimitz, Commander in Chief of the Pacific Fleet, announced: "Pearl Harbor has now been partially avenged."

The U.S.S. "Lexington" goes down in the Battle of the Coral Sea. She dodged nine torpedoes before her luck ran out.

JUNE 22 **THE SCORE:** Now that the returns from the Coral Sea and Midway are in, these facts seem clear:

¶ Japan has lost much of her Navy's striking power at sea. Without that power, Japan cannot bring the war to the U.S., or even to the remaining U.S. strongholds in the Pacific: Pearl Harbor, Midway, Australia, the endangered (but by no means conquered) Aleutians and Alaska.

¶ Japan has not lost her defensive power, her power to defend what she has already won in Malaya, the Indies, the Philippines, and to defend her home islands and cities.

LEXINGTON LOST: As U.S. dive-bombers dipped and the torpedo-planes flew low and level at the massed Jap ships in the Battle of the Coral Sea, the attacking pilots swore and yelled into their phones in excitement. From three attacks that day, every U.S. plane returned to the mother carriers—the *Lexington* and another, unnamed—waiting 100 miles south of Tulagi with a covering force of cruisers and destroyers.

Three mornings later, U.S. scout-bombers spotted the Japs in the biggest force yet: three carriers, with accompanying cruisers and destroyers. Off went the planes, into history's first carrier-v.-carrier combat. The U.S. planes apparently struck first. Their bombs and torpedoes left the

14,000-ton, 45-plane *Syokaku* flaming and listing so badly that the U.S. pilots doubted her survival. When she was hit, the *Syokaku*'s flight decks were bare; her planes were attacking the *Lexington.*

Against the *Lexington* and her unnamed sister carrier came 108 Japanese planes. [When censorship was later lifted, it was revealed that the other carrier was the *Yorktown,* which was sunk in a subsequent battle at Midway.] Forty were shot down. The *Lexington* dodged nine torpedoes, could not dodge two others. Three bombs also hit her. Nevertheless her crew took aboard most of her planes, had three fires under control and another nearly out when an internal explosion (apparently of escaping gasoline fumes) rent the *Lexington.* At 5:07 p.m., her commander gave the sailor's saddest order: "Abandon ship!"

Before they slid overside into the sea, to be picked up by destroyers and cruisers, all the men lined their shoes in orderly rows on the flight deck. As the last of the crew went overboard, another explosion shook the ship. A little later, lest she fall into Jap hands or endanger other ships, a U.S. destroyer torpedoed the *Lexington*'s flaming hulk.

THE FIRST OFFENSIVE: For the first time since Dec. 7 a price- AUG. 17 less intangible asset finally came into U.S. hands: an attack on the Solomon Islands had snatched the offensive from the Japanese in the Pacific. The blow was struck from Down Under at the exotic Solomons, a fringe of volcanic peaks strung for 600 miles across the northern end of the Coral Sea. The Navy was out to take the Solomons from the Jap— and with them the threat they held to the supply line from the U.S. to Australia. The attack's first objective was Tulagi, one of the best harbors in the Solomons, which the Jap had held since early June for a jump-off place if he should decide to head south again. Around Tulagi are other rings of the Navy's target. Most important of them passes through the island of Guadalcanal, said to be the only spot on the Solomons where a big system of U.S. airdromes could be established. For the rest, the Solomons are precipitously mountainous, bordered with mangrove swamps, inhabited by natives with an incurable habit of roasting and eating white visitors.

For weeks, news of the campaign in the Solomons was hidden behind a heavy security blackout. The first sparse accounts of how the fighting was going were optimistic; then gradually U.S. citizens began to learn of the bitter seesaw struggle for an island they had never heard of. Its name was Guadalcanal.

SEPT. 7 **CARLSON'S RAIDERS:** The night of August 17, when the Marines landed on Makin Island in the Gilbert Islands, was dark and rainy. The surf was high. Captain James N. M. Davis of Evanston, Ill. lost his pants in the waves. Major James Roosevelt of Washington, second in command to Lieut. Colonel Evans F. Carlson, cut his left index finger on a piece of coral. But the Marines, their faces and hands daubed green to blend with the foliage, all got ashore.

Colonel Carlson had led the main group of Marines toward the heart of the island. They crept into several shacks, found them empty except for such things as a piano and a roll of sacred music (the Marines found no trace of several Catholic nuns who had been on the islands). The clatter of a Jap machine gun told Colonel Carlson that his landing had been detected. Then the Marines heard the flat crack of snipers' bullets from the palms.

During the fighting, Sergeant Jim Faulkner of Red Oak, Tex. got shot through the hand.

"Goddamit, they got me," Sergeant Faulkner cried, and went on fighting.

Then he was hit in the head.

"Goddamit, they got me again," Sergeant Faulkner yelped.

He was hit in the side. His howl rang through the palms.

"Goddamit, they got me!"

He was hit in the leg.

"Goddamit," Sergeant Faulkner announced, "they got me!"

Finally persuaded to return to the beach and his ship, he awoke after an hour and a half on the operating table, then sat up and had a bowl of soup.

The native chief of the islanders gave pantsless Captain Davis a sarong. Other friendly Micronesians ignored the Japanese fire, plied the Marines with coconuts, told them where the Japs were concentrated. Toward the end of the fighting, the natives told Colonel Carlson that only eight Japs were left alive. They were all snipers, strapped in the trees. Marines killed six, but never did find the other two. Colonel Carlson figured that he and his raiders had killed 198 of the 200 Jap marines on the island. Said Colonel Carlson: "We wanted to take prisoners, but we couldn't find any."

HOW TO TAKE ISLANDS: As details of the Solomon campaign filtered through, it was obvious that U.S. forces had mastered a new technique of warfare which had caught the Japs flat-footed. Warships screening the transports first shelled the islands; carrier-based dive-bombers and long-range Army bombers from New Caledonia or Australia also softened up the Japs. Then the Marines streamed toward the beaches with new assault equipment. They had self-propelled, steel-walled barges. They had amphibious tanks. They had amphibious tractors, bearing combat engineers and equipment ashore with the first assault waves. They had Jeeps, wheeled machine guns, mortars, light artillery quickly trundled to the beaches from the barges. It was a brilliant demonstration of mobilized, concentrated fire power.

The Marines greatly outnumbered the Japs. This advantage they compounded by complete surprise and complete ruthlessness. For once the advantages were nearly all on the U.S. side. The Japs apparently had no planes on their almost-completed airdrome on Guadalcanal Island; they failed miserably with their air attacks when planes finally arrived from the upper Solomons and Rabaul. U.S. carrier planes constantly swarmed over, quickly based on Guadalcanal's airport after it was captured the second day. Guadalcanal fell with only minor resistance from snipers. Many of the Jap troops were sick with malaria. Great stores of trucks, ammunition and guns fell undamaged into U.S. hands.

NO PEACE IN THE SOLOMONS: How the Japanese behave SEPT. 21 when they have lost face—as they did when the Marines took their Solomon bases—was told last week when correspondents were allowed to describe a powerful Jap counterattack made on Aug. 24. It was a naval engagement on a scale only slightly smaller than the Battle of Midway.

On a morning as bright as a picture post card, a Japanese carrier force of some 40 warships appeared north of Tulagi, approaching in a great arc spread out over almost 1,700 miles of the tropic sea. U.S. ships and U.S. planes went out to meet it. The sky was soon filled with U.S. planes and the bombers and fighters of the enemy, wheeling around each other in no-man's-cloudland while once more the opposing surface fleets never once came in sight of each other.

With a grandstand seat on the bridge of a warship, the New York *Times*'s Foster Hailey watched the battle, listening to the disjointed radio talk of the young U.S. pilots at the scene of action:

"Here they come, Hank." . . .

"I see them. Very good. I think you got him, Lou." . . .

"There are about 26 bombers." . . .

"Peel off, Barney." . . .

"Here I go." . . .

The cold voice of a squadron leader ordered: "Hit the sons-of-bitches."

Meanwhile, on Guadalcanal itself, U.S. Marines fought off Zeros and bombers that were attacking there. This was only one Jap attack. A week later the persistent Japanese returned and under the cover of darkness put men and supplies ashore on the northern tip of Guadalcanal, to reinforce their guerrilla bands in the interior. Day after day, vengeful Jap bombers with their fighter escorts drummed overhead, dropping their explosives. Even submarines crept in close to Tulagi, tried to shell the Marines. The seizure of the Solomons had been only the beginning of a long and stubborn campaign.

SEPT. 28   **THE FIGHTINGEST SHIP:** The mighty *"Y"* is gone. Last week, three months and nine days after the carrier *Yorktown* sank near Midway, the Navy chose to announce her passing. How many men went down with "the *York"* the Navy did not say, but photographs of the survivors at Honolulu eloquently told of suffering and heroism.

At 2 p.m. on June 4, at the height of the Battle of Midway, Jap bombers found the *York*. Her planes had already been in furious battle. They had helped to sink three Jap carriers and were preparing to attack a fourth. At some 18,000 feet, the Jap planes looked like tiny match sticks. They dived for the *Yorktown*'s heart. Every gun of the carrier and her escort began to blaze. Tiny planes hesitated in their dives, made brief flowers of flame, fell into the sea. But a few kept coming at the *Yorktown*. The bombs slashed through the decks, started fires over the fuel tanks and magazines.

Crews worked frantically to control the fire and patch the twisted deck. But more Jap planes caught up with the limping carrier. They came in two waves: bombers and torpedo planes. Of more than a dozen torpedo planes, half were shot down before they neared the carrier. But eight came on, 50 feet over the water. The *Yorktown* tried to twist away, but two planes roared through the barrage and dropped their fish. The first torpedo hit squarely amidships. The second seemed to strike in the hole made by the first. Thick yellow smoke and flame vomited up with the spray. The 19,900-ton hull appeared to leap out of the water.

"I can't bear to look at her," said a young ensign, watching from an escort. Slowly the *Yorktown* turned on her side. Two planes clung like beetles to her slanting deck. "My God, she's going to capsize," an officer said, almost in a whisper. Then up went the blue & white flag: "Abandon ship."

Aboard the carrier two carpenter's mates and a petty officer were trapped in a compartment five decks below. The telephones were still working. Somebody called down: "Do you know what kinda fix you're in?" "Sure," they called back: "We know you can't get us out, but we got a hulluva good acey-deucey game goin' down here right now."

SOMETHING THEY ATE: The U.S. forces that had taken over OCT. 5 the South Seas island were in a hurry. An airfield had to be built and there was a lot of work to do. Native labor on the island was short. So Captain Martin Teems sent a sergeant to a nearby island to round up help. When the sergeant landed, the natives, attired in loincloths and belts of coconut husks, were in the midst of a happy community feast. Main dish: the ten wives of a neighboring tribe's chief. The sergeant waited around until the barbecue was over. Then he had no trouble getting his recruits. Explained Captain Teems to his nervous soldiers: "They only eat each other."

OCT. 12 **CAVIAR:** Last week a Navy officer revealed the report that the U.S. submarine *Sturgeon* radioed to its flagship after sinking its first Jap ship: *"Sturgeon* no longer virgin."

NOV. 2 **THE SINKING OF THE "WASP":** At 3:09 p.m. there was a mighty explosion; a whole piece of heaven seemed to catch fire. Jap torpedoes had hit near the U.S. carrier *Wasp*'s gasoline system, which was particularly vulnerable because the carrier's planes were then being refueled. Gasoline fires spread to the magazines; bombs and gasoline caused the explosion.

Before sending more torpedoes into her to put her out of her misery, accompanying U.S. destroyers had crept near, risking fire from burning gasoline on the water. They saved 90% of the *Wasp*'s crew.

Watching helplessly from a nearby ship, an old hand with greying hair and a cynical look said: "Well, that's three I've seen go—the *Lex*, the *Yorktown* and now this baby." Another officer said: "We'll just have to develop better methods of detection."

"NO TIME TO WRITE": A quiet, middle-aged man sat down to write his wife a letter. He began: "Have been so busy last few days, no time to write. . . ." The author of the terse sentence was Major General Alexander Archer Vandegrift, Commander of the Marines in the Solomons, and he certainly had been busy. He had lowered his high rank into damp foxholes. He had eaten captured Jap rice for want of anything better. Like his men, he had slapped mosquitoes, swum naked in the Lunga River. He had, moreover, led the U.S. Marines in the toughest job they ever did—the effort to hold Guadalcanal against a fierce Japanese counterattack.

How could it be so important to battle for a three-by-eight-mile patch of meadow, jungle and coconut grove in an economically worthless island? The Marines' beachhead on Guadalcanal is a geographic key. If the U.S. loses Guadalcanal, the Japanese can press on with relative ease, take the whole chain of islands down to New Caledonia, and then have only the narrow moat of the Coral Sea between them and Australia. But if the U.S. holds Guadalcanal, and can force its way up the chain as far as Rabaul, then the Allies will have a series of bases from which to build a major offensive. To the U.S., therefore, Archer Vandegrift's tiny patch of warfare is destiny.

THE SCORE ON ZEROS: The first Zero was easy. Smitty sent a burst into the Jap's rear and the plane fell into the sea off Guadalcanal. Then Smitty spotted another, banked sharply, caught the Zero full in his sights and that was two down in almost as many minutes. Telling about the exploit, Smitty was carefully casual:

"My third Zero came right up under the belly of my plane, sowing bullets up & down the fuselage. I dropped the nose of my plane and came at him head-on. One of his bullets hit my windshield right in front of my nose, but it missed me. My own bullets were tearing him apart. We tore past each other less than 15 feet apart. When I looked over my shoulder, he had lost control and was spinning down." With only a few rounds of ammunition left, Smitty headed home. As he skimmed over coconut palms he ran onto a hedgehopping Jap. "It wasn't even a fight," he said. In 15 minutes he had knocked down four Zeros.

This was a fast and dangerous life for Squadron Leader John Lucian Smith, accountant-trained son of an Oklahoma rural-mail carrier. But nineteen planes shot down in half as many months by the 27-year-old flyer probably made Major

Fighter pilot John Smith. Four Zeros in 15 minutes give him an edge.

General Stilwell: Hard of face, fast of foot and mind. Page 86.

John Smith the No. 1 U.S. war ace. Just behind Smitty as a Zero killer is Captain Marion Carl. Captain Carl lost five days' flying to Smith when he was shot down. He bailed out at about 15,000 feet, hit the water four miles from shore. He struggled four hours before a native picked him up in a canoe. The native hid Carl until he was strong enough to start back to camp on foot. But the Japs had landed between the Marines and the native village. "I fixed up an old motorboat the native had and went back by sea," Carl said, without explaining that he had had to putt-putt past Japanese-held beaches, where he was subject to fire.

"What's Major Smith's score?" was his first question when he reached his base. Told that Smith was further ahead than ever, Carl begged: "I was away five days. Ground him for five, General." Smitty was not grounded, but Carl got himself another fighter and went at it again.

NOV. 30   **HIT HARD, HIT FAST, HIT OFTEN:** Reports showed that the stubborn Japs had organized everything which they thought necessary to retake Guadalcanal once & for all. They formed a powerful bombardment task force, which was to come in with the most terrifying kind of attack. Then convoys of transports with over 20,000 troops with tanks and heavy artillery were to effect landings.

But Friday the 13th was not lucky for the Japs. At 2 a.m. a U.S. task force of cruisers and destroyers drove in on the Jap bombardment group. It was almost a Nelsonian stroke. At first Rear Admiral Daniel J. Callaghan led his task force right between two Japanese groups, so that when he pulled out the Japs fired on each other. In running the gantlet, Callaghan's flagship had crippled a Jap battleship, but a 14-in. salvo found the cruiser's bridge and killed the admiral.

On all the ships in the Fleet, Admiral "Bull" Halsey's battle cry was memorized: "Hit hard, hit fast, hit often." The few times the Japs had been hit, while reinforcing the Solomons, they had been hit and run from. But this time there was a new spirit in the U.S. task forces. The Americans came in slugging again and again. Another U.S. unit under Rear Admiral Norman Scott took part. He, too, was killed.

Altogether in the final engagement, the Japs suffered the

following sinkings: one battleship, another battleship or a very large cruiser, eight cruisers, six destroyers, eight troop transports, four cargo ships. They also lost a huge number of ground troops who had been taking their last ferry trip— between 20,000 and 40,000, Admiral Nimitz estimated. Halsey's battle had saved Guadalcanal.

Battle of Asia

"HELLO, SINGAPORE": On Nov. 18 the British War Office mysteriously announced that it had reserved a "special appointment" for Lieut. General Sir Henry Pownall. Last week, after an embarrassing hiatus, Sir Henry arrived at Singapore and the War Office specified: he was to replace sleepy, overconfident Air Chief Marshal Sir Robert Brooke-Popham as Commander in Chief of British forces in the Far East. The first thing Sir Henry did when he got to Singapore was to sit down with his staff to find out what had happened. He heard plenty: JAN. 5

The Jap was on a line roughly 300 miles above Singapore, but scattered patrols were already within 175 miles of the vital British base. The enemy had at first been grossly underestimated, not only as to numbers but also as to ability. It had never occurred to the British that little men in shorts and gym shoes could actually filter through Malayan jungles. Moreover, the British had not scorched the earth as they should have to make the Jap attack harder. At Penang, strategic island base on Malaya's east coast, they had left warehouses full of rubber, several months' supplies of rice, and —incredible blunder—all utilities working like a charm. At week's end the Japs had gone on the unscorched Penang radio and had repeatedly broadcast: "Hello, Singapore, how do you like our bombings?"

HONG KONG DIES: Hong Kong, born of opium and piracy, fat with a century's pleasure and profit, died last week in a blaze of glory. Only a few months ago had the British really begun to equip Hong Kong to meet a growing threat. They sent Canadian and British troops, new supplies and artillery. But when the Japanese struck, Hong Kong was still far from ready.

On Dec. 8 a few thousand men—English, Scottish, Canadian, Chinese, and Indian troops—faced two full Japanese divisions (30,000 or more). The first Japanese attack pierced the mainland line within 24 hours. Japanese artillery pumped streams of shell into the island positions. One by one British batteries went silent. British searchlights winked out. On Dec. 18 the Japanese burst across from mainland China to the island itself. The British fought on.

But by Dec. 23, there was only one day's supply of water left. On Christmas military authorities told the Government that no further effective resistance could be offered with the 6,000 exhausted troops still fighting. In the afternoon Sir Mark Young, Hong Kong's cricket-playing governor, crossed the blue strait to the mainland, met the Japanese in the swank Peninsula Hotel, where he surrendered. For the first time Britain had lost a Pacific outpost.

JAN. 12 **REPORT ON A GRIMNESS:** Somewhere in eastern Asia a good man reported to this chief this week on one of the shortest, strangest and grimmest commands ever held by a British general. The good man was General Sir Henry Royds Pownall, who only a fortnight earlier had become Britain's Far Eastern Commander. Now he was being promoted out of the job. One cause of the crisis at Singapore, General Pownall reported, was that the Japs were as good as animals in the jungle. With their bare hands they made rafts of logs and rode down rivers. They climbed in the trees and dropped, like monkeys, on passing patrols. Every hardship which a hungry animal could tolerate and many an ingenuity it could not conceive, they experienced and used. The British defenders had been too civilized for this sort of thing. They defended the airfields, stood at the bridges, guarded the cities, gallantly did everything the manuals said to do.

It is not clear whether General Pownall's predecessor, Air Chief Marshal Brooke-Popham, understood this problem. Although it was the Singapore custom to take an afternoon nap, he began to drop off at odd and inconvenient hours—in conference, at dinner parties. The result was that the Japanese quickly got command of the air over Malaya, and last week the Japanese bombed, not only the forward posts of land power, but the base of sea power, Singapore.

CITY FACING THE SEA: Like Hong Kong and Manila before FEB. 2 it, Singapore awaited its fate. It has been an Asiatic paradise for Occidentals and it was built to withstand attack from the sea. Its main reservoir of water is across the Strait in Johore and although there are emergency reservoirs on the island itself, the Jap might be able to thirst out the city's 600,-000 inhabitants. This week the enemy was within 40 miles of the main water supply.

The Jap has already bombed the city. Heavier raids are yet to come and Singapore is not ready for them. Its clammy soil is too wet for underground shelters. In Tokyo, over his shortwave radio, the Jap announced that the fall of Singapore was scheduled for Feb. 10.

As one base after another on the Asiatic mainland fell to the advancing Japanese armies, defending Allied troops were forced back. The most effective resistance was provided by a small force of mercenary fliers who operated out of Burma and China. Officially known as the American Volunteer Group but popularly called the "Flying Tigers," they were in the pay of Chinese Generalissimo Chiang Kai-shek and were commanded by a former American Army officer, Claire Chennault.

TIGERS OVER BURMA: Last week a young man from Chipley, FEB. 9 Ga. fell 17,000 feet through the Burma sky. His Curtiss P-40, shot out of control by a Jap, hurtled past him. At 7,000 feet he pulled his parachute cord. The young man and his parachute plopped into a rice field. A Burmese farmer spewed mouthfuls of water on his bloody forehead. Others fed him, sped him back to his airdrome at Rangoon. Said the young man from Georgia: "I got back so late the skipper didn't have me down on the next day's flying schedule. That's how you caught me loafing now."

But the American Volunteer Group in Burma and China did little loafing. At Rangoon, on the ocean entry to the Burma Road, at Kunming, on its inner terminus, at many an airdrome between, A.V.G.'s 100-odd U.S. pilots brightened last week's dark record of war in the Pacific with great valor and victories. Said a spectator in Rangoon: "It looked like a fleet of rowboats attacking the Spanish Armada."

A.V.G.'s spark plug from the start, its commander in Burma now, is a famous U.S. flyer: lean, dark Brigadier General Claire L. Chennault of Water Proof, La. Claire Chennault flew for the U.S. in World War I, was a major when he retired from the U.S. Air Corps. In the early '30s he organized a fabulous Army team of aerobats ("Three Men on a Flying Trapeze"), thrilled thousands of air-meet spectators.

Claire Chennault quit the Air Corps (officially he was retired for deafness), and became a consultant to the fledgling Chinese Air Force in 1937. Last year Claire Chennault came home and began to organize his new group. Air Corps and Navy pilots and flying students were allowed to resign to go to the defense of the vital Burma Road. Their promised pay: in action, $600 per month and a $500 bonus for every plane shot down (which with last week's total bag would run their take well past $60,000).

FEB. 23 **THE END FOR SINGAPORE:** It fell to an unfortunate young major named Wilde to carry the white flag toward Japanese headquarters. He reached Lieut. General Tomoyuki Yamashita at 2:30 p.m. and asked for conditions of surrender. General Yamashita had the conditions written out. At 4:15 Major Wilde left for the British lines inside Singapore. He promised to be back with an answer by 5:30. And so, what with the comings & goings, Major Wilde's commander, Lieut. General Arthur Ernest Percival, had less than an hour in which to make his decision.

The decision was inevitable because the Japanese had captured Singapore's reason for existence, the Naval Base. They had captured its means of subsistence, the reservoirs. They had flanked the city and destroyed or seized the airfields. They had cut off its rear by knocking out evacuating ships. And so General Percival made the hard, the humiliating choice. He went, as directed, to a Ford Motor plant where, earlier that day, there had been bloody fighting. There, at 7 p.m. on Feb. 15, he signed away large pieces of the land, the power and the pride of the British Empire.

STIFF UPPER LIP: From Fort Changi, Singapore, now an in- ternment camp for British Imperials, a wide-eyed Japanese correspondent wrote last week:

"At one place along the way we passed a band of Scottish Highlanders marching toward internment, blowing lustily all the while on bagpipes. A monocled officer led them, sporting a cane in place of his saber. Not one face carried a shadow of sadness. The more I see of them the more these men amaze me."

CHINA'S AMERICAN: Generalissimo Chiang Kai-shek last week appointed a U.S. Army officer his Chief of Staff. The officer: peppery Lieut. General Joseph W. Stilwell. When General Stilwell arrived in Chungking a fortnight ago, the Chinese welcomed an old friend who literally spoke their language. Off & on, he has spent 15 years in China and has perfected his Chinese dialects. General Stilwell is a soldier's officer, whose one passion is leading and training troops. His mouth is thin, his face hard and decisive beneath greying black hair. Fast of foot and mind, General Stilwell is forever barking: "Yah-Yah!" when his thoughts leap ahead of a companion's words. When they jump far ahead, he barks in triplicate: "Yah-yah-yah!"

BURMA SURGEON: Outnumbered 10-to-1 in the air, 3-to-1 on the ground, the Allies all but conceded the loss of Burma last week. As the retreating British prepared to demolish the oilfields and refineries in their rear, TIME Correspondent Jack Belden visited the front where Chinese troops defended Burma under U.S. command. His dispatch follows:

"I found a British liaison officer driving a bus, trying to pick up wounded from the fires. He brought five Chinese soldiers to a makeshift hospital. There, in a palm-treed courtyard on an open, unroofed stone porch, I saw a muscular white man, stripped to the waist, making swift jabs with a surgeon's knife in a struggling Chinese soldier's arm. Three 90-lb. Burmese nurses were holding down the soldier. Gas lamps strung on wires provided the only light.

"The soldier grew violent. The Burmese girls were unable to hold him down. The surgeon held with one hand and cut with the other. The soldier moaned in Chinese: "*Ma ma,*" calling his mother in the same sounds we use. The doctor, his body gleaming with sweat in the tropic night heat, finished the operation, picked up the patient, carried him off in his arms, laid him on the floor in an inside room, picked up another Chinese soldier and resumed operating. The nurses rushed out to the courtyard and washed towels in a pool beneath the palm trees.

"I gasped: 'Who are you?' He answered: 'My name is Seagrave,' and turned back to operating. He was Burma-born Gordon Seagrave of the American Baptist Mission. Seagrave called to the British liaison officer: 'Try to get us some food. Some of these soldiers have not eaten for three days.'

"As I went out ambulance units were bringing in more Chinese wounded in American Jeeps; all of them would be handled by Seagrave, who was the only surgeon there. The house was full of wounded. When he buried two dead, under the moon, he said: 'Now that the shooting has started, we have got to get down to work. Nobody's doing enough.' " [Dr. Seagrave remained in Burma after the war and in 1950 was arrested on charges of aiding tribesmen in a rebellion against the Burmese government because he donated medicine to them. He was found guilty of treason, but later cleared. He died in 1965.]

MAY 11 **FAREWELL TO MANDALAY:** From Burma this week TIME Correspondent Jack Belden sent the following report on the campaign that came to an unhappy end with the fall of Mandalay:

"This is probably my last message. I'm staying with General Stilwell and a small command post directing the rearguard action. The Japanese are driving with incredible speed, swinging wide of both our east and west flanks and somehow we have to get the troops out of this closing-in trap. They are moving forward 25 miles a day. It is this terrific Jap pressure, plus food and water scarcity and the lack of roads to India, that makes the task so difficult.

"In the midst of writing these words, I heard a sudden roar, looked overhead at a transport plane circling in low to land. 'Don't that plane look good. Go kiss it,' cries an American enlisted man. Someone sings *God Bless America.*

The list is now being made out of those who will evacuate. At any rate I won't go, and 'Uncle Joe' Stilwell will stay to the last to direct his troops.

"Now everyone at Stilwell's Headquarters but Headquarters' doctor and myself has gone. We will set the houses afire with all diaries, documents and anything of value as soon as it gets dark, and leave early tomorrow morning to try to catch Stilwell. I have just come from the tank corps with a thousand rounds of machine-gun ammunition and we hope this is enough to last out our small unit on what promises to be a long journey through an uncharted area. The doctor and I killed a sheep which we put in a burlap bag, for emergency, but someone has stolen this already and we will have to manage to get along on a can of cheese we discovered in the litter. I must close and try to rush this off. All about me there is nothing but utmost misery. Roads are lined with belongings abandoned by refugees, 20,000 of whom crossed the Irrawaddy only yesterday, hoping to get to India, but their chance is very slight.

"Must go. Goodby."

TIGERS' LAST LEAPS: The most terrifying battle cry of World War II will soon be heard no longer on the headquarters' radio. British pursuit pilots will still call to one another their sporting "Tally-ho" as they sight the enemy; the serious Germans will still rasp their guttural *"Achtung! Achtung!"* But the gallant, hell-for-leather professional pilots of the American Volunteer Group suddenly glimpsing a Jap formation will no longer have reason to exchange their gleeful call: "Certified check!"

The Army has decided that it was no longer good business that some U.S. fighting men paid by the Chinese Government should get $600 a month plus a bonus of $500 per enemy plane downed. Perhaps more important: all A.V.G.'s battle-won know-how on the technique of destroying Japs was far too precious to keep concentrated—it needed to be spread through the U.S. air forces. So Chiang Kai-shek's light-hearted U.S. mercenaries will soon be back in Federal service along with their seam-faced leader Claire L. Chennault.

It was fun while it lasted.

JUNE 1 **THE GISSIMO'S WAR:** "Let them come," Generalissimo Chiang Kai-shek said in the summer of 1940, when Chungking morale reached an all-war low, "let them drive me back into Tibet. In five years I will be back here and I will conquer all China again."

But today the Gissimo, usually a monument of calm confidence, makes no secret of the fact that he is more worried than at any time in five years. To a man of 54, who since 23 has devoted every waking moment of his life to making his country one, the current Japanese invasion of south China threatens the worst possible personal calamity.

Chiang the soldier says very little to his men. He listens to their reports, their suggestions or their fears. Then, with a single grunted word, *hao* (good) or *pu* (no), he makes his decision. He is a stern disciplinarian, and keeps his army taut. When he visits the fronts, he blurts words of praise or of withering criticism on the spot, in public hearing.

No matter how much he educated his peasant army, Chiang would never be able to stamp out all its superstitions. One is that Chiang is the reincarnation of a great sea beast which used to live in the waters near Fenghua and sun himself on the sands. They say that if it rains when Chiang goes out to battle, he will win; if it shines, he will lose.

There is shrewd reality in this peasant superstition. If Chiang goes out to fight in rainy weather, the enemy cannot use his planes. Since Chiang has almost no planes himself this makes a difference. In Chungking last week, a government spokesman explained that embattled China has three needs: "1) bombers and pursuit planes; 2) bombers and pursuit planes; 3) bombers and pursuit planes."

UNCLE JOE TURNS UP: Out of the wreck of Burma last week came Lieut. General Joseph W. Stilwell. When the outside world had last heard of him, "Uncle Joe" and his Chinese Fifth and Sixth Armies were cut off, and had swung north in a ferocious slash at the back of the Jap. There was no more word until he turned up at the northeastern India frontier leading a motley column.

Later, to correspondents at New Delhi, Uncle Joe said: "I claim we got a hell of a beating. We got run out of Burma and it is humiliating as hell."

CHENNAULT'S SHACK: Tokyo Radio complained that Brigadier NOV. 16
General Claire Chennault's U.S. flyers in China fought un-
fairly: they zipped into target areas, dropped their bombs
and zipped right out again before the Japs had a chance to
fight back. Unless Chennault changed his tactics, said the
Japs, they would take stern measures.

Last week they did. For the first time in many weeks, the
Japs bombed one of General Chennault's airdromes. The
Japs zipped in and zipped right out, but not before they
had lost one bomber and three fighters. Chennault reported
the U.S. loss: "One Chic Sale shack."

Battle of the Atlantic

A GRIM THING: Twelve hours out of New York, 60 miles off JAN 26
Long Island's fingerlike tip at Montauk Point, the Panamian
tanker *Norness* pressed toward Halifax. She carried 10,000
tons of fuel and a 40-man Scandinavian crew. Suddenly a torpedo ripped into the tanker's hull on the port side. Ten
minutes later another direct hit was scored from starboard.
A third, final torpedo struck again from port side. A fishing
boat, U.S. destroyer and Coast Guard cutter picked up the
38 chilled survivors. Said Skipper Harold Hansen: "I thought
we were just as safe there as in New York harbor."

Less than 36 hours later torpedoes caught the 6,768-ton
British tanker *Coimbra* a scant 20 miles from Southampton,
L.I., only 100 miles east of New York City, and left it sinking. Off the North Carolina coast the heavily laden U.S.
tanker *Allan Jackson* swerved desperately to avoid a torpedo
that broke water 150 yards short of its mark, then scored a direct hit amidships. Only 13 of the crew of 35 reportedly
survived. Also off North Carolina the tanker *Malay* was torpedoed but limped to safety. The Battle of the Atlantic is,
in 1942, a grim thing.

DOENITZ'S WAR: The Battle of the Atlantic was awesomely FEB. 2
close to the U.S. coast, and the man most interested in the
fate of German subs in Yankee waters was thin-lipped, seam-
faced, British-hating Vice Admiral Karl Doenitz, creator

and Commander of Germany's U-boat fleet. Win or lose his end of the war, Karl Doenitz will never lose the dubious historical honor of being the man who laid the groundwork for the greatest submarine fleet in history, in utter defiance of the Versailles Treaty and under the very noses of Allied investigating missions.

At 50 he has devoted half his life to submarines. He is a master of every phase of his subject. He perfected a liaison system between plane and submarine. His training of submarine crews emphasized democratic relationships between officers and men to avoid the difficulty with mutinous officer-bullied crews which helped break down the German U-boat service in World War I. He supervised every detail of submarine construction, and was responsible for the dispersal of factories throughout occupied Europe to escape British bombings.

Two years ago Karl Doenitz declared that "it makes no difference to the present-day German U-boat fleet whether British ships sail alone or are convoyed." But as U.S. strength showed up in British convoys, Karl Doenitz changed his mind, emerged with a new, radical offensive technique known as the "wolf pack": several submarines attack the center of a convoy, preferably at night, loose torpedoes in every direction, slip away at top surface speed.

Some, though by no means all, of Germany's sub commanders in the last war were dashing, romantic figures, ruthless in their destruction of merchant tonnage but usually solicitous over welfare of survivors. But Doenitz has not trained his men for gallantry. His victims are in Davy Jones' locker.

MARCH 16 **"JAKIE" TO DAVY:** Destroyers are built to hand out punishment, not to take it. If a lurking submarine gets in the first punch, they have not much chance, especially old four-pipers like the *Jacob Jones*. The "Jakie," as her crew called her, was off Cape May, N.J. when the first torpedo crumpled her bow, probably killing every officer and man on the bridge and most of the men in the forward sleeping quarters. Less than a minute later, a second torpedo blew in the stern, exploding some of the destroyer's own depth charges.

The bow and stern of the *Jacob Jones* broke off and

sank, leaving the center section afloat. The rest went down with a mighty explosion that tossed nearby swimmers into the air like popcorn. The sun was high in the sky when a rescue boat found the survivors; eleven enlisted men out of a complement of 122 officers and men. *Jakie* was the first U.S. warship ever torpedoed in her own coastal waters.

SOLE SURVIVOR: From a hospital in the Canal Zone last APRIL 6 week came one of the grisliest tales of the war. It was told by a haggard, wan-eyed, bearded sailor, who looked like a man of 50. He was a mess boy named Robert Emmett Kelly, aged 17, sole survivor of a middle-sized tanker that a Nazi sub potted somewhere in the Caribbean.

The torpedo struck at dusk. The cargo of petroleum was ablaze in an instant. On the stern of the tanker, Kelly and ten shipmates struggled frantically with a lifeboat. In launching, the lifeboat turned over, and Kelly and his shipmates hid under it when the sub cut loose with deck guns. When things quieted down, they righted the boat and bailed it out, found that they had eleven cans of condensed milk, some hardtack and chocolate, a compass and a small dictionary with a map of the Western Hemisphere.

After that it was all bad. Somebody stole the milk and drank it. Without water, the men were afraid to eat the hardtack and chocolate. They ate seaweed and some of them drank sea water.

Hunger, thirst and the Caribbean sun began to madden and kill them. The cook, with $163 in his pockets, stepped casually over the bulwarks, remarking: "I'm just going across the street to get some pineapples." Another shipmate ate a jellyfish and jumped screaming over the side. Another, in demented fury before he died, tossed the one bucket of rain water overboard.

By the third week only Kelly and another mess boy were left. When his side-kick gave up, Kelly waited 36 hours before he tossed him overboard to make sure he was dead. "After that," he said, "I laid down and tried to make myself comfortable, hoping that I could die without any more trouble." He was lying there waiting for death when his lifeboat nuzzled into a small steamer. His open-boat voyage had lasted 21 days.

AUG. 31 **INVITATION TO DESTRUCTION:** The U.S. cargo ship's skipper ordered his radio operator to relay the S O S he had picked up which reported another ship in distress some 30 miles distant in the South Atlantic. Soon night closed down over the unruffled sea and the third officer spotted lights about three miles away. Swiftly the lights grew closer. At three-quarters of a mile the approaching ship opened fire. Shells from 8-in. guns tore into the cargo vessel and torpedoes from the deck tubes of the attacker plowed through the sea.

It was a Nazi trap, baited with cynical confidence that a U.S. merchant ship would observe the law of the sea and relay a distress signal, thereby revealing her own position. As the lifeboats were lowered, machine-gun fire forced the occupants to leap into the sea and swim for a raft. Within half an hour the cargo ship went down. The few survivors of the sinking were the first eyewitnesses to confirm the presence of an armed Nazi raider in the South Atlantic.

Battle of Europe

JAN. 12 **FIFTEEN MINUTES:** "Norwegians, your fellow-countrymen are here, and with them your British allies. We wish you a good Christmas and a happy New Year. We bring you this greeting from all free men."

Cheery as a birthday sing-o-gram, that message boomed through the loud-speaker of a British ship, one of several anchored brazenly last week off the German-held Lofoten Islands on Norway's jagged northwestern coast. Bearers of the greeting were Britain's tough Commandos, bent on destruction of radio equipment guiding German shipping along the Axis sea route to the Arctic fighting front in Russia.

The raiders took over in 15 minutes flat, destroyed a radio mast and transmitter, shot down a lone plane offering resistance, sank a German patrol boat, took several prisoners including six quislings. The Commandos did not lose a man. Simultaneously another Commando unit made successful raids on Vaagsoy and Maaloy islands, assembly points for German troop and supply ships. There 95 Germans and nine quislings were collared. In Commando-weary Vidkun Quisling's official newspaper there later appeared an angry complaint: other Norwegians had painted signs on the quislings' homes to identify them for the Commandos.

PADDY DOWN: Londoners sometimes see him on his infrequent MARCH 2 play nights, striding through the restaurants and bars with an air of careless majesty. There, the onlooker instantly feels, is somebody. He is somebody: Brendan ("Paddy") Finucane, Irish leader of Australia's famous No. 452 Fighter Squadron. To 21-year-old Squadron Leader Finucane's credit, up to last week, were 25 German planes shot down, scores of fighter-bomber attacks on Nazi shipping in the Channel and on Nazi targets in Occupied France. In compiling this record, Paddy had had a lot of luck. His plane had been badly shot up only once. He limped for awhile, but not from enemy bullets: he fell off a wall at Croydon, while celebrating an R.A.F. victory. Last week Squadron Leader Finucane's luck turned.

Two Focke-Wulfs attacked him and Pilot Officer Richard Lewis while they were harrying a Nazi steamer. One of the Focke-Wulfs riddled Finucane's plane and wounded him in the leg and thigh. By radio he ordered Lewis to run for home. Lewis disobeyed. He hovered behind Finucane's tail, fought off repeated Focke-Wulf attacks while Finucane and Lewis scurried back to their home airdrome. Squadron Leader Finucane (pronounced Fin-YOU-kin) taxied his fighter up to the line and then collapsed at the controls.

PADDY BACK: All through a winter of dirty flying weather— MARCH 23 too dirty for big-scale raiding—British airpower had been bristling, waiting. Now the open season was on. One night a force of more than 100 British heavy bombers bore down on Cologne (chemicals, munitions, transportation). The raiders saw scores of fierce fires knitting a red blanket for the city. Equally devastating attacks were made on Essen (home of the vast Krupp works) and the vital port of Kiel.

With fighter protection, R.A.F. day raiders hammered factories, ports and rail yards in northern France, Nazi airdromes in France, Holland and Belgium. Famed Squadron Leader Paddy Finucane, his leg wounds mended, returned to action, downed two more Nazis, raising his score to 27.

MAY 4 **"ON TARGET":** In an antiaircraft station in the south of England the siren murdered sleep. Eight girls of an ATS (Auxiliary Territorial Service) crew slapped on tin hats, raced for the gun pit. Jerry was upstairs. The detectors had him pegged. Turning the little knobs on her gun predictor, 18-year-old Private Nora Caveney cried: "On target." As the guns spat, came the high whine of German bombs, a crash. A hot, jagged bomb splinter ripped through the sandbags and struck Nora Caveney in the chest. Another girl jumped into her place; another treble cry went up: "On target."

In a village churchyard nearby, Private Nora Caveney was buried last week, the first ATS girl to die in action against the enemy. Said her C.O.: "Seasoned soldiers could not have behaved better." From all over England came polite letters asking for Nora Caveney's picture.

JULY 6 **IKE LANDS:** The man who may wear the mantle of Pershing in World War II landed in England last week and took over a new command: U.S. forces in the European theater. Army men cried "Amen" to his appointment. A colonel only nine months ago, 51-year-old, Texas-born "Ike" Eisenhower is no flash in the pan. Since he left West Point in 1915 he has been pushing along. Made a lieutenant colonel in 1918, he was dropped back to a captaincy after the war.

Eisenhower. Nine months ago a colonel, he takes command in Europe.

Paddy Finucane. The ace calls, "This is it, chaps," and is gone. Page 96.

The big chance came when he went to the Philippines as Douglas MacArthur's assistant in 1935. The reputation he made there and in the 1941 Louisiana maneuvers (as Chief of Staff of the Third Army) carried him to Washington, where he soon became head of the vital Operations Division of the General Staff.

PADDY UP: "Positively no alcoholic beverages," says a sign in a U.S. officers' club, "will be sold to Air Corps lieutenant colonels under 21 unless accompanied by their parents."

The U.S. Army Air Forces' accent on youth (which has brought up two brigadier generals at 36) had not yet made this jest a verity last week. But Britain's R.A.F. came close to it. Upped to the rank of Acting Wing Commander was Britain's top fighter pilot, wavy-haired, blue-eyed Brendan Finucane. With a rank corresponding to lieutenant colonel, Paddy Finucane was 21. Officially credited with 28 German ships, Finucane for months has led a squadron made up of Australians, Czechs, French, Irish, Scots, Welsh, Canadians, South Africans, Hollanders and Britons. Few R.A.F. men doubted that, as lead man in a wing (two or more squadrons), Paddy Finucane could make his elders hop to his command.

PADDY GONE: Behind his Spitfire, with the green sham- JULY 27 rock on its side, thundered the other ships in the command of the R.A.F.'s leading ace (32 planes): Brendan Finucane. Paddy was on his last sweep. As he led his wing low over German installations on the French beach, his second-in-command saw something Finucane did not see: a small machine-gun post perched about 20 feet above the beach on a ridge of sand. Finucane's second-in-command, whose name was Aikman, saw a burst from the machine gun go through Paddy's starboard wing and radiator. Aikman called on his radio: "You've had it, sir—in your radiator."

Finucane replied: "I shall have to get out of this."

Aikman followed him as he turned out over the sea, trying to get as near England as possible with his failing engine. Ten miles from the French coast Aikman saw the Spitfire with the green shamrock level off, drop its tail, hit the sea. Just before it crashed he heard Paddy's voice on the radio: "This is it, chaps." The ship sank like a stone.

AUG. 31 **REHEARSAL AT DIEPPE:** It was a hot, muggy night on a lifeless Channel. Before dawn His Majesty's destroyers, transports, and launches and a mile-long string of invasion barges laden with troops and tanks were off the French seaside resort of Dieppe, hidden in the night's retreating skirts.

The strategy was simple. The British Commandos were to land by stealth and distract German forces while the Canadians carried the main show, with flanking attacks against the chalk cliffs on both sides of Dieppe and a frontal assault on Dieppe's beaches. As they came in, the Germans raked them. Many a Canadian soldier never reached shore. Many died in the sand where English honeymooners once frolicked or fell on Dieppe's pretty esplanade. But in other sectors Canadians in tanks and afoot cut their way through barbed wire; stormed into the city; occupied the casino, which the Germans had turned into a fortress; blasted snipers out of boarded-up resort hotels; destroyed gun emplacements and a radio-locator station; rounded up Nazi prisoners; staggered, wounded, back to the shore. Throughout the whole chaotic morning some 1,000 planes, flown by British, U.S., Czech, Polish, Canadian, New Zealand, Norwegian, Belgian and Fighting French flyers, fended off the *Luftwaffe,* dropped more than 200,000 lb. of destruction on enemy positions.

This week the Canadians licked their wounds. Losses in manpower were known to be high—probably two to three thousand. The Allies confessed that they had met unexpected resistance. Said the British: "The raid was a reconnaissance in force, having a vital part of our agreed offensive policy." That offensive policy presumably was an eventual second front, for which the Canadians had staged a costly rehearsal.

SEPT. 14 **GREMLINS:** The R.A.F. first learned about the little creatures and called them gremlins—probably from the obsolete Old English transitive verb greme, meaning: to vex. The R.A.F. also learned that a female gremlin is a finella and that the babies are widgets.

Usually gremlins are about a foot high. They wear soft, pointed suede shoes (occasionally spats), tight green breeches, red jackets with a ruffle at the neck and stocking caps or flat-topped tricorn hats with a jaunty feather. The R.A.F.

Coastal Command believed at first that the gremlins climbed aboard in mid-air from the wings of sea gulls. It is generally believed now, however, that the gremlins have wings on their shoulders.

Fighter pilots often are bothered by gremlins who sit on their shoulders and make a noise like a knocking motor when the motor is running smoothly. When a pilot has been flying for a long time through clouds, a gremlin may whisper into the pilot's ear: "You fathead, you're flying upside down!" The pilot then hurriedly turns over and flies upside down while the gremlin laughs and laughs, silently. Another favorite gremlin trick is to climb into gun barrels and deflect bullets. (But usually this is done by widgets.) Sometimes a gremlin puts his finger over a carburetor jet and makes the motor sound for a moment as if it were conking out.

Bomber pilots say that the most annoying gremlins are those which like to use the ship's compass for a merry-go-round while the pilots are trying to fly blind. The most dangerous gremlins are those which delight in covering bombers' wings with ice or slide down the radio beam when a plane is making a landing.

For nearly three years the gremlins devoted themselves exclusively to the R.A.F. But recently Sergeant Gunner Z. E.

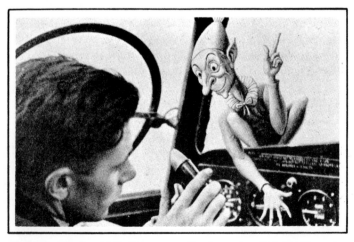

A gremlin visits the cockpit. They are usually about a foot high and like to use the compass for a merry-go-round.

White of Dallas, Tex. had the guns on his Flying Fortress jam just as he got a German Focke-Wulf in his sights over the North Sea. When White reported what had happened, Pilot Oscar Coen, who had flown with the R.A.F., nodded his head sagely. A noted gremlinologist, Coen knew then that the gremlins had now joined the U.S. Air Forces.

OCT. 19 **PHYLLIS THE FABULOUS FORTRESS:** Phyllis is a Flying Fortress. She had been sent to bomb an aircraft factory in France and had just roared over her target when the 30 Focke-Wulfs pounced on her. Two of Phyllis' gunners fainted as shells smashed their oxygen equipment. Cannon shells knocked out one of Phyllis' engines. Pilot Charles Paine headed Phyllis downwards to revive the two gunners. The Nazi fighters closed in for the kill.

The coast was a solid wall of antiaircraft fire but Phyllis got through it. Lumbering along, minus another engine now, she wobbled out over the Channel. There was a shell hole in Phyllis' wing, three shell holes in her rudder, three in her stabilizer. Half her controls were shot away, her landing gear was wrecked, her upper turret was shot away, her fuselage was a sieve. But she shot back and in mid-Channel the pursuing Nazi fighter fled.

Like a weary, wounded bird, Phyllis took a long dive for England. The nearest airdrome in England was too small for fat Phyllis, but Pilot Paine decided to try it before Phyllis collapsed. She was going too fast over the pocket-size drome and neither of her remaining engines would cut out. Paine lifted her up again, knocking some bricks from an airfield building. He careened around and headed back. This time he let Phyllis brush the tops of some trees to slow her down. Her flaps refused to work, her wheels would not come down. She landed on her belly. Phyllis had to be patched and her gunner had to go to the hospital for a head cut. But the rest of her crew were back on duty last week.

OCT. 26 **"NOTHING TO SPEAK OF":** The Dieppe story of Canadian Corporal Joseph A. Gregory, 42, as told to TIME Correspondent B. T. Richardson last week:

"My buddy, Silver Stewart, we worked together. Stew would kick in a door while I covered it with my tommy gun. Stew sure kicked in them doors. Jeeze, he was a good guy. Then he took a wounded man down to the beach and I lost him. He got hit and died on the last boat going back to England. I worked on alone.

"About 11:45 a.m. I heard the orders shouted for evacuation. I went back to the beach. There was an assault boat stuck, so I ran out to help push it off. A ricocheted bullet smacked me on the forehead, knocking me into the water. I couldn't see out of one eye.

"Jeeze, there was a lot of stuff flying around. I got on another landing boat, but it sunk in a few minutes. I swam out to this boat, kicking off my tunic, and caught hold of a rope. There was a guy hanging to each of my legs and I couldn't move. The Jerries were firing at us from the top of the cliff and lots of the fellows were getting wounded all over again.

"I let go that boat and made for a gunboat. Mac pulled me aboard, that's Sergeant Major McEvoy, a grand guy. He told me my eye was gone and he bandaged my forehead. We got orders to transfer to a destroyer and Mac practically carried me up those ropes. I was pretty weak. He put me in the sick bay and said: 'You'll be all right now, Joe.'

"Then we got dive-bombed and a big hole was blown in the sick bay. The water poured in and the backwash washed me right out through that hole. Another gunboat came steaming in and picked me up. We finally pulled out, and had a few engagements going home, but nothing to speak of."

Battle of Africa

Italian troops had invaded North Africa in 1940 to secure the Mediterranean, conquer Egypt and gain control of the Suez Canal. They had done so badly, however, that German units under General Erwin Rommel had gone to their rescue in February 1941. Now the British were fighting both.

TOUGH SPONGE: The spongy little island of Malta, 60 miles APRIL 6 south of Sicily, is the most heavily and frequently bombed stronghold of World War II—and therefore in the history of the world—and from the impatient Axis last week it got its heaviest raids of the war.

Not only does Malta straddle the Axis supply route to Libya; it also threatens the left flank of any Axis drive along the African coast toward Egypt. Submarines glide in & out of the harbor at Valletta. Bombers and fighters come out of hiding in hangars dug deep in the limestone and take off from rocky fields in the hills. The British believe that Malta's concentration of antiaircraft guns is the heaviest in the world, not even excepting Moscow's.

Recently the Germans sent the *Luftwaffe*'s Field Marshal Albert Kesselring to Sicily, already bristling with German airpower. Kesselring had a blueprint ready for Malta; he cocked his fist and let fly across the short gap of blue water. Wave after wave of *Stukas* came over, hour after hour, day after day.

After 1,600-odd air attacks, the 270,000 people of Malta are hardened to raids, and so are their goats and donkeys. Between attacks, movies and markets are crowded. But when the bombers come, the people take to the caves and catacombs.

These shelters have been enlarged so that every civilian in Malta can go underground. The soft limestone and coral rock is easy to excavate, but when exposed to air it hardens like concrete.

Geologically, Malta is a sponge. Militarily, it is a rock.

APRIL 27 **ALL-MALTESE CROSS:** All the 270,000 people of much-bombed Malta last week were awarded the George Cross, which is given for spectacular feats of civilian bravery. It was the first time ever that a British King had thus decorated a fortress, an island, a whole people.

MAY 18 **TIGER ON DUTY:** Appointed British Governor of Malta, General the Viscount ("Tiger") Gort, 55, onetime Chief of the Imperial General Staff, arrived at Malta in the teeth of a heavier-than-usual air attack.

Sworn in while bombs were dropping, by a chief justice whose hand was bleeding, Tiger Gort fell on his face when a bomb crashed close by.

*The campaign along the North African coast was one of lo-
gistics. As the British, attacking out of Egypt, confidently
pushed the Germans farther and farther to the west, their supply lines were stretched increasingly thin. At the port of
Tobruk in Libya, Rommel struck back.*

ROMMEL MARCHES ON: For the British it was utter, humiliat- JUNE 29
ing defeat. Tobruk, the same battle-scarred port that last
year held out for eight months against Axis besiegers, suc-
cumbed quickly, squashily, to the planes, tanks and guns of
Germany's Erwin Rommel. The Axis announced that it
took 28,000 Allied prisoners in the garrison, including "several generals."

Rommel was well known to be a demoniac master of desert
war, but neither the British nor the U.S. public was prepared
for Tobruk's fall. One thing Rommel did was to let the British exhaust themselves winning their "victories," then throw
in his reserves to take the real victory. Moreover, he changed
the pattern of desert warfare by stepping up the role of artillery. When the British, confident of equal armor and equal or
greater air strength, attacked Rommel's line, the German sur-
prised them with a massive assembly of 88-mm. antitank guns
and the British tanks took a dismal mauling.

HOTHOUSE TRAINING: When Hitler decided in 1940 to put JULY 13
Rommel in charge of the *Afrika Korps* and send him to
strengthen the stumbling Italians in Libya, Rommel began
to train the kind of army that could fight a successful desert
war. His carefully picked soldiers lived in overheated bar-
racks, learned to get along on dried food and vitamins,
little water. Wind machines blew up artificial sandstorms.
Rommel acclimated himself in a private hothouse.

Once his men were in Africa, Rommel made them as comfortable as possible. Rations included beer, coffee, tinned
and fresh meat, lemons, potatoes, onions. At the rest camps
in the rear there were beer gardens, brass bands, playing
grounds, movies. Rommel never tells his men that the British are pushovers. He tells them that the British are tough—
and that they, the thin, hard young elite of Germany, must
be tougher. As a successful man, Rommel is vain, arrogant

The Afrika Korps' General Erwin Rommel shares lunch in the Libyan Desert. He is arrogant, autocratic—and able.

and autocratic. When things go awry in battle, he showers everyone around him with a stream of vituperation, usually beginning with "*Schweinehunde!*"

One lesson that many British generals have yet to learn from him is adequate reconnaissance. Rommel leaves nothing so important as reconnaissance to others, if he can help it. At the risk of his life and of capture, he haunts the front lines at night. When he makes decisions they are based on facts. Rommel demands results from those who work for him and he doesn't care what the results cost. A new aide-de-camp (fifth in a few months) recently arrived to report to him. "Let me wish you luck," the Marshal snapped. "Your four predecessors were killed."

Seizing the initiative at Tobruk, Rommel counterattacked, driving the British back 300 miles before they were able to dig in at El Alamein.

AUG. 19   **BIRTHDAY:** Il Duce had expected to celebrate his 59th birthday in Egypt. When Tobruk fell he rushed through the air to North Africa to lead the victorious march into Alexandria. On the way, R.A.F. pilots knocked down a convoying plane, killing his personal chef and personal barber. Loss of the barber was not so bad, since Il Duce is as bald as a monkey's bottom, but loss of the cook was dismal. Furthermore, Rommel was not getting to Alexandria, and there could be no triumphal procession. Il Duce returned to Rome, where the subject of his birthday was not mentioned.

NEW COMMANDER: Britain's new commander in the Middle AUG. 31 East, General Sir Harold Rupert Leofric George Alexander, once had a conversation with a literary friend. The author stared at the soldier, and said: "Tell me something I have always wanted to know, Alex. You're really very intelligent, aren't you?" Alexander winked. "I am," he said.

The British last week put their hopes in General Harold Alexander's intelligence and in his reputation as an aggressive fighting man. At 50, he is the youngest full general in the British Army. Under him, in direct command of the Eighth Army in Egypt, he has Lieut. General Bernard Law Montgomery, a 54-year-old Ulsterman who is also a veteran of the retreat from France.

ROMMEL STALLED: This week Rommel began his long-awaited SEPT. 14 action with feints toward the north, then a jab at the southern front. With his entire *Afrika Korps* of four divisions he struck at the British lines, penetrated some distance into British mine fields, swung toward the seacoast. But Alexander and Montgomery were ready for him. This time the British broke Rommel's drive before it got fully under way and kept pressing him back on his heels until he grudgingly edged back from a battlefield littered with his demolished tanks and motor vehicles.

"DESTROY ROMMEL": The British preparations for battle at El NOV. 2 Alamein had been on a scale indicating an effort to retake all of conquered North Africa. On the 40-mile line near the Mediterranean, the Germans had a fixed and deeply fortified front. Before and between their positions they had planted thousands of land mines, barely covered by the sand, in wait for British tanks, artillery, trucks and troops. On the Eighth Army's side of the line, the British also had permanent fortifications and mines. Patrols from each side constantly

This map, from the October 26 issue of TIME, shows the British base of Malta under heavy German bombardment and indicates the chief areas of activity along the coast of Africa. Field Marshal Rommel's Afrika Korps, supplied by ship and plane from Italy and Greece, controls the cities of Tripoli, Bengasi and Tobruk, and is moving against Egypt. But the British have already begun their counterattack, and by November will be pushing back along the coast to Bengasi. That month the Allies will also invade French North Africa, causing the port cities of Algiers and Oran to surrender almost immediately. Bizerte would not fall until 1943.

wormed into the mine fields, cautiously uncovered the buried boxes of T.N.T., neutralized them with a twist of a screw and threw them aside. But there were always more.

As Rommel learned when he felt out the British positions in September, El Alamein was no place for the sweeping tank tactics of the open desert. To break either the Axis or the British line, the attacker needed artillery and more artillery, supporting and opening the way for infantry and tanks. Aircraft could—and did—function as flying artillery. So the R.A.F. and the growing U.S. bomber and fighter forces in Egypt concentrated on Rommel's airdromes for two weeks before the battle opened.

For weeks, Lieut. General Montgomery had been incessantly touring his positions, forever popping up in a slouch hat which he had grabbed from the head of a startled Australian infantryman. He had personally marched with the new troops, fired every new gun and tried out every new tank as they arrived.

Now a piper skirled a march for the Highlanders in the British front line and hell broke over El Alamein. From hundreds of hidden positions artillery laid down the heaviest barrage yet seen in the desert. After six hours infantrymen moved toward the Germans' shattered positions. R.A.F. bombers and fighters attacked with the ground forces. Montgomery's order of the day: "Destroy Rommel."

LIKE COCKROACHES: Bernard Law Montgomery, the son of a NOV. 16 clergyman, is an abstemious, godly and implacable man. Famous are his orders to his staff at the beginning of a conference: "There will be no smoking. For two minutes you may cough. Thereafter coughing will cease"; nor does he drink. This month, with the zeal of the godly, he went to work as his Eighth Army surged against every foot of Rommel's defense at El Alamein. The constant pressure had its effect. Dazed and shell-shocked Germans surrendered, turned and ran, or died in the sand beside their 88-mm. guns. Rommel's dam had burst.

A British squadron leader described the carnage: "As we came in to drop the first stick of bombs, trucks careened madly off the road. It looked absolutely crazy. I saw one overturn and troops run like cockroaches—colliding, jumping headfirst into patches of scrub or any hole they could find."

The capture of El Alamein was only one objective of the Allies. In order to convert all of North Africa into a base from which they could later invade Southern Europe, Allied troops also had to invade and occupy French North Africa, to secure that territory as well.

THE DAWN'S EARLY LIGHT: Algiers in the dawn of Nov. 8 was a white, triangular wound against the dun hills behind the harbor. Beyond its jetties, well out in the Mediterranean, a great naval concentration stood in from Gibraltar: Royal Navy battleships, an aircraft carrier, cruisers, destroyers and transports laden with U.S. troops.

The first Allied bombers bore leaflets, imprinted with the American flag and a proclamation from Lieut. General Dwight David Eisenhower to the 252,000 Frenchmen, Arabs and Berbers of the town. A destroyer darted up to one of the docks, disgorged a small force of U.S. Rangers. Unfolding at Algiers that morning was a plan for the conquest of French North Africa. Its initial objective was the seizure of the principal ports: Algiers and Oran on the Mediterranean, Casablanca on the Atlantic and Rabat, the capital of Morocco. These cities are more than ports and naval bases: they are also the keys to the political control of French Morocco, Algeria and Tunisia. With them in hand the larger objectives of the U.S. entry into North Africa could unfold: the joining of the U.S. forces with the British in Libya, the destruction of Rommel's *Afrika Korps,* the re-establishment of Allied mastery over the southern Mediterranean and finally an assault on southern Europe.

At 7 p.m. on Sunday, 16 hours after the U.S. troops landed, General Alfonse Juin, Vichy's military commander in North Africa, and Admiral Darlan agreed to surrender Algiers.

NOV. 23 **DANGEROUS MISSION:** Last week the U.S. learned of a daring expedition which laid the military and diplomatic groundwork for the invasion of French North Africa. The time was mid-October, three weeks before the U.S. Army planned to go ashore. Cloaked by the North African darkness, eight men watched breathlessly for the signal light. At the appointed hour no light showed. In grave danger of capture, possibly of execution as spies, the men waited on. Finally, at a second prearranged hour, the light gleamed from a darkened house. Breathing more easily, the eight strode forward into the light and into the house jammed with French Army officers.

Towering, raw-boned Major General Mark Wayne Clark, fresh from a submarine, had led his men to the house on a dangerous mission: to extract as much information and win as much support from the French Army garrison as possible. All that night and all next day Mark Clark and his men talked and argued with the French officers. All went well until word came that Vichy-controlled police, informed by an Arab servant, were nearing the house.

"I never saw such excitement," said General Clark later. "Maps disappeared like lightning. A French general changed into civilian clothes in one minute flat, and I last saw him going out of a window." The Americans hid in a wine cellar, Clark with a revolver in one hand and 15,000 francs in the other, "to shoot them or bribe them." After an hour the police left. The Americans escaped, their deal made.

THE PAYOFF: The occupation of French North Africa was accomplished with *Blitzkrieg* briefness, utilizing expert coordination of planes, ships, tanks, trucks, guns and courageous men. Near Algiers two U.S. Ranger officers scrambling ashore with the first assault force were met by a friendly French officer. Twenty minutes later, still dripping with surf, they were inside the fort shaking hands with the garrison commander, who showed them instructions received the previous evening for cooperating with the Americans.

Fighting was more bitter for Oran, 130 miles west of Algiers. U.S. pilots flying British Spitfires hammered at the French while armored ground forces moved in on key airdromes. On the second day Brigadier General James H. Doolittle arrived to command the air assault. Planes peppered Oran with leaflets from General Henri Giraud urging Frenchmen to "save your bullets for the Boche." U.S. ground forces broke Oran's resistance on the day that Darlan, terming himself commander for all North Africa, signed a general armistice with Lieut. General Dwight D. Eisenhower.

In Morocco tough, muscular Major General George S. Patton Jr. ran into just the kind of opposition for which he had prepared. Months ago, on the deserts of southeastern California, he had drilled his men to fight in blazing heat over terrain such as they would meet in North Africa. Patton had insisted that they keep their sleeves rolled down, that they get along on a minimum of water. Not long after his men reached Africa, their grumbles turned to praise for what the Old Man had taught them.

Casablanca managed to put up the stiffest of all resistance to the U.S. invasion. Foresighted George Patton shoved three tank columns ashore east and west of the sprawling city and hit first for an outlying reservoir. With that in his hands, he could cripple Casablanca if necessary. Soon parachutists seized the city's main airdrome and the tank force advanced. By the time Patton's tank columns had pierced through to Casablanca, all coastal French Morocco was in American hands.

NOV. 30   **THE BELLS OF TOBRUK:** TIME Correspondent Walter Graebner last week cabled from Cairo: "I have witnessed one of the war's greatest spectacles—the dash of the victorious Eighth Army and R.A.F. over the Western Desert. At sundown on the first day we reached the former no man's land at El Alamein. The area was littered with German and Italian guns and shells, helmets, clothing, food, maps and other things, smashed and torn by the Aussies as they crashed through. Old tins of British-made 'Kiwi' shoe polish lay side by side with empty bottles of Italian Chianti.

"We viewed freshly made graves of Aussies and Germans across the road from where we slept. The bodies were simply laid out and covered with sand. Fresh graves dug by the Germans rarely bear the usual inscription 'He died for Hitler,' but are now marked 'He died for Germany.'

"On our last day we saw the ruins of Tobruk. The main church is badly damaged but three bells in the tower still ring. Every Tommy who enters yanks the ropes."

CLOSING TRAP: Rommel's African days were growing shorter. The strung-out columns of his army steadily shredded away as he frantically dragged westward along the Libyan coast. Ahead lay the El Aghéila bottleneck, the most logical place for Rommel to try to make a stand. Beyond that lay the long (600 mi.) and weary route to Tripoli which, by the time Rommel gets there, may be only the other end of a trap.

Last week Rommel abandoned Bengasi. Short of Tripoli itself, Bengasi was the last port left to him and the last chance he had to evacuate by sea. But British were hot after him and evacuating from Bengasi would have been a Dunkirk in reverse, a disaster which Rommel elected to put off. Britain's Montgomery almost caught him south of Bengasi. But the intercepting column was just too late. By the time it had battered down a holding force which Rommel left along a 50-mile escarpment, Rommel's main army had slipped past, desperately wriggling on along the seacoast.

YOICKS!: The Desert Fox lost his tail last week. Rommel let DEC. 28
Montgomery overtake him and, before he knew it, Montgomery had bitten off his brush. Erwin Rommel's latest
retreat had begun with an orderliness that was almost sedate. He sprinkled his trail with land mines and booby
traps and loped off along the coast.

But presently there were signs that the fox was in distress.
Allied planes pounded him. Rommel began to stumble and
duck. It was then that Montgomery got on his flanks. As
Rommel moved along the three-lane coastal highway, British
tanks, light artillery and motorized infantry drew abreast of
his rear guard. Near Wadi Matratin the British sliced in
and cut off part of a German *Panzer* division.

Westward Rommel continued to flee and, at week's end it
appeared that he might retreat all the way to Tunisia. There
he could make a stand behind the Mareth Line, the "Little
Maginot" of pillboxes and concrete forts strung along the
hills. There was even a report (from Berlin) that Rommel
himself had left to go "elsewhere on another job." The report
obviously was put out to save the fox's face, now that he had
lost his tail. [Later intelligence indicated that Rommel had
been called home to Germany in late November for consulta-
tion with Hitler. He then returned to Africa, but went home
again in March 1943 for medical treatment. The *Afrika Korps*
was defeated in Tunisia two months after that.]

Battle of Russia

BITTER PILL: Like it or not, Adolf Hitler had to write off his JAN. 19
winter campaign as a dead loss. For last week was the sixth
of German retreat in Russia. Hitler had apparently planned
to be in Moscow early in the autumn, firmly entrenched before winter set in. He had relied on an attack of paralyzing
speed. But Leningrad, encircled, has withstood over four
months of siege; Moscow threw back three gigantic of-
fensives.

When, contrary to plan, winter found the Germans deep
in Russia, Adolf Hitler vetoed the plea of his generals that
a winter line be established, and tried twice to keep the of-

fensive. But German aerial operations over Russia dwindled to the merest trickle. Tanks and trucks, oil frozen, bogged in the deep snow and were abandoned in wholesale lots.

JAN. 26 **APOPLEXY IN RUSSIA:** Nazi spokesmen last week announced the death from apoplexy of lean, athletic Field Marshal Walter von Reichenau, 57, Commander of Germany's Sixth Army in the Ukraine, who was so stiffly Prussian that his friends said he wore his monocle in bed.

APRIL 20 **WINTER IS OVER:** A.P.'s famed Correspondent Eddy Gilmore was sitting in a Kuibyshev hotel with a friend one night last week when they heard a noise: *crack, crack, boom.*

"What's that?" Gilmore asked.

They dashed into the lobby and asked a girl at the desk. She shook her head, looked worried. They ran outside. There the noise was louder, but they could see no searchlights, no shell bursts.

"What are the guns shooting at?" they asked an old man. "Have you heard a plane?"

"*Nyet, nyet,*" he replied, "*lyod tronulsya*—the ice is on the move."

"Winter is over," said the friend.

Gilmore and his friend walked home. All along the Volga, they heard the noise of spring, like the noise of guns: *crack, crack, boom.*

JUNE 22 **THE MEAT GRINDER:** The worst news for Russia last week was not the peril to Sevastopol, nor a new Nazi advance below Kharkov. For the U.S.S.R. and her Allies, the worst news was that on the two fronts where the Germans attacked in strength last week they had more men, more planes, more tanks, more everything than the Russians had. It was proof that, after all the agonies and losses of the Russian winter, the German armies were still strong and fresh. And it was proof that in this new year of war Russia will need all the aid the Allies can give her.

"The August City" is what the Russians call Sevastopol, their great port and naval fortress on the Black Sea. It is a majestic town with cathedrals, palaces, a mighty harbor where all the warships in Europe could anchor, a holy "Common Grave" nearby. That grave holds the dust of 127,000 Russians who died at Sevastopol in 1854-55, when Britain and her allies in the Crimean War besieged the city. Nine miles south of Sevastopol is the town of Balaklava, where the Light Brigade's 600 rode against the Russian batteries in that area. Last week many times 600 Nazis died near Balaklava, but the Russians called their defensive maze of gunpits and tank traps nothing so poetic as "the valley of death." They called it "the meat grinder."

Hitler's General Fritz Erich von Manstein had thrown some 100,000 men into this effort to smash Russia's last stronghold on the Crimea, to abolish the southern anchor of the long Russian front, to win command of the Black Sea, to open one gate to the oil-rich Caucasus. This week, on the eve of Hitler's second year in Russia, the only question at Sevastopol was how much Nazi meat it would take to choke the grinder.

AFTER EIGHT MONTHS: For days, the fall of Sevastopol had JULY 13 been near. But the Russians had been stubborn. German artillery blazed point-blank at the concrete, steel and limestone of Maxim Gorki Fort. When the Germans at last swarmed over the fort, a Nazi radio reporter's voice crackled with epic exasperation:

"Although the upper stories of Maxim Gorki Fort are in our hands, Soviet soldiers deep under ground in the lower stories continue to resist. We have sent negotiators to explain to them that further resistance is useless, but they won't come out."

In the Crimean War the British, French and Turks besieged Sevastopol for 329 days before the city fell. Last week, eight months after the Germans first approached Sevastopol, Berlin announced: "Sevastopol has fallen."

"MOT PULK": Russia was in mortal peril, and with her the JULY 27 whole Allied cause. It was not so much the German advances, although they were great enough; nor the Russian retreats, although they were foreboding enough. It was the total pattern of retreat and defeat in the valley of the Don that chilled the hearts of Russia's allies and sharpened Moscow's cry for a second front.

A new and terrible form of offensive pressed the Russians back last week. The Germans had discarded *Blitzkrieg,* given their new technique a new name: *Mot pulk* (motorized mass movement). The Germans, who once scorned weight and mass for the lighter, faster *Panzer* technique, had now gone whole hog for mass. Unprecedented concentrations of very heavy, semi-mobile artillery are the newest feature of *Mot pulk.* The Germans also use heavier tanks than they used before, and armored trains on the Russian model.

The *Luftwaffe*'s front-line role has been intensified beyond anything seen in previous German campaigns. Chief change: the number of dive-bombers on a given front has been tripled, and even quadrupled, to hurl the maximum weight from the air at Red troops, artillery and tanks.

AUG. 24 **MOSCOW AWARE:** Not since the Nazis stood on Moscow's threshhold last October had the city been so preoccupied with war:

¶ No foreigners could engage a Russian in conversation for five minutes without mention of the need for a second front.

¶ Men & women from shops, offices and hotels were drafted to bring in wood for winter fuel. Before a performance of the ballet it was announced that Première Ballerina Merserer would not appear. She was stiff from chopping wood.

¶ More women replaced men at heavy tasks: truck driving, street car operation, trench digging, munitions manufacturing. Nearly all women not in essential services were in uniforms.

¶ Women on subways stood to give their seats to soldiers.

SEPT. 7 **STALIN'S CHOICE:** Concentrated in the hands of Joseph Stalin is more wartime authority, both political and military, than is wielded by any of his allies. As Premier, Defense Commissar and Secretary of the Communist Party, Stalin is shouldered with domestic and international responsibilities which grow with each German step into Russia. Last week, as German armies threatened the city which is named for him, Stalin sought someone to share his burdens. As First Deputy Defense Commissar he chose General Georgi Konstantinovich Zhukov.

Of peasant origin, solemn, brooding Georgi Zhukov joined the Red Army in 1918. His military career was unpublicized abroad until 1939, when he won recognition for effective use of tanks against the Jap on the Khalka River.

BUNKER BY BUNKER: Stalingrad was in mortal danger. Herds of Nazi tanks gored a gaping wound in Russian defenses between the Volga River and the Don. Day by day they dug deeper toward Stalingrad and Russia's Volga artery, clamping a giant pincers around the strategic city. Thousands of factory workers laid down their tools and streamed westward to take up guns with the embattled Red Army. Bunker by bunker, from every concrete pillbox and every swallow's nest hollowed hastily from the earth, the Russians were putting up a defense of Stalingrad that would rank with Leningrad and Moscow—prizes that once were within the enemy's grasp, but never taken.

Every Russian knew what it would mean to lose Stalingrad, to lose control of the Volga, to have the Red Army cut off from the Caucasus with its oil, steel and supply route to sources outside. Over Moscow radio came this meaningful message to the Russian people: "Not only can we not afford to retreat any farther, but we must, at all costs, throw the enemy back. Hitler must be destroyed and destroyed this year. There is no alternative."

"THEY WILL LIVE FOREVER": Field Marshal Fedor von Bock, SEPT. 21 the German commander in south Russia, would have esteemed Vassily Kochetkov, a junior lieutenant of the Red Army. Bock commanded 1,000,000 or more men, fighting for Stalingrad, the Volga and the Caucasus. Junior Lieut. Kochetkov commanded 16 Red Guardsmen holding a hillock before Stalingrad.

At dawn twelve of Bock's tanks climbed the hillock toward the trenches and light fortifications where Kochetkov and his men lay. The Guardsmen had only rifles and hand grenades. Kochetkov was wounded. Four of his Guardsmen fastened grenades to their thick leather belts. Each chose a tank, ran down the hill, and dived headlong. Eight tanks were left. Six of the eight tanks turned and retreated. The two others crawled on toward the Guardsmen's nest. By then only Kochetkov and three Guardsmen were alive. The three soldiers placed Kochetkov in a trench, laced more grenades to their belts, and ran to meet the tanks. Junior Lieut. Kochetkov was alone when a Red detachment found him. He told the newcomers what his men had done, and said: "They will live forever." Junior Lieut. Kochetkov then died.

OCT. 5   **FROM STALINGRAD'S RUINS:** This report of a trip through battle-torn Stalingrad was written by Author Konstantin Simonov [who would later write a distinguished novel about the battle, *Days and Nights*]:

"It is evening and we are standing on the outskirts of the city. Before us is the battlefield: smoking hillocks and flaming streets. Everywhere there is a bluish-black smoke cut by fairy arrows of mortar fire from our guards. Ashes float in the air. White German flares light up the long circular front. First we hear the Nazi bombers, then the explosions of their bombs. Next comes the roar of our bombers sailing west. They drop yellow flares to illuminate the German position, and a few seconds later they drop cargoes of death.

"On the east bank of the Volga we see the supply system in operation. Our ferryboat is overloaded with five trucks full of munitions, a company of Red Army men and a number of nurses. Bombs are whistling all around. Next to me sits a doctor's assistant, a young Ukrainian woman named Victoria Tshepnya. This is her fifth crossing. As the ferryboat approaches the landing stage, Victoria confesses: 'You know me, always a little frightened to get out. I've already been wounded twice, once very seriously. But I don't believe I'll die yet because I haven't begun to live.'

"It must be frightful to have been wounded twice, to have fought for 15 months, and now to make a fifth trip to a flaming city. In 15 minutes she will pass through burning buildings, and somewhere under the rain of shrapnel and bombs will pick up a wounded man and bring him back to the ferryboat. Then she will make her sixth trip.

"We are in the city. Near the river the streets are still black, except when bombs land. In that moment the outline of the buildings is silhouetted against the sky and reminds one of a fortress. Indeed Stalingrad is a fortress. Under-

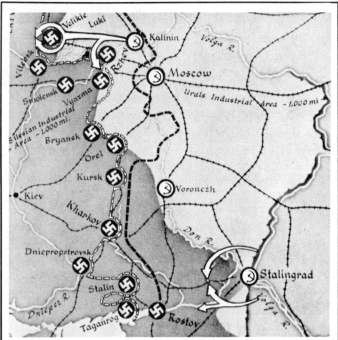

This map, from the December 14 issue of TIME, shows the situation along the most active sector of the Russian front. The broken black line indicates German advances the previous winter, when Hitler's troops moved within 25 miles of Moscow. The broken white line indicates Russian gains during the same period. In the north the Russians have held onto these gains; in the south the Germans have pushed the Russians back to capture the area shown in dark grey. The bitterest fighting is at Stalingrad, where Soviet units inside the city are holding off a massive German attack. Russian armies coming to the rescue will soon encircle the German positions (see arrows) and in February of 1943 the Germans will surrender at Stalingrad and begin their long retreat back through Russia.

ground we enter the staff headquarters. Telegraph girls, their faces pale from sleepless nights and explosion dust, tap out dots and dashes. I try to light a match, but it is quickly smothered. Here underground there is not enough oxygen.

"Now we are riding through the streets in a dilapidated gazik [old make Soviet car] to a command point. We pass a gate through which roll squeaking wagons loaded with fresh bread. Evidently the building houses a bakery. The city is still alive."

DEC. 7 **HITLER'S LOST GAMBLE:** Hitler had lost the gamble. Instead of consolidating his eastern front he had gambled on the capture of Stalingrad. But Stalingrad had held out and now began striking back at his advanced columns. In the midst of Herr Hitler's frantic preoccupation with Africa the Russian winter offensive exploded. Under cover of sub-freezing nights thousands of Russian soldiers had crossed the icy Volga on ferryboats, fishing boats and rafts, carrying with them the artillery, tanks and weapons they would need for a massive counterattack.

First the Soviet artillery awakened. The cannonading kept up without break for two and a half hours, pouring destruction into the German lines. Under its cover Russian sappers swept forward to "delouse" German mine fields. Over the frozen earth rolled Russian tanks, some of them dragging artillery. Mobile cannon followed, operating in massed groups, blasting holes in German positions that had already been spotted by Russian guerrilla intelligence.

As the attack started from the south, Soviet troops north of Stalingrad also launched an assault. Their purpose was to swing west and south, meet the southern columns and close a ring around the Germans. Inside the ring the battle became a melee. Distracted Axis troops faced in all directions at once. *Panzer* divisions dug in, using their tanks as pillboxes. Across the steppes galloped Cossacks in their black capes. Around gutted villages roared Russian tanks, swift motor-borne Siberian infantry. Axis troops in suddenly hopeless positions gave up. According to Moscow communiqués, 66,000 were seized in ten days of fighting. [Total German capitulation at Stalingrad came two months later. Hitler's stubborn determination to take the city is regarded as one of the major military blunders of the war. The effort cost the Nazis 150,000 dead and 91,000 prisoners—of whom only 6,000 ever returned to Germany.]

FOREIGN NEWS

Great Britain

ANOTHER YEAR: London was tar black as the war year of JAN. 12
1942 began. The eddying, nearly solid crowd in front of St.
Paul's could scarcely see its own faces as it waited for the midnight bells. When the clock struck the crowd sang *Auld
Lang Syne.* Then the people began to scatter, walking in
pairs or groups past the gnarled skeletons of bombed-out
houses. Most of them, men & women, were in uniform.
They shouted "Happy New Year!" to strangers half seen in
the dark, and they sang *She'll Be Comin' Round the Mountain.*
The Yankee tune was the latest craze.

CHURCHILL FACES UP: Winston Churchill last week finally MARCH 2
faced up to what the British had begun to call the "Winston
Crisis." To those who said that his Cabinet was too stupid
or too stiffly Tory, or both, he responded with a general Cabinet reshuffle in which some of the stiffest Tories went out of
the window and Britain's most eminent Socialist, Sir Stafford
Cripps, came boldly in the front door. The appointment of
Cripps as Lord Privy Seal was sensational, since he was
also to replace the Prime Minister as the Government's representative in the House of Commons.

One of Britain's ablest corporation lawyers, Sir Stafford
quit practice in the '30s, saying that he was tired of "taking
large sums of money from one capitalist to give it to another capitalist." Thereafter he became even better known
for his Christianity, vegetarianism (he was nicknamed "Christ
and Carrots") and socialism. Like Winston Churchill, he constantly foretold war before it came, attacked the Munich
men. As Ambassador to Russia, he favored a British-Rus-
sian coalition against Hitler.

REGRET, REPLY, SALUTE: Three times in three years Lady Mac- MARCH 16
Robert was handed one of the tiny yellow envelopes. Inside

Lady MacRobert loses sons, names a   *Sir William Beveridge. His plan is*
bomber "MacRobert's Reply."   *called "A bit of all right." Page 123.*

each one was a telegram beginning: "The Air Ministry regret...."

The first advised Lady MacRobert that her son Sir Alasdair, 25, had crashed in England. The second told her that son Sir Roderic, 26, had been shot down in Iraq. The third reported the loss of son Sir Iain, 24, who was known as "the perfect Coastal Command pilot." With no more sons to give to her country, Lady MacRobert sent Air Minister Sir Archibald Sinclair a check for £25,000 to buy a bomber. "It is my wish," she said, "to make a mother's immediate reply in a way that I know would be my boys' reply—attacking, striking sharply, straight to the mark." The R.A.F. promptly named one of its giant Stirling bombers "MacRobert's Reply."

Last week Lady MacRobert took out her pen and checkbook again. She sent Sir Archibald Sinclair £20,000 to purchase four fighter planes for use "on fronts where they could aid Russia." She asked that three of the planes be named for her sons, that the fourth be called "MacRobert Salute to Russia (Lady)." "Had I been a man, I, too, would have flown," said gallant Lady MacRobert.

JUNE 8   **COMMANDO COMMANDER:** On their rounds of London last week, visiting U.S. Army chiefs sought out a very lean, very tall (6 ft. 4 in.) Englishman with a graceful name, royal blood, and one of the key posts in warring Britain. If, as some people thought, the U.S. officers were in London to sell the Imperial General Staff a second front, they did well to look up Vice Admiral, Lieut. General and Air Vice Marshal Lord Louis Mountbatten.

For, to Britons a-clamor for Continental action, Lord Louis personifies the second front. They know him as the chief of their savage specialists in hit-&-run invasion, the Commandos. Actually, he is Chief of Combined Operations, directing not only the Commando troops themselves but the naval and air units which share the labor, glory and death of Commando raids.

The Commandomen have a friendly, free-&-easy comradeship unique in the British Army. They must learn to catch, kill, dress, cook their own meat. They must know how to stalk, unseen, in woods, fields, mountains. If a man is spotted on his first stalking practice, he is warned. On the second, a blank round is fired at him. On the third, a live bullet spats close by him. Said a onetime Commando officer now on duty in the U.S.: "It certainly teaches people quickly."

Above all, Commandomen must learn to kill. They prefer to kill quietly. A favorite Commando weapon is a long, straight knife, both edges sharpened razor-keen, carried in a trouser sheath. Some have metal kneecaps, fitted with metal spikes, to be driven into enemy crotches and spines. They can devise their own daggers, clubs, knives. They know the uses of spiked brass knuckles. All must know a Commando equivalent of jiujitsu. Fiercely, without quarter, they battle each other in practice combat, often break each other's bones.

As Lord Louis supervises the training of his troops, Londoners often see him at about 9:30 each morning, driving himself to work in his four-seater Ford. Nowadays, he has almost no club or social life. Often, he lunches on sandwiches in his headquarters office. "All tickety boo," he says when everything is as he likes it, in apple pie order.

MR. BULLFINCH TAKES A TRIP: Bit of a dandy Winston Churchill is, always dashing about somewhere. Now it was a 10,000-mile trip to Egypt and Moscow. The flight to Egypt found AUG. 31

him in "the office" (control cabin) of the four-motored American B-24 bomber, chattering with the American crew.

"Nasty terrain!" exclaimed the Prime Minister, looking down on some of the desert of French North Africa. "What would happen if we couldn't go on?"

"Knock the kite around a bit, but nobody'd get hurt," Copilot Jack Ruggles guessed.

"But if we had to land there," Churchill mused, "we'd probably be made prisoners. I've an idea the Nazis would like to get their hands on me. Probably they'd shoot me."

When he reached Moscow, Churchill's first meeting with Stalin lasted three hours and 40 minutes. W. Averell Harriman, representing President Roosevelt, sat in on the conferences with instructions that Roosevelt would be in agreement with "all decisions taken here by Mr. Churchill." Afterward at a banquet in the Kremlin's huge Catherine Hall, Stalin sat with Churchill on his right and Harriman on his left. Wine, vodka and champagne washed down 26 courses, beginning with caviar and ending with bonbons. After 25 toasts, count was lost. Guests left as the morning sun struck the Kremlin's eastern battlements. Churchill, who has dressed for dinner virtually every night of his adult life, wore his zippered overall "siren suit."

After he had finished his business in Moscow, Tripper

Prime Minister Churchill takes the controls on a fighter. To an Australian soldier, "Mr. Bullfinch" hands over a cigar.

Churchill was not yet ready to go home. From second-front talks with Stalin he returned once more to North Africa, where a United Nations' second front may be opened. He had an audience with King Farouk, a chat with the Shah of Persia. And the old (67) war horse could not be kept from the front. He flew west into the desert, changed into an armored car, got within four miles of no man's land near El Alamein. Through binoculars he saw Rommel's fortifications, watched Messerschmitts fighting with Spitfires two miles away.

The chief censor had insisted that Churchill be known as "Mr. Bullfinch." But soldiers soon discovered who Mr. Bullfinch was. "Blimey, it's Winnie," they said. "Winnie's come out into the bloomin' desert." "Hey, Winnie," shouted an Australian, "have you got a spare cigar?" Winnie handed over a fragrant Hoyo de Monterrey.

PEACETIME CLAMOR: Since June 1940, every British family NOV. 23 has kept its shotgun and poker, pitchfork and flatiron ready to use against invaders whenever the church bells rang. This week the bells broke their long silence. Over tattered city streets and the camouflaged tin huts of army encampments the rolling echoed, celebrating with propriety victory in Egypt.

No clamor came from some 1,200 parish churches, either because their old grey stones had collapsed under bombs or because partial damage had left the bells insecure in the belfries. At Coventry the cathedral bells, all that were saved in a night of concentrated blitzing, sang out at special length, to observe the victory and to commemorate the second anniversary of the raid which destroyed the cathedral and the town.

To an old nursery rhyme:

> *"Gay go up and gay go down,*
> *"To ring the bells of London town,"*

London urchins sang a new verse, added during the blitz:

> *"Now come the incendiaries to light you to bed,*
> *"Bring out the sandbags and kill them all dead."*

DEC. 2   **ITALY'S CHOICE:** Over the world's short waves, Winston Churchill gave another of his full-dress oratorical performances, launched the first big broadside in a new war of nerves against Italy. To the "fair land of Italy," he guaranteed "prolonged, scientific and shattering air attack." To Italians he offered the choice "to say whether they want this terrible thing to happen to their country or not." To Benito Mussolini he applied a fresh epithet: "The hyena in his nature broke all bounds of decency." (Previous Churchillian labels for Il Duce: "jackal," "lackey," "serf," "utensil.")

DEC. 14   **REFRESHING BEVERIDGE:** Not since the day of Munich had the British press given such play to any single story. War news has all but pushed from the pages of London's war-curtailed dailies as Sir William Henry Beveridge's report, virtually a blueprint for postwar socialization, ran to 200,000 words and proposed a comprehensive, compulsory system of social insurance for every man, woman and child, regardless of age, income or class, with premiums to be paid by the individual, his employer and the State.

First reaction of press and public to the Beveridge Report was one of almost unanimous approval. Said the London *Times:* "A momentous document which should and must exercise a profound and immediate influence on the direction of social change in Britain." Said the man in the street: "A bit of all right."

DEC. 28   **THE PLAN AND THE SPIRIT:** Benign, witty Sir William Henry Beveridge by last week was second only to Winston Churchill as Britain's most popular man. Britons had bought more than 200,000 full texts of his plan for postwar social security. The Ministry of Information was bringing out a threepenny *Beveridge Report in Brief* and every Army officer was to be supplied with this brief for the instruction of rankers.

Sir William, 63, punch-pleased with the way things were going, broke off his lectures explaining the plan long enough to marry his former secretary, Mrs. Jessy ("Janet") Philip Mair, grandmother and economist in her own right. The marriage, performed by the Archbishop of Canterbury at Caxton Hall, was Sir William's first. Chirped he: "Though I have known the lady for many years, marriage must always be an adventure. Yet my critics say that social security kills that spirit."

France

"HELP ME!": France was in pain. Cold and the want of food JAN. 12 and fuel were painful. And if millions of Frenchmen were anguished by collaboration with Germany, so was collaborating Marshal Henri Philippe Pétain. He virtually begged Germany for mercy. "In partial exile to which I am subjected," said he from Vichy, "I strive to do all my duty. Each day I endeavor to wrest this country from the stagnation that threatens it. Help me!"

FOR A SMALL FEE: When the Germans hacked prostrate France JAN. 19 into two parts the line of demarcation placed the tiny village of Cérilly in Unoccupied France. Its cemetery, half a mile away, was in Occupied France. By special dispensation, the Germans permitted funerals to cross and recross the line without the usual formalities.

Funerals became strangely frequent. Always first in processions was Pierre Guichard, dignified beadle of the Cérilly church. Next, the curé, sprinkling holy water with an energy suggesting joyous abandon. Behind him came the coffin bearers, their spirits lighter than the heavy box they bore. Then the black-veiled mourners, bearing their grief with an odd furtiveness.

For more than a year M. Guichard led his villagers back & forth. Then someone talked. German authorities checked up, found that as many maidens walked on moonlit lanes as ever before, as many men plowed the fields, as many oldsters sat in the sun, drinking the wine and upbraiding the quality of the bread. With Teutonic thoroughness Nazi statisticians calculated that Cérilly had celebrated so many funerals that virtually every living soul in the village should be dead by now. Revealed at last was M. Guichard's sly scheme.

By interchanging mourners at the cemetery he had been

smuggling Frenchmen back & forth across the "border," had even handled mass movements by arranging particularly magnificent funerals. All this he had done for the pleasure it gave him and, of course, a small fee.

APRIL 27 **"THAT FLABBY HAND, THAT EVIL LIP"**: Pierre Laval came back to power as "Chief of Government" in Vichyfrance last week and the world felt in its bones that the war had taken some great new malevolent turn. Cried a De Gaullist spokesman in London: "Think of that flabby hand, that evil lip, that shifty glance, that sneer of the executioner—and tell yourself that for 30 years France has not shed a tear without Laval gaining by it."

In Vichy a somber crowd of 2,000 waited for two hours for the return from Paris of Hitler's No. 1 French servant. Laval came heavily guarded in a fast, dark limousine followed by two police cars. Not a sound came from the crowd. They were not there to pay tribute. They were there out of morbid curiosity. They knew his return was bad news, for many a French patriot is now in danger of the concentration-camp horrors which the Pétain Government had so far spared them.

Laval devotes much time to his toilet, but he is one of the untidiest political figures on earth. The cigaret drooping from his lip is always stained with spittle. His teeth are crowded and ugly. His hair insists on its greasy disarray. He is a heavy, un-French eater and uses his fingers as a fork, his fork as a toothpick.

MAY 11 **GREAT EMBARRASSMENT**: Never since the flight of Rudolf Hess had the Nazis' faces looked so red. But was it anger? Was it embarrassment? Or was it pride in a successful hoax?

The Nazis' No. 1 French war prisoner had escaped from Germany, reached Vichy and talked openly with Marshal Pétain. Presumably the Nazis could yank him back to Germany again. But this was not the first time General Henri Honoré Giraud had escaped from the Germans. In 1914, aged 35, he was wounded in a French bayonet attack near Charleroi and left for dead on the field. Captured by the Germans, he made his first escape via Holland to England, variously disguised as a butcher, stableboy, coal man, and magician in a traveling circus. At one point he was helped by Nurse Edith Cavell. In 1915 he was back with the French Fifth Army.

This young man's feat paled by comparison with the elderly General's recent escape as it was recounted last week. Captured by the Germans at Sedan in May 1940, Giraud was imprisoned in Saxony's grim, moated Königstein Fortress on a mountainside 750 feet above the Elbe. There, from gift boxes, he assembled a suit of civilian clothes. As to the actual escape, a version attributed by Vichy to the General himself was that his wife had sent him lengths of thread in every gift package, and these he had woven into a long rope. One night the General is supposed to have let himself down on the rope. It was too short. He (a 63-year-old) climbed up again, wove some more, later let himself down 60 feet. Posing as a traveling salesman, he spent eleven days on obscure roads and railroads leading to Switzerland, Occupied France and Vichy. His closest call came when the Gestapo searched a train on which he was talking with a German officer. He got the German into such a hot argument that the Gestapo did not wish to interrupt the officer with inquiries.

Speculation was high this week as to why General Giraud had reported to Marshal Pétain, whom he has always disliked; why Vichy publicized the almost incredible details of an old man's escape with a young man's techniques. Perhaps General Giraud had the unlikely theory that Vichy might be able to give him a command. Or perhaps the Germans and Vichy had some other use for General Giraud.

THE CASE RESTS: The mystery of France's big, beloved old JULY 6 General Henri Honoré Giraud was no longer a mystery. When the 63-year-old general said he had escaped from Germany's Königstein Fortress by letting his ponderous body down a self-made rope, the outside world raised an eyebrow.

The general's rope trick was, however, no illusion. He wanted to help France. But when he reached Vichy he found a France quite unlike anything he had heard about within Königstein's walls. Marshal Pétain gave him a paper to sign, which among other things pledged him never to take up arms against Germany. General Giraud balked.

Then Pierre Laval slyly suggested that the general could do France a mighty service by offering to return to prison in exchange for 400,000 married French war prisoners. General Giraud was amenable until he met Laval's bosses, the Nazi occupation authorities in Paris. Then he blew up, said he would trust no Nazi word on anything.

The Nazis, of course, had the general at their mercy, but the general also held cards. The French people held him close to their hearts; Laval dared not turn him over to the Germans. Finally the Nazis had to content themselves with a promise by the general that he would not interfere in Vichy-German affairs. Last week the general was living with his sister in Lyons. General Giraud, and his case, rested.

SELLING PETAIN: Pierre Laval decided the Vichy government OCT. 5 needed a new image, so he tried a super-duper advertising campaign to sell 85-year-old Chief of State Marshal Henri Philippe Pétain to every Frenchman. The Marshal's profile, slogans and symbols appeared on stamps, china, ash trays, badges, hatbands, blotters, coins, bijoux and shaving mugs. The Marshal's colors and cheerful slogans about healthy children appeared on milk bottles. Frenchmen wryly remembered World War I, when the Kaiser's picture had adorned the bottoms of chamber pots.

Pierre Laval (right) sells Marshal Pétain (left) to Frenchmen by putting him on ash trays, hatbands and shaving mugs.

THE FLESH EXCHANGE: A special train carrying 452 pallid, ca- OCT 19
daverous, sick and wounded French war prisoners ground
into the Gare du Nord last week, bringing a stench of decaying, living flesh to Paris. At the same time, six trainloads
of healthy French flesh on the hoof left France for Germany.
Pierre Laval's plan of exchanging three French workers for
one war prisoner was functioning. Frenchmen had become
domestic animals, weighed and traded and shipped.

The plan was worked out with German thoroughness and
handed to Laval. German factory requests for labor were
sent to recruiting service bureaus, in both Occupied and
Unoccupied France, which referred them to French factories.
Here lists had already been made up of all men between 18
and 50 with fewer than three living children. For every 25
workers, a foreman was taken; for every 50 workers, an engineer. The entire group then proceeded to Germany to
take over the operation of a factory or shop. French indus-
trialists were instructed to replace deported workers with
unskilled recruits. After a period of training this raw labor
would be ready to take its turn in the Reich. Continuous
labor exchange would tend to standardize industrial technique in the two countries.

Last week several hundred thousand French workers had
received notices designating them to go to Germany, with
contracts to be signed within 24 hours. Recruits underwent
medical examinations. Germany wanted only healthy meat.

"THE ENEMY GASPS AND WAVERS": As U.S. troops swarmed NOV. 16
over French North Africa last week [see page 108], the men
of Vichy gave the impression that they were ready to crum-
ble. The totalitarian old figurehead, Marshal Pétain, quavered
in a letter to President Roosevelt: "It is with stupor and sadness that I learned tonight of the aggression of your troops.
You have taken such a cruel initiative."

The leaders of the French millions who hate Vichy were
quick to seize the political weapons the U.S. had given
them. Broadcasting from London, General Charles de Gaulle
called to French North African troops: "Forward! The
great moment has come. Help our allies. Everywhere the
enemy gasps and wavers."

Over the Algiers radio came the most surprising and inspir-

General Giraud: "We have one pas- *General de Gaulle: "Everywhere the*
sion—France; one aim—victory." *enemy gasps and wavers."*

ing French voice of all. It was that of big, spirited General Henri Honoré Giraud, idol of France, Germany's No. 1 war prisoner and escapist. Cried he:

"Germany and Italy want to occupy North Africa. America forestalls them and assures us of her loyal and disinterested support. We cannot neglect this opportunity of recovery. I take up my action station among you. We have one passion—France; and one aim—victory." Commander in Chief of Allied forces in North Africa Lieut. General Dwight D. Eisenhower announced that General Giraud had arrived in Algeria "to organize a French North African Army and again take up arms side by side with forces of the United Nations for the defeat of Germany and Italy." At the time of Giraud's escape, General de Gaulle had declared that he would be glad at any time to serve under his senior.

NOV. 23 **THE INHERITORS:** Behind the battle lines in North Africa emerged the specter of French politics. Shifty Admiral Jean François Darlan, ex-collaborating Premier, heir-designate of Marshal Pétain and Commander in Chief of all French sea, land and air forces, had come to Algiers before the invasion, ostensibly to visit his sick son. In the Allied attack, Darlan the opportunist saw the great chance of his career.

He ordered the surrender of Algiers, followed this up

with the "cease fire" order to all French troops in North Africa. Then he took over the civil administration of the colonies in the name of Marshal Pétain—and with the approval of the U.S. authorities. He set up his own military command under stanch old General Henri Honoré Giraud. Still in the name of Marshal Pétain, still with the approval of the U.S. commanders, an administration took form in North Africa under this former collaborator with Germany and in the rear of the Allied armies sweeping on toward Tunisia.

The Fighting French under General Charles de Gaulle were at first bewildered, then indignant at the news that their movement, for over two years the recognized rallying point of free Frenchmen, was being ignored while former Vichyites gained control in North Africa. For nearly a week De Gaulle was silent. Then he issued a blistering statement:

The Fighting French, he said, "were taking no part whatsoever in, and assuming no responsibility for, negotiations in progress in North Africa with Vichy representatives."

DICTATOR LAVAL: The name Pétain might keep for many a NOV. 30 touch of magic—a legendary gleam that shone out of the mud of Verdun. But the man Pétain, watery-eyed and old, and his regime, for months largely fictional, seemed indisputably through. No longer able to maintain the fiction of personal power, Pétain handed over the destinies of the country he professed to love to the hands of a man abhorred throughout France. To Pierre Laval, Adolf Hitler's Auvergne shyster, Pétain gave a dictator's power to rule by decree.

THE ADMIRAL EXPLAINS HIMSELF: Nearly everybody else had DEC. 28 already had his say on Admiral Jean François Darlan, when last week the Admiral decided to have a say for himself. He took great pains to repair his reputation. At the exotic *Palais d'Eté* in Algiers, where he received correspondents, the Admiral was wearing sharkskin civvies with a white shirt, a brown polka-dot tie and black shoes. His grey-green eyes peered brightly through his horn-rimmed spectacles. Said he:

"In 1940 I believed an Axis victory was possible. In 1941 I believed no victory could be achieved by either side. But for several months now I have been convinced that Germany would lose."

He added: "There is no question that the French Army and Navy are anxious to wage war again on the side of the United Nations on one condition."

The Admiral paused. He evidently had in mind General Charles de Gaulle and the Fighting French—who had not imposed conditions. The Admiral's condition apparently was that the French must fight under "recognized leadership"— meaning himself. Said he: "French soldiers will follow me because I am a man whom Marshal Pétain appointed to take his place. That is the only reason French West Africa came into the new entente under my authority." [On December 24, shortly after making this statement, Darlan was assassinated in his headquarters at Algiers by a young Frenchman who called himself an anti-Fascist.]

LAVAL'S WAY: Swart, pig-eyed Pierre Laval could have things his own way now in France. With dictatorial powers, with the Gestapo by his side in a country now fully under German occupation, he felt he could thumb his bulbous nose at public opinion. At a press conference last week he said: "I want Germany to win. An American victory would bring in its train the triumph of Jews and Communists."

Germany

MARCH 2 **HESS'S SUCCESSOR:** Adolf Hitler appointed a successor to Rudolf Hess as second in the Nazi line of succession, following porcine Hermann Göring. The world had heard little of the appointee, Martin Bormann, but he was soundly qualified for the job. Short, crop-haired, 42-year-old Bormann was a schoolboy bully in Halberstadt near the Harz Mountains. After World War I he joined a murderous anti-Republican gang whose pastime was beating workmen as they left their beer halls. This connection led him into the German Workers Party, predecessor of the Nazis.

In 1923 Bormann was arrested for taking part in Hitler's attempted Munich *Putsch,* got a year in jail. Later he proved himself a nimble manipulator of Party funds, rose to be Hess's administrative right hand. Since Hess's flight, Bormann has seen Hitler regularly and Hitler has given Martin Bormann greater powers than any Party official ever had before. He can (theoretically) veto any law, must countersign all official appointments.

In addition to his financial services to Nazidom, Bormann has made ideological contributions in the field of religion. Recently he told Party leaders: "Our National Socialist world picture stands far above the teachings of Christianity." [Martin Bormann was with Hitler when the Führer killed himself in his underground Berlin headquarters in April 1945. Bormann disappeared, and has not been seen since.]

Martin Bormann. A former schoolboy bully is now the No. 3 Nazi. *Hermann Göring blames the weather for bad crops, rationing and Russia.*

GÖRING'S WEATHER REPORT: Hermann Göring did more than JUNE 1 report last week what Adolf Hitler had said last March: that Germany was no longer crusading for world domination, but was fighting for its very life. He confirmed reports that Europe is facing the worst crop failure in years—that not only subject peoples but the *Herrenvolk* may taste real starvation. Göring blamed the weather ("Nature really has treated us very unkindly") for crop shortages and the need for a new "temporary reduction" in ration cards.

Göring also blamed the weather for much of Germany's

military difficulty in Russia. "The Russians were able to break through in the night over frozen rivers, lakes and morasses. Guerrillas blew up our railways and ambushed our supplies. Our troops nearly froze to death in the cold."

NOV. 16 **WEARINESS IN MUNICH:** The deep voice, weary, almost with a touch of resignation, boomed out of the loudspeakers in millions of German homes. Germans wondered. The radio had told them only a few hours before of Americans landing in force on the coast of French Northwest Africa, the first major attack of the great enemy whose coming they had dreaded in World War II. What would the Führer say?

If they expected clear-cut, reassuring statements, they were disappointed. Adolf Hitler's brightest predictions were that Germany would hold her lines and some day strike back:

"When Roosevelt today carries out his attack on North Africa with the remark that he wants to protect it from Germany and Italy, I don't have to reply to the lying old scoundrel. The last word will certainly not be spoken by Herr Roosevelt. We will prepare our blows, thoroughly as usual, and we have always arrived at the right time so far. I assure you the hour will come when I will strike back with compound interest. They will get an answer which will knock them deaf and blind."

Occupied Europe

During this critical year of the war, much of Europe was almost invisible to the rest of the world, blocked from view by a wall of Nazi oppression and censorship behind which entire towns could disappear and their citizens be massacred. Resistance continued, however, and occasionally a report would reach TIME *telling what was really going on—in places like Paris or Denmark or the little Czechoslovakian village of Lidice. The following section contains a selection of these reports.*

FEB. 9 **HUNGRIEST COUNTRY:** Britain last week broke its own Mediterranean blockade by announcing that Britain and the

U.S. together would send 8,000 tons of wheat to the hungriest country in the world, Occupied Greece.

Bread was priced at $15 a loaf in Athens last week and there was no bread. There were no potatoes, no figs, no raisins, no tomatoes. There was, in short, famine. The sight of wasted men & women fainting in the street was so common that no one thought anything of it.

In Athens and Piraeus alone, between 1,700 and 2,000 men, women & children are dying each day. Not all starve to death. Cholera, typhus, typhoid and dysentery run like a licking brush fire through the weakened population.

Hunger has fostered a new profession. When the Athens powerhouse shuts down at nightfall to save fuel, grave robbers prowl the dark cemeteries, stripping the dead. Some of the lucky ghouls find rings and necklaces on the corpses. With jewelry they can sometimes buy a mouthful of bread from Italian soldiers.

REBELLION: Everywhere in Occupied Europe there were people FEB. 23 who could not stand the humiliation of the New Order, who had to fight back to keep their souls intact. In France attacks on German personnel and property amounted to a terror against the terror. In Norway two railway stations and the National Theater in Oslo were set on fire, bombs were tossed into the House of Parliament. In Czechoslovakia a workman called "Old Vacek" ran a crane at the great Skoda munitions works at Pilsen. One day a big ladle of molten lead being carried on Vacek's crane suddenly flipped over. It happened that a posse of German Army commissioners were passing beneath: 14 of them were burned to death. Old Vacek did not try to pretend accident. He dived out of his cab, 60 feet head first to the concrete floor.

To combat rebellion in Europe, it seemed logical that Germany should choose its bloodiest man. Reinhard Heydrich is six feet tall, lean, trim, yellow-haired, 37. He is pale, thin-nosed, thin-lipped. Most Germans call him simply *der Henker* (the Hangman).

At the Gestapo headquarters in Berlin, foreign diplomats who used to visit him to plead or protest for fellow nationals found him polite, attentive, even affable. But they noticed one thing about him—he never smiled.

Until three or four years ago he stood in the shadow behind the lurid light of Heinrich Himmler, head of all the German police. But Heydrich knows everything that Himmler knows and he has spies everywhere, even in the lairs of his closest associates. A onetime official of the Berlin Gestapo, now a refugee in England, described the situation thus: "Without Heydrich, Himmler would be just a senseless dummy. Heydrich is young and intelligent, brutal, despotic and merciless. Himmler betrays loyalties and friends, Heydrich annihilates them."

JUNE 1 **WHERE DEMOCRACY WAS BORN:** When their relatives die, the Greeks no longer bury them in cemeteries. The cemeteries are full now. Instead the bodies are placed unmarked in garden plots. By avoiding mortuary declarations, the living can keep and use the dead's ration cards.

Starvation in Greece. In the birthplace of democracy, the cemeteries are full, tuberculosis is rampant and 300,000 people live on herbs.

Tuberculosis brought on by undernourishment is now rampant in Greece. In the Aegean islands 300,000 people forestall starvation by eating herbs. Thousands of islanders, their skin hanging in folds about their hunger-dulled eyes, have fled to Turkey in small boats. "Trying to halt them," said the mayor of Chios, "is like trying to drive clouds against a strong wind."

*Late in May, on a road outside Pilsen, Czechoslovakia, as-
sassins tossed a bomb into Reinhard Heydrich's car. He died
of the wounds a week later.*

NOT GOOD ENOUGH: The Nazis could not do enough for JUNE 15
Hangman Reinhard Heydrich. His bomb-gutted body was
borne through torch-lit streets; it lay in state in gabled
Prague Castle. Four Black Shirts stood as a guard of honor
at each of the four corners of a coffin scarred by a huge swas-
tika. In courtyards and alleyways the volleys of retributory
gunfire were like the spitting of angry cats. At each spatter another Czech fell. In ten days the Germans admitted 216
Czechs shot.

In the greatest man hunt in modern history, Nazi police
moved from house to house, sniffing out new victims for
the Heydrich funeral pyre. But they did not find the two patriots, possibly Czech parachutists dropped from British planes,
who had struck down the No. 2 Gestapoman.

A cortege, with all the outward signs of oldtime Nazi ar-
rogance, stalked through Prague streets lined with sullen
Czech workers. Then the body was shipped to Berlin for a
princely funeral ordered by Adolf Hitler. What happened to
Heydrich's soul, no one knew.

*Hangman Heydrich. What happened
to his soul, no one knows.*
    *King Haakon. On his birthday the
Nazis get the surprise. Page 138.*

JUNE 22   **LIDICE:** In the small town of Lidice, not far from Prague, there lived 1,200 human beings. Some worked in the orchards, gardens and fields which they owned; others were woodworkers and coal miners; still others walked 45 minutes every day to toil in the munitions plant at Kladno. Lidice had a church—St. Martin's—which was nearly five centuries old and to which the people of four nearby villages flocked on Sundays.

Last week the Nazis removed Lidice from the map. German soldiers surrounded the village at dusk, moved in, sorted out all adult males and killed them. The women were packed off to slower death in concentration camps, the children to "educational institutions." Then the Germans burned Lidice to the ground, left nothing but a great black scar in what had been green fields.

This was the worst atrocity committed by a civilized nation in modern times. The Germans did it with the cool expression of a concentration-camp guard kicking a prisoner in the groin. There was no need of the grapevine to get news of Lidice to the civilized world: the Germans themselves announced it in official radio broadcasts from Prague and Berlin.

The Germans accused the onetime people of Lidice of routine subversive activities, such as hiding arms and hoarding food. But the deadliest charge was that they aided and sheltered the killers of the Gestapo's hangman, Reinhard Heydrich. Besides the slaughter in Lidice, the Germans by week's end had shot 400 Czechs in reprisal for Heydrich's death.

JULY 27   **MASSACRE IN ZAGREB:** On market day in Zagreb's sun-washed square townspeople used to haggle with bright-costumed peasants who had spread out their wares. From sidewalk cafés men would banter with the pretty peasant girls. One day last week the shadow of hated Major Helm, Gestapo chief for the puppet state of Croatia, swaggered in the sun across the square. Somewhere a rifle's muzzle nosed from a window. A shot clapped. Gestapo Chief Helm flopped down on his shadow, dead. Enraged and terrified, his bodyguard swung their pistols on the crowd, hurled hand grenades among the tables of a close-packed sidewalk café. When screams and explosions died out, the wounded lay moaning all around the square and some 700 were dead.

EPIDEMIC: Near Lublin, Poland, guerrillas killed Franz Wald, local Gestapo chief, and four of his men. A fortnight ago another Gestapo chief, "Little Butcher" Erich Guttart, had been killed in the same district. The assassination of Reinhard Heydrich two months ago had started an epidemic.

NEXT!: A Yugoslav barber, shaving Lieut. Gustav Stuher, Deputy Chief of the Nazi Gestapo in Zagreb, let the razor slip. Now a new Deputy Chief is needed. AUG. 3

FLOWERS VERBOTEN: Last week in London, Norway's exiled King Haakon VII observed his 70th birthday. Said the King: "Today the home front in Norway is united like a strong wall. All Norwegians are thankful for the courage of the people who will not yield to Nazi demands." AUG. 17

From the Royal Palace in Oslo the unassuming King used to pedal his bicycle almost every day. Now the palace is the home of Major Vidkun Quisling. Early in the morning, on the King's birthday, Nazi Gestapomen and Norwegian police began patrolling Oslo streets. But there was no trouble until the Nazis noticed that hundreds of Norwegians were wearing flowers in their buttonholes and tried to pluck some of them out. Then arrests and riots began. In the center of the town beflowered crowds gathered, sang the national anthem and the royal song. Hastily the Nazis chased the flower sellers off the streets and padlocked all flower shops. But there were far too many flowers. And in each flower was hidden a razor blade.

BARBER'S ITCH: Last week the fingers of a Polish barber, shaving Nazi General von Killinger, began itching to let the razor slip. They itched so hard that it did. This was the second time in three weeks that a Nazi bigwig had got his last shave.

"LILLE GOEBBELS": To Gulbrand Lunde, Propaganda Minister and second in command of Vidkun Quisling's Government in Norway, Joseph Goebbels was a man to be admired. In NOV. 9

mannerisms, gestures and work, the small, blue-eyed Norwegian tried to emulate his Nazi friend. First of the Quisling Cabinet to get a uniform, he copied his so closely from Goebbels' that in photographs it was hard to tell Lunde from Goebbels. Norwegians nicknamed Lunde "*lille* Goebbels," and knew him as a vain, ambitious, foolish man who had been an outstanding research chemist when he joined the Quisling Party in 1933.

Last week Norwegians heard their Propaganda Minister no longer. The last to see him were the villagers of Vage, a tiny hamlet on the Norwegian coast. In the dark of a Sunday evening, Lunde, with his wife and a district party leader, arrived in Vage to take the little ferryboat that went across the fjord to Andalsnes. The chauffeur drove the limousine out on the slip, got out and strolled aboard the ferry. An instant later, slip and ferry parted. The car teetered, plunged into the icy water.

The skipper of the ferry dived into the fjord, came up gasping, dived again. But it was not until 7 o'clock the next morning that the bodies were hauled up with the car. In their homes Norwegians heard of the Propaganda Minister's death from the German-controlled radio. Their grim jest: the ferryboat skipper had "made those dives to be sure the car doors were locked."

Lookalike propaganda ministers, Joseph Goebbels of Germany (right) and Gulbrand Lunde of Norway. Lunde visits the bottom of a fjord in his car.

India

*The Japanese invasion of Malaya and Burma as the year
opened posed a military threat to the British colony of India,
and precipitated a political crisis within the country.*

ONE MAN'S WORD: It was late, Japan's armies were near, and APRIL 6
at last, after all the painful years, Britain turned the page of
history. Standing in a sun-splashed conference room in
New Delhi, Sir Stafford Cripps solemnly read to correspondents Britain's offer of full Dominion status to India
after the war, including the right to separate into two or
more Dominions and even to secede from the British Com-
monwealth. He spoke for the British Government, but the
offer had unmistakably the sound of his own voice. He was
the only top member of the British War Cabinet who had
long & loudly advocated such an offer.

The quick, smiling, 52-year-old lawyer is a man not only
of stabbing intellect and wit but also of transparently high sin-
cerity. The British Government had customarily approached
India down marble stairs and along crimson carpets. Sir Stafford hustled out of an R.A.F. Lockheed with a briefcase, three
small bags and a portable typewriter.

The British-Indian problem was 300 years old, but Sir Stafford said he hoped he could iron things out in two weeks.
It seemed astounding, but he knew what he had in his bags.
He did not have tropical clothes, and he sweated hard
through a rush of interviews with all manner of Indian po-
liticos. When newsmen began to draw optimistic deductions
from the smiles of callers as they left Sir Stafford's bungalow,
Sir Stafford cracked that he always asked everyone to smile
as he left.

Then, after six Conference-jammed days Sir Stafford called
in the press, read them India's Magna Charta. When he
was asked who would guarantee Britain's declaration, he replied: "You must trust me; it is only on my word."

BOGGED DOWN: After two weeks of brilliant and painstaking APRIL 13
labor, Sir Stafford Cripps looked years older. So great had
been his confidence in the plan that he had expected to be

on his way back to London this week. It was almost inconceivable to him that his beloved Indians would not readily and cheerfully accept his English version of Christian idealism.

But then the offer bogged down in the morass of Indian politics. No sooner had Sir Stafford reached India than rumors spread that Mohandas Karamchand Gandhi, spiritual head of the potent Indian National Congress Party, would come to New Delhi to see that his party vetoed Sir Stafford's plan. Sure enough, the wily Saint arrived, in loincloth and carrying a staff, after a 24-hour rail journey from his mud hut in central India. On the way he acted as his own press-agent, handing notes (it was his day of silence) through the train window to newsmen at the stations.

However much Gandhi longed for India's "freedom," he balked at any plan which would involve India more deeply in the war. For two hours Sir Stafford did his Christian-Socialist best to sway the Hindu Saint. The little man with the minxy smile merely kept repeating: "India cannot be conquered by the Japs so long as we do not cooperate with the invaders." After the interview Sir Stafford was tired and exasperated. And presently the Holy Man went off home.

If Sir Stafford Cripps could swing Pandit Jawaharlal Nehru, active leader of the party, away from Gandhi, there was still hope of a favorable Congress vote. But Nehru represents only a large minority of Sir Stafford's problem. Another great minority Sir Stafford had to deal with was India's 80,000,000 Moslems. His proposal for them: the opportunity to form a separate state. This proposal was not disliked by the Moslem League's President Ali Mohamed Jinnah. But it was much disliked by Nehru and other Congress leaders: they feared Moslem secession, cried that Indian unity should not be destroyed.

APRIL 20 **GOOD-BY, MR. CRIPPS:** "We have tried, by the offer I brought, to help India along her road to victory and freedom. But, for the moment, past distrust has proved too strong to allow a present settlement."

On the New Delhi radio, Sir Stafford Cripps's voice was level and controlled. But his self-control could not hide his enormous disappointment. With the Japanese on the road to Mandalay and their bombers already roaring over the Indian coastline, India's political factions had been unable to resolve their suspicions of each other and of Britain.

GANDHI IN HIGH: It was so hot in New Delhi last week that airplane pilots clad only in shorts said they were still comfortable at 20,000 feet. Was Mohandas Gandhi crazy with the heat? Under the blazing sun, Gandhi's faith in the nonviolent noncooperation which he urges for India's defense reached such furnace temperature that he wrote in the journal *Harijan:* "The presence of the British in India is an invitation to Japan to invade India. Their withdrawal would remove the bait." Wildly exaggerated as Gandhi's faith in his own defense technique may be, it is not beyond possibility that the British-Indian Army's fighting may be aided to a degree by Gandhi's nonviolent noncooperation. Armies of nonviolent noncooperators might be a considerable obstacle to a Japanese invasion. Gandhi's policy is anything but pacifism. It is organized mass resistance whose nearest U.S. equivalent is the sit-down strike. Gandhi's followers would obstruct

MAY 25

This cartoon from the Newark "Evening News" shows Mohandas Gandhi trying to stop a Japanese invasion with nonviolence.

Japan by refusing the invader their labor; they would not work in factories, run trains, operate telephones or telegraphs, draw water or grow crops for Japan. If Japan killed them for their resistance, it would not help. And followers of Gandhi have sometimes proved their willingness to die—in front of streetcars or police, or in hunger strikes—for their cause.

JUNE 29 **THE MIND OF GANDHI:** This interview with Mohandas Gandhi was cabled from India last week by TIME Correspondent Jack Belden:

"I found Gandhi flat on his back on a white mattress laid on a clean-swept floor made of cow dung. About his body was a simple cotton loincloth, the thread of which was spun by his own hands. In one hand he held a rag, which he constantly dipped into a bowl of water by his side and wiped over his shiny bald head. Gandhi looked old as wisdom, skeleton-thin, sharp, bird-like; all his teeth are gone. He seemed in remarkable spirits.

'So you've come to vivisect me. All right, I'm at your disposal.'

"Gandhi insisted that nonviolence against Japan was the only course open to him. Said he: 'We have no army, no military resources, no military skill, and nonviolence is the only thing we can rely on. Of course we can't prevent invasion: the Japs will land, but they will land on an inhospitable shore. We do not need to kill a single Jap; we simply give them no quarter.'

"Gandhi added: 'I do not want to help the Japs, even in order to free India. Remember, I am more interested than the British in keeping the Japs out. For if Japan wins, India loses everything.'

"Finally, he summarized his demand to Great Britain: 'For heaven's sake, leave India alone. Let us breathe the air of freedom. It may choke us, suffocate us as it did the slaves under emancipation, but I want the present sham to end.'"

JULY 27 **"BRITAIN, WITHDRAW":** Monday was Gandhi's day of silence, but Tuesday morning the silence was broken. Correspondents were summoned to receive the decision of the Congress

Party Working Committee. In a high-pitched, whistling voice, the 90-lb. arch-enemy of the British Raj declared that, from now on, the people of India would be in open, nonviolent rebellion against British rule. The Congress resolution demanded that Britain withdraw politically from India, and threatened to use all the possible nonviolence of the people to compel Britain to withdraw.

"I think this may be illegal," said one British official after he finished reading the resolution. There was no doubt that, by the law of India, Gandhi and every member of Congress was subject to arrest.

"DO OR DIE!": Monsoon skies were slate-grey overhead. The AUG. 17 oppressive heat gave added pungency to the smell of human filth in the Bombay slums. Shopkeepers moved listlessly; talk dribbled in the bazaars. Suddenly everything changed. Word sputtered from mouth to mouth that the British Raj had jailed Mahatma Gandhi.

No longer listless, Bombay Hindus ran riot. Foreigners were stoned. So were police, who answered with tear gas, then fired directly into the crowds.

Thus last week did a tragic hour come to India. The British struck first. In the dawn's early light, Bombay's police commissioner arrested Gandhi at the home of a wealthy Indian industrialist. The elderly Pied Piper, who had been up until 2 a.m. writing memoranda, was sleepy but good-humored. He was given an hour to get ready. During that time he had a breakfast of orange juice and goat's milk. He heard a Sanskrit hymn and a few words from the Koran, read by a young Moslem girl. He scrawled a last-minute message to his followers: "Every man is free to go to the fullest length under *ahimsa* (nonviolence) for complete deadlock by strikes and all other possible means. *Karenge ya Marenge!* (Do or Die!)."

Then, with a copy of the Bhagavad-Gita (sacred Hindu poem), the Koran and an Urdu primer under his arm, a garland of flowers around his wizened neck, he was taken in the commissioner's car to Victoria station. "Nice old fellow, that Gandhi," the commissioner said. The train chuffed on to Poona. There the Mahatma was imprisoned in the rambling stone "bungalow" of the rich Aga Khan.

Nearly 200 party leaders were rounded up and jailed including white-capped Pandit Jawaharlal Nehru, Gandhi's leading disciple and right-hand man, and white-bearded Maulana Abul Kalam Azad, President of the Congress party. A few minutes before his arrest Azad smuggled out a message: if party leaders were seized, "every Congress member becomes Congress President."

This message, coming before Gandhi's, set off the first riots. Spreading from Bombay, the disorder took on increasingly serious proportions. In New Delhi a small crowd fought its way past a barricade at the foot of the hill leading to the Viceroy's palace, but later was turned back. Whites said: "It's here," kept close together for mutual protection.

OCT. 5 **MACHINE GUNS:** So serious were disturbances in India last week that General Sir Alan Hartley announced that it had been necessary "on five occasions to use airplanes to deal with mobs by machine-gun fire from the air."

NOV. 23 **NO LIQUIDATION:** Winston Churchill had been commenting on Allied successes in North Africa, but Great Britain's Prime Minister was obviously thinking about India when he said:

"Let me make this clear, in case there should be any mistake about it in any quarter: we mean to hold our own. I have not become the King's First Minister in order to preside over the liquidation of the British Empire."

Ireland

APRIL 20 **IRE IN IRELAND:** In Northern Ireland, relations between the Irish and the predominantly Midwestern U.S. troops recently stationed there were somewhat strained. Illogical to the Irish mind was the troops' complaining of the lack of supplies while they absorb all the surpluses in sight, especially beer. Stopped by a small-town constable for passing a red light, a U.S. trooper rudely exclaimed: "I've never seen traffic lights in a cemetery before." Another, asked his opinion

of Irish girls, glumly replied: "At home, we bury our dead."
The Irish have a tendency to resent such remarks. When a
U.S. technician in a bar grumbled audibly about "having to
come over to look after this little island," an incensed Irish-
man flashed back: "Faith, you don't seem very good at
looking after your own little islands."

The Irish were still Irish.

Italy

*Although the German-Italian Axis was still doing well mil-
itarily, the Italians themselves had little stomach for the war.
Mussolini's prestige had already begun to decline as wartime
hardships grew, and there was increasing sentiment for peace.*

MORALE: "My mouth brushes against his and I say: 'And   MARCH 16
you, Benito—do you know I love you?' "

With such sultry passages did the onetime French gossip
columnist, Magda Fontanges, reveal the story of her passion
for Italy's aging (58) Mussolini. Last week, two years later,
she would scarcely have recognized her onetime lover. In
his private study at the Palazzo Venezia, Mussolini no longer entertains visitors. In deep gloom he sits alone, reading
Dante and Virgil, while his people faint on the streets from
hunger.

For the first time since Italy declared war on the U.S.
came a firsthand account last week of how recent months
have affected Mussolini and the humble *paesanos* he exhorted
to "live like lions." It tallied in most respects with information smuggled out by secret societies. All accounts told of
hunger in Italy, of disillusionment, of despair.

So hungry was Venice that the thousands of pigeons in
famed St. Mark's Square had been eaten and were almost
gone. Bread was scarce, fats almost nonexistent. Vegetables
were being exported to Germany to pay for coal. But there
was so little coal that convalescent soldiers shivered miserably
in the hospitals.

As Italy's food grew scarce, down went Italian morale.

The quip of the moment was: "If England wins, we are losers; if Germany wins, we are lost."

DEC. 14 **HONEST DUCE:** The hour had come when the truth was more useful than propaganda. With his back to the Alps, Benito Mussolini last week ladled out the truth. He did it sparingly, and he mixed it with apologies and name-calling. To Churchill's latest description of him as a "hyena," Mussolini replied: "I, Mussolini, rate myself a thousand times more a gentleman than this man Churchill—intoxicated with alcohol and tobacco."

Later Mussolini attacked "that hyena Roosevelt," declared Britain's history for 300 years has been "one long list of acts worthy of hyenas."

"This is not a speech," Mussolini told the National Council of Corporations in a voice that wheezed but did not falter. "I am going to review the first 30 months of war with statistics. We are the only country which gives exact figures of losses."

If this were a matter of pride to Mussolini, then the statistics he gave of war losses for a nation of 44,000,000 were not. They totaled 445,000 Italians killed, missing, wounded or captured.

Japan

JAN. 19 **FOOTNOTE TO CONQUEST:** Slipping the news into a week of spectacular victory, the Japanese Government told its people that starting Feb. 1, in the six most populated provinces, each person would have to get along with only 35 "handfuls" of rice per month—just over a handful a day. To the rice-dependent Japanese, a handful is not a stomachful.

JUNE 22 **TOUGH JOB:** Wrote a frank and unawed Japanese to a TIME correspondent: "You may wonder why the emperor wears a bad-tailored cloth. The reason is the simplest one: since he is a living god, no one can touch him, so the tailor judges his body by photo or otherwise. Indeed, the emperor's tailor is one who has the most difficult task in the world."

Russia

"LET US CUT DOWN THE ORCHARD": From a Russian cor- SEPT. 7
respondent of the London *Times* last week came this typically
Russian account of scorched-earth tactics in the Cossack
country:

"A burning haze hovers over the dusty street of the Cossack village of Starominskaya. In each courtyard stands a
wagon to which a pair of sturdy horses is harnessed. Villagers take only the most essential belongings; the rest will
be buried under cover of darkness where the German invaders will never discover it. All that is left is the poultry,
which the children are now chasing in the courtyards, while
their mother, tears streaming down her cheeks, cuts the
throats of cocks and hens. As the column leaves, the night
sky is illuminated by the glare of burning villages and gunfire flashes. With the baggage go the old men and women,
mothers and small children, the sick and crippled. The able-
bodied will remain behind and fight side by side with the
Red Army troops.

"An old Cossack took up his ax and called his 13-year-
old grandson from a neighboring house: 'Come here, grandson, and let us cut down the orchard and smash the beehives.'
Apple, pear and apricot trees laden with still unripe fruit
fell one after another. 'Pile it up in the street,' the old man
said. 'Let anybody who wants take it, and what is left the armored tractors will crush to pulp when they come by.'

"Tonight Red troops poured through en route to the
front. Later in the quiet village the sound of plane engines
presaged German parachutists. The Cossacks dashed out
from their huts, hastily arming themselves with shotguns, sa-
bers, axes and even fire irons. Scattering among the yards
and orchards, concealing themselves behind fences and in
ditches, they spied out the position of the enemy force. A report was dispatched to the commander of the nearest Red
Army unit. 'Kill wherever you can and any way you can,'
he ordered, and the Cossacks began operations. A German
coming to a well for a drink was shot. Another got a brick
on his skull. When the Red Army troops reached the village, only about a score of German parachute men still
survived. The rest had been annihilated by villagers."

Yugoslavia

From the time of the Nazi invasion of Yugoslavia in 1941, the outside world heard so many stories of the brave resistance being put up by a group of patriots called Chetniks under the leadership of General Draja Mihailovich that it appeared he was the most effective fighter against the Nazis. It was later learned, however, that an even more effective resistance movement consisted of an army of Partisans under the leadership of a Communist soldier known as Tito.

JAN. 26 **UNSUNG HERO:** The most unsung hero of World War II had last week gained control of 20,000 of the 96,000 square miles of a nation which Adolf Hilter imagined he had conquered early last spring. The Nazis had quit trying to dislodge Yugoslavia's General Draja Mihailovich from the cold mountains southwest of Belgrade and had retired to that city to await warmer weather.

Draja Mihailovich's fiery army of 145-150,000 former Yugoslav regulars, Serb *Chetnik* guerrillas, Croats, Slovenes, Jews, Bulgarian and Austrian deserters usually fights in small, separated groups like guerrillas. But General Mihailovich has a radio sending station. His forces have countless portable radio receiving sets of the former Yugoslav Army. His war is thus an organized, continuous raiding operation—mobile, swift, deceptive—which in years to come will undoubtedly rank as an epic.

When Hitler's *Panzers* began rolling into Yugoslavia last April, General (then Colonel) Mihailovich led his regiment into the mountain fastnesses near the Albanian border and let the enemy roll on to Greece. The collapse of the Yugoslav Army meant that thousands of soldiers, fully and modernly equipped, rushed to Mihailovich. Soon he began systematically harassing Nazi units.

Draja Mihailovich, 47, is a stocky, jovial father of five who with equal spirit plays the mandolin and fights. Born in Ivanjica, Serbia, in the territory he now holds, he was wounded fighting the Turks in 1913 and the Austrians in 1915. After World War I he became an expert on Nazi fifth-column activity. In London last week the Yugoslav Government-in-Exile did General Mihailovich proper honors; they made him Minister of War.

"KIND HEARTS": The Nazis threatened last week that if brave APRIL 20 General Draja Mihailovich and his 150,000 guerrillas did not surrender within five days, 16,000 Yugoslav hostages, including many relatives of the guerrillas, would be executed. Responses came at once from the 20,000-square-mile "Island of Freedom" where General Mihailovich has for months fought off and made raids against as many as seven different Nazi divisions. One response was a "spring offensive" against the one remaining Nazi division and the Bulgarian troops which have replaced the others.

Last week, over a clandestine radio transmitter, a simple, peasant voice appealed to Yugoslavs with another answer:

"Be patient, for patience alone will save our mother Serbia and our great Yugoslavia. You can help us and our chief in two ways: by joining us with your rifles or by giving us food, clothing, shelter and news. Rifles are not the only weapon. We also need kind hearts."

MIHAILOVICH ECLIPSED: "They emerged like cats from every- DEC. 14 where, knives between their teeth. Flares did not frighten them. They broke into our right flank. Then the terrible thing happened that froze the blood of all of us. Men, women and children flung themselves into the attack."

Thus wrote a German war correspondent. He was not describing Allied Commandos, or even Russian guerrillas. He was talking about Yugoslavia's Partisans, who, he added, "are not wild hordes, but strictly organized units which print their own newspapers in the forests and manufacture their own bombs and munitions."

The emergence of the Partisans last week as the main anti-Axis force in the Balkans opened a new phase in the complicated, triangular Civil War that has alternately smoldered and flamed in Yugoslavia ever since the German invasion nearly two years ago. The Partisans had organized an army and a state; they were operating on a front 100 miles long and had already destroyed one Nazi *Panzer* column.

Many a U.S. citizen had come to identify General Draja Mihailovich and his *Chetniks* with the resistance of the peo-

Draja Mihailovich. His Chetniks get the credit for resisting the Nazis.

Josip Broz ("Tito"). His Partisans are doing most of the fighting.

ples of Europe to Nazi invaders. By last week it was clear that the Partisans had eclipsed Mihailovich. Axis military communiqués referred consistently to the resistance of the Partisans, rarely mentioned Mihailovich. As might be expected, Axis propaganda described the Partisans as cutthroats, Communists and bandits. In London Yugoslav officials connected with the Government in exile used the same epithets.

In November 1941, General Mihailovich's heterogeneous band had suffered a serious defeat near Valjevo at the hands of German mechanized columns. The *Chetnik* Army splintered. Whole units under Mihailovich's former subordinates joined the Italians. Others went back to their farms. Mihailovich himself retired to relative inactivity, somewhere in Montenegro, avoiding action except for a sharp attack last June against a Partisan army fighting the Italians in southern Montenegro. Montenegrin Partisans charge that in certain instances Mihailovich collaborated with the Italians.

Those *Chetniks* who wanted to continue active resistance filtered through the lines and joined a Partisan band which became the largest and most active of half a dozen Partisan groups who fought steadily and bitterly against the Germans and Italians.

The Partisans prepared systematically for major military operations. They trained their ever-growing armies, not for pinprick sabotage, but for a major campaign to drive the Axis from Yugoslavia. And they prepared politically, by adopting democratic methods almost unprecedented in the Balkans. Town councils were elected by ballot. Medical services were instituted. Theaters were opened in the liberated territory, featuring well-known actors and the entire orchestra of the Zagreb National Theater, which had joined the Partisans. The new State even had a Foreign Office and a radio station whose English-language newscasts come over in a sharp Yankee accent. [The role of Tito's Communist Partisans gradually grew in importance until Tito himself became the recognized leader of the resistance. Using this prestige, he became Prime Minister of the country after the war. In 1953 he was elected President.]

MILESTONES

BORN: To Anne Morrow Lindbergh, 35, and ex-Colonel Charles Augustus, 40; their fifth child, fourth son; in Detroit. Their other living children are: Jon Morrow, 10 (born six months after the kidnap-slaying of two-year-old Charles Augustus Jr.); Land Morrow, 5; Anne Spencer, 2.

DIVORCED: Cinemactress Mae West; from Vaudeville Dancer Frank Wallace, from whom she had been separated since a few weeks after their marriage in Milwaukee, 31 years ago; in Los Angeles. Said Divorcée West: "He has been a pain in the neck for a long time."

DIED: Tony, the late Tom Mix's famed "wonder horse"; of euthanasia; in San Fernando, Calif.

DIED: Charactress Edna May Nutter ("Edna May Oliver"), 59, long-faced, purse-mouthed player of acid old maids; of an intestinal ailment; on her birthday; in Hollywood. Born into a well-to-do Boston family that went broke, she was originally a singer but ruined her voice giving outdoor concerts, turned to playing in theatrical stock companies. In Hollywood she was a deft scene-stealer, won a reputation as a character actress. She lived alone, rarely took part in Hollywood's whoop-te-do.

MISCELLANY

SHOT: Near Pomona, Calif., Ranchman C. E. Foote shot at a crow. The shot frightened his horse, whose shoe struck sparks from a rock. The sparks set a fire that burned 25 acres of land. The crow escaped.

CLEAN SWEEP: In Shutesbury, Mass., the Army at one swoop drafted the chairman of the Selectmen, the chairman of the Board of Public Welfare, the principal of the Center School, the chairman of the Board of Health, the director of old-age assistance, the chairman of the Civilian Defense Committee, the president of the Teachers Association, a trustee of the library, the library's janitor, the school department's janitor, the town identification officer, and a voters' registrar: all the same man, Henry Dihlman.

PEOPLE

"Names make news." In 1942 the following names made the following news:

TALLULAH BANKHEAD offered her blood for her country. "I told them that I was so damned anemic," she reported, "my blood would kill a good American soldier. I told them that I'd give them quarts of the stuff if they would put it into the right places—into Japanese soldiers."

Soldiers at California's Camp Callan whose mothers were to be absent on Mother's Day chose a "proxy mother" to visit them. The proxy: RITA HAYWORTH.

KING GEORGE VI of Great Britain cut down on fuel and light in Buckingham Palace and Windsor Castle by: 1) limiting bathers to five inches of water in the tub (warning lines were painted at the five-inch levels); 2) allowing only one light bulb to a bedroom; 3) forbidding the use of fireplaces in bedrooms except on doctors' orders.

Out of the ring four years, former welterweight boxing champion BARNEY ROSS, 32, was still all right in defense and attack. A Marine private on Guadalcanal, Private Ross looked up and beheld an advance guard of Japs approaching. Ross got two wounded men into a shell hole and dived into a six-foot crater, started throwing grenades. Every time he lifted his head machine-gun bullets whanged his helmet: before the night was over there were 30 creases in it. Out of ammunition, the men in the crater crouched and prayed. At dawn the prize fighter jumped out under cover of a cloud of smoke and helped get the wounded to the rear. His purse: shell shock, malaria, minor shrapnel wounds, promotion to corporal, recommendation for a distinguished service award. His only complaint: "No referee to break the clinches."

Muscleman Charles Atlas (left) offers to build up the physique of that "poor little chap," India's Mohandas Gandhi (right) for nothing.

MOHANDAS KARAMCHAND GANDHI, leafing through a muscle-building magazine, set eyes on an article by CHARLES ATLAS in which the Muscle Mahatma expressed pity for "the poor little chap" Gandhi and offered to build him up, for nothing. Exclaimed Gandhi: "I have met some inventive Americans, but Atlas takes the first prize. Mind you, I would be delighted to have him work on me—if I could find someone to pay his passage to India."

QUEEN WILHELMINA of The Netherlands, on a visit to the U.S., went shopping in little Lee, Mass. "Good morning, Queen," said the drugstore man. The ruler bought a sponge. "I am old-fashioned," she explained. "Everybody else uses a washcloth, but I like a sponge for my bath." She moved on to the furniture store, bought an inexpensive grade of linoleum for the bathroom floor; her granddaughters had been splashing it with water. Then she departed as she had come, in a big armored car, a carload of guards in front, another behind.

SPORT

JAN. 19   **NAVAL BATTLE:** For the first time in U.S. ring history, a champion risked his title for charity last week. Joe Louis knocked out Heavyweight Buddy Baer in exactly 2 min. 56 sec., and kept his title, but his purse went to the New York Auxiliary of the Navy Relief Society. That night, Joe was notified that he had been drafted into the U.S. Army.

MARCH 30   **BIG RED'S 25TH:** If ever a U.S. horse attains the immortality of Pegasus or Don Quixote's Rosinante, surely it will be Samuel D. Riddle's Man o' War. This Sunday, at Faraway Farm in Lexington, Ky., "Big Red" reaches the grand old age of 25—an age comparable to three-score and ten for a man—and without a grey hair to show for it.

Big Red leads the life of Reilly, in Kentucky's lush, warm Blue Grass country, is stalled in a luxury stable, with attendants to come a-running at his every sneeze and snort. Since settling down at stud some 20 years ago, he has attracted visitors on the scale of the Dionne Quintuplets.

Big Red has money in his genes. Having a mare served by him costs the mare's owner $5,000 and through 1941 he had sired 335 registered foals. Some of his more brilliant off-spring: Crusader, War Admiral, Mars, Scapa Flow, Genie and Battleship. Big Red was the famed Seabiscuit's grandpa. Though his weight is up a little and his back has sagged a trifle, he still has plenty of life in him: this year he will take care of from ten to a dozen mares.

APRIL 6   **PAYOFF IN APPLES:** For the 21st time since he won it from Jim Braddock in 1937, the incomparable Joe Louis successfully defended his title by knocking out vast (255 $\frac{1}{4}$ lb.) Abe Simon, who looks like a worried cigar-store Indian, in 0:16 of the sixth round last week in Manhattan's Madison Square Garden. Joe had bought some $3,000 worth of tickets to the fight for his fellow privates at Fort Dix, and turned

Joe Louis v. Buddy Baer in a title match. After knocking out Baer to help the Navy, Louis gets drafted into the Army. Page 155.

his purse, estimated at $45,000 over to the Army Emergency Relief Fund. Promoter Mike Jacobs rewarded him with a dozen eating apples.

SPRING AGAIN: *"Should an air-raid siren sound while you're* APRIL 20 *watching a game, don't leave the ball park. A sticker on the back of your seat will tell you what to do. If you are to move at all, red and green arrows will direct you beneath the stands. You'll probably be sitting in the best bomb shelter in the neighborhood."*

Except for this wartime note, broadcast by big-league clubs, the 1942 baseball season opened this week much as usual. Some headliners were missing—notably Detroit's Hank Greenberg, Cleveland's Bob Feller, Washington's Cecil Travis, Philadelphia's Sam Chapman—and many another great ballplayer will follow them to war before the season ends.

But draft or no draft, U.S. baseball fans were down with their perennial spring fever.

IMMORTAL SIDESHOW: In the pitcher's box was the one & AUG. 31 only Big Train, at the plate the one & only Bambino, the greatest pitcher of all time *v.* the greatest swatter of them

Man o' War. At the grand old age of 25, "Big Red" lives in Blue Grass luxury and hasn't a grey hair on his body. Page 155.

all. Between games of a war-chest doubleheader—New York Yankees *v.* Washington Senators—Walter Perry Johnson (54) and George Herman ("Babe") Ruth (47) stepped out of the Hall of Fame this week to take one last crack at each other.

Walter Johnson—whose blazing antitank ball had won 413 games (113 shut-outs) and struck out 3,497 batters in 21 years with the Senators—pitched his last game 15 years ago. Babe Ruth—whose magnificent coordination had chalked up 714 home runs in 22 years with the Red Sox, Yankees and Braves—retired seven years ago. Yet both managed to squeeze into their old uniforms last week.

To 70,000 fans it looked like the good old days. The Babe stepped up to the plate with choppy little strides of his matchstick legs. Johnson shuffled awkwardly around the mound, his long right arm winding up the historic side-arm delivery.

The first pitch was low and inside, the second a called strike. Ruth popped the third into right field, the fourth was ball two. Then the crowd let out a mighty roar as the Babe walloped the ball up, up, up into the right-field stands. Fourteen pitches later, he clouted another, trotted around the bases and called it a day. Old Barney had got only three strikes on him.

ARMY SAYS NO: Up spoke the Secretary of War, Henry L. OCT. 5 Stimson: "I have determined that Sergeant Barrow and Corporal Conn shall be returned at once to their military duties. The standards and interest of the Army do not permit the proposed contest to be carried out." Thereupon Sergeant Joe Louis Barrow returned to his chores at Fort Riley, Kans., Corporal Billy Conn to his at Fort Wadsworth, N.Y. Off for the duration were heavyweight championship prize fights.

WHITEWASH: If there was one outstanding hero of last week's OCT. 12 Series, it was the St. Louis Cardinal Southpaw, Ernie White. With the help of two miraculous one-handed catches by Outfielders Enos ("Country") Slaughter and Terry Moore, White whitewashed the Yankees, 2-to-0—something that had not happened to them in a World Series in 16 years. Another hero was long-legged Johnny Beazley, 23, only Cardinal pitcher to win two games in this year's Series. He grips the ball so hard his hand quivers for a half hour after each game. But the Beaze has plenty on the ball.

In winning the fifth and final game, Beazley turned in a masterful performance. In the fifth inning, trailing by one run, with the bases loaded and two Cardinal errors behind him, he calmly retired Roy Cullenbine and Joe Di Maggio. He kept his head until Whitey Kurowski broke up a nerve-racking ninth-inning tie with a home run to bring in an extra run and give the Cardinals the game (4-to-2) and the championship, four games to one.

MILESTONES

MARRIED: John Hay ("Jock") Whitney, 37: and Betsey Cushing Roosevelt, 33; both for the second time; in Manhattan. Handsome, enthusiastic Jock Whitney, heir to a $27,-000,000 trust fund, has been an art patron, six-goal polo player, owner of a famed racing stable, is now a dollar-a-year man with his friend Nelson Rockefeller's Committee on Inter-American Affairs. Blonde Betsey Cushing Roosevelt, daughter of late famed Surgeon Harvey W. Cushing, got her divorce from Captain Jimmy Roosevelt in 1940.

MISCELLANY

SYSTEM: In Fairview, Okla., Farmer Ben Sorge explained why he had worn his shoes on the wrong feet every other day for the past ten years. Said he: "It wears the heels and soles down even all the way around."

THE THEATER

FEB. 16 **ONE OF THE WORST:** Since Christmas night, not a new show—and only one revival, *Porgy and Bess*—had really managed to click on Broadway. It has been one of the worst seasons in a generation.

Easiest explanation of the trouble is the war. The war, to be sure, has had a somewhat wavering effect on box office. But no show has perished which deserved to live. The war has also had a slightly paralyzing effect on playwrights, who have found the world's present plight too big to cope with.

There also exists the feeling that in wartime standards can be lowered and the public will amiably make allowances. So far, the public has agreed to do no such a thing.

APRIL 27 **"WITHOUT LOVE"** by Philip Barry offers the public its latest chance to see Katharine Hepburn defrosted. This time she is a prominent young Washington widow whose memories are too sweet for her ever to want love again. She meets a jilted young economist (well played by Elliott Nugent) whose memories are too bitter for him ever to want love again. So, at the end of Act I, they coldly set forth on a marriage of companionship. It is not till the end of Act III that Playwright Barry lets them avow their blatantly self-evident love for each other. Meanwhile Actress Hepburn, with her glacial purr, her arctic charm, her sudden dazzling flashes of girlishness, her usual knock-out white evening dress, is the play's best attraction.

JUNE 8 **THE GREAT PROFILE:** John Barrymore liked living in glass houses—and in a way was concealed by their glare. The world saw all his poses, heard all his wisecracks, without ever really knowing what he was like.

In 1903, when he was 21, he went on the stage, following the footsteps of his father, mother, sister Ethel, older brother

Lionel, Uncle John Drew and grandparents and forbears for over a century. At 34 he found himself, and fame, in Galsworthy's *Justice.* Seven great years followed: *Peter Ibbetson, Redemption, Richard III,* and then a *Hamlet* that became legendary. At 43 John Barrymore was the greatest actor on the English-speaking stage. But he never, except once long after, appeared on the stage again.

He went Hollywood with a bang. There were great parties, great Barrymore flareups. "All the Barrymores," said playboy John once, "have tempers. What do you think we are, book ends?" In any encounter, he usually got in the last word. "Thank God," said Katharine Hepburn to him when they finished a picture, "I don't have to act with you anymore." Cooed John: "I didn't know you ever had, darling."

Slowly The Bottle began to win out over The Profile; even what Barrymore called "the left, or money-making side of my face" stopped throwing women into dithers. In 1939 Barrymore made his only return to the stage, in an embarrassing burlesque of his own life, *My Dear Children.* Then he went on the air, majestically insulting himself on the Rudy Vallee hour. Shattered in health, he often could not go on, lived in & out of hospitals. Fortnight ago he turned up, staggering with pain, for a rehearsal, finally said: "I guess this is one time I miss my cue."

Rushed to a Hollywood hospital, he lay mostly in a coma, suffering from myocarditis, chronic nephritis, cirrhosis of the liver, gastric ulcers. When his great friend, Author Gene Fowler, visited him, Barrymore stage-whispered weakly: "Lean over, Gene, I want to ask you something. Is it true that you're an illegitimate son of Buffalo Bill?" Last week, at 60, with only his brother Lionel at his bedside, John Barrymore died.

"THE EVE OF ST. MARK" is the first successful U.S. war play. OCT. 19 Playwright Maxwell Anderson has contrived no elaborate plot, essayed no vaulting rhetoric, embraced no queer philosophy. He has simply set down the ubiquitous story of the U.S. today—a kind of *Everyman* in khaki. He has told of young Quizz West (William Prince), a farm boy who leaves his girl (Mary Rolfe) and his family to become a soldier. Quizz goes to training camp and then to war, and, on a tiny island in the Pacific, is part of a gallant, malaria-ridden remnant that face war's horror, enact its heroism and succumb to its fate.

The play—which takes its rather far-fetched title from a legend that on St. Mark's Eve a young girl standing at a church door may see the ghosts of all those who will die within the year—is dedicated to the author's nephew, Sergeant Lee Chambers, "one of the first to go, one of the first to die that we may keep this earth for free men." It is the thought of some other Sergeant Chambers in every spectator's mind that accentuates the poignancy of Maxwell Anderson's drama.

John Barrymore. Slowly The Bottle wins out over The Profile.   *George M. Cohan. "Great actors are born. I know. I was born."*

NOVE. 16 **GREAT SHOWMAN:** When Death, the prompter, as it must to all actors, called exit last week, George M. Cohan did not have to wonder what his notices would be like: his career had been vividly reported to millions while he lived. Songwriter, actor, dancer, vaudevillian, playwright, Cohan was never equaled for sheer versatility. But his many talents had a single showman's air: to please the crowd. "First think of something to say," his formula ran, "then say it the way the theatergoer wants to hear it—meaning, of course, that you must lie like the dickens."

The child of troupers, Cohan was born in Providence July 4, 64 years ago, when Jerry and Nellie Cohan had $1 between them. At eight he was fiddling in the orchestra. Cocky and conceited, he was a hellion in his youth. "Great actors are born," he said once. "I know. I was born."

Cohan hit Broadway at 23, was soon tossing off song hits like *You're a Grand Old Flag, Yankee Doodle Boy, Give My Regards to Broadway.* Sometimes he had six or seven productions a year—writing one while rehearsing another and acting in a third.

He shone again in the '30s as the father in Eugene O'Neill's *Ah Wilderness!* and in *I'd Rather Be Right,* in which he impersonated Franklin Roosevelt. When he went to the White House in 1940 to receive a medal, the President greeted him with: "Well, how's my double?"

"THE SKIN OF OUR TEETH"—In *Our Town* Thornton Wilder NOV. 30 abolished space and expanded Main Street into the universe. In *The Skin of Our Teeth* he has annihilated time and turned the Antrobus family of Excelsior, N.J. into the story of mankind. But where *Our Town* was a warm and human allegory nourished with crackerbarrel wisdom, *The Skin of Our Teeth* is a cockeyed and impudent vaudeville littered with asides and swarming with premeditated anachronisms. Dinosaurs collide with bingo; the Muses jostle the microphone. In showing how man through the ages has escaped destruction by the skin of his teeth, the play tweaks his nose, barks his shins, musses his hair, gives him the hotfoot.

The characters are humanity's archetypes. Mr. & Mrs. Antrobus (Fredric March & Florence Eldridge) are the eternal Mr. & Mrs.; their maid Sabina (Tallulah Bankhead) is Lilith, the eternal floozy; their son Henry (Montgomery Clift) is Cain, the eternal Dead-End kid. Their story is the eternal struggle between good & evil, the eternal seesaw of progressing and falling back. Mr. Antrobus comes home excitedly from the office, having invented the wheel and fixed up the alphabet—but the Ice Age has arrived. Finally he comes home, exhausted, from war to another battered world. "This is where you came in," Sabina tells the audience. "We have to go on for ages & ages yet. You all go home. The end of this play isn't written yet."

$$\boxed{\textbf{MUSIC}}$$

FEB. 23   **DOUGH-RE-MI:** The highest-paid musician in the U.S. is Singer Nelson Eddy. He has pocketed $7,000 for a single concert, generally gets $3,000-$3,500. His take last year: better than $200,000. So reported *Variety* last week. Second-best box office, said *Variety,* was petite, vivacious Coloratura Lily Pons, who averages $3,000 an appearance.

MARCH 30   **BRIGHT STARS, DEEP BLUES:** Two songs that are poles apart are now vying for top popularity among U.S. song hits. Biggest hit of the moment is the novelty handclapping number *Deep in the Heart of Texas.* Its childishly simple but rollicking tune has only 30 notes; to fill out a 32-bar chorus, the melody has to be repeated. Opening lines:

> *The stars at night are big and bright (clap, clap, clap, clap)*
> *Deep in the heart of Texas.*

The other smash hit is a meandering, rhapsodic flowering of the old-fashioned W. C. Handy type of blues, *Blues in the Night.* Unlike the Handy songs, it did not spring from Mississippi Valley soil, but was machined to order by Composer Harold Arlen and Lyricist Johnny Mercer for a Warner Brothers movie. To sing it from start to finish is a tricky job for an amateur, but almost any man in the street can take a whack at the lines:

> *My mama done tol' me....*
> *A woman's a two-face,*
> *A worrisome thing who'll leave ya t' sing*
> *the blues in the night.*

JULY 20   **SHOSTAKOVICH & THE GUNS:** "When guns speak the muses keep silent," says an old Russian proverb. But last winter, as he listened to the roar of German artillery and watched the sputtering of German incendiaries from the roof of Leningrad's Conservatory of Music, Fire Warden Dmitri Shostakovich snapped: "Here the muses speak together with the guns."

This Sunday afternoon the U.S. will hear the proof of his assertion, when a special NBC Symphony broadcast will give the Western Hemisphere its first chance to hear what Shostakovich's Marxist muse has to say in his *Seventh Symphony,* his biggest, most ambitious orchestral work to date—the work that he wrote last year between tours of duty digging trenches in the outskirts of Leningrad and fire-watching on the Conservatory roof.

Last month a little tin box, no more than five inches around, arrived in the U.S. In it were 100 feet of microfilm—the photographed score of the *Seventh Symphony.* Before the first strip of film had gone into the enlarger, three top-flight U.S. conductors—sleek, platinum-haired Leopold Stokowski, the Cleveland Orchestra's Artur Rodzinski, Boston's Serge Koussevitzky—were locked in a polite battle royal for the glory of conducting the première.

But a fourth, Maestro Arturo Toscanini, was very well connected—with National Broadcasting Co.—and NBC has been exceedingly forehanded. Last January, before a note of the symphony had been heard in rehearsal in the Soviet Union, NBC started dickering, through its Moscow correspondent, for first Western Hemisphere performance rights. By April the rights to conduct the *Seventh* were tucked away in NBC's pocket.

SHOSTAKOVICH PREMIÈRE: After 73 minutes of nonstop conducting, Arturo Toscanini looked as if he had just come through the siege of Leningrad. The audience jumped up and cheered, as if it had just heard news of a Nazi defeat. Thousands of radio listeners sighed and turned their dials. The great event had happened at last. Manhattan's music critics were inclined to do little tearing down. But most of them were cautious. JULY 27

Possibly the *Sun*'s Oscar Thompson best expressed the general reaction. Said he: "It does thunder—and for a particular time of war and the emotions of war it thunders very well."

Dmitri Shostakovich. The muses and the guns speak simultaneously.

Harry James. Twanging heartstrings catapult him into Bigtime.

SEPT. 28 **HORN OF PLENTY:** Swing fans milled around the Boston Theater's stage door, clamoring for autographs and drying the tears in their eyes. Glenn Miller had played one of his last stands for the duration; within the fortnight he will be gobbled up by the Army. But fans were fickle. Already they had picked a new favorite: the six-foot-one, wavy-haired son of a circus bandleader and circus bareback rider, Trumpeter Harry James. Already the "modern Gabriel" and his band had pied-piped away the followers of many hotter orchestras.

Three years ago, Benny Goodman gave his dark-haired, blue-eyed trumpeter a friendly shove toward bandleadership. A semi-failure at first, Bandleader James began tasting success only when he laid away his ambitions as a "hot" man, and developed a simple sweet style that features the clear, cool James trumpet against a mass of soft strings. His biggest Success Secret is the astute James theory that wartime fans, tired of pure heat, now want their heartstrings twanged. It was his revival of Al Jolson's 1914 hit, *You Made Me Love You* (I didn't *want* to do it, I *didn't* want to do it) that catapulted him into Bigtime.

OCT. 5 **HOT CLASSICIST:** Two shapely brown shoulders and a round, roguish face, framed in a triangle of white light, showed above the grand piano's shining ebony. From the keyboard Chopin's *Minute Waltz* flowed fleetly, ripplingly. Then watchers saw an impish flicker of a smile, an insinuating movement of a shoulder. Came the first suggestion of a hot lick; another, and another. Then Hazel Scott began to "break it down," and was off in a wild mélange of pianistics, sweet, hot, Beethoven and Count Basie.

Her fans had known all along what was coming. Hazel Scott, star Negro entertainer of Manhattan's Café Society Uptown, was doing what she does best, the thing that has made her this season's Manhattan sensation: swinging the classics. But where others murder the classics, Hazel Scott merely commits arson. Classicists who wince at the idea of jiving Tchaikovsky feel no pain whatever as they watch her do it. Then she may do just the reverse: into *Tea for Two* may creep a few bars of Debussy's *Clair de Lune.* Says wide-eyed Hazel: "I just can't help it."

WHITE CHRISTMAS: NOV. 23

> *I'm dreaming of a White Christmas,*
> *Just like the ones I used to know*
> *Where the tree tops glisten*
> *And children listen*
> *To hear sleigh bells in the snow.*

Tailored by Tunesmith Irving Berlin for the suave, sleepy voice of Cinemactor Bing Crosby, this song (from Paramount's *Holiday Inn)* originally expressed the longing for sleet and ice of an Easterner marooned among the palm trees of Hollywood. But with thousands of U.S. servicemen facing snowless Christmases from North Africa to Guadalcanal, *White Christmas* has unexpectedly become the first big sentimental song hit of World War II. Result: a sale, up to last week, of 600,000 copies—more (for a similar ten-week period) than any previous hit in Irving Berlin's hit-studded career.

ARMY & NAVY

JAN. 19 **CINCUS TO COMINCH:** Admiral Ernest J. King is the new Commander in Chief of the U.S. Fleet, but he will not be called CINCUS, the traditional Navy abbreviation of this big title. At his own stern, thin-lipped request, CINCUS (pronounced "sink-us") was abandoned. Official new nickname for the job: COMINCH.

APRIL 13 **ANSWER:** Landlubbers may wonder what a battleship band does when it is not tootling and drumming. The Navy told them last week. The 21 men in the band of the *Arizona,* sunk at Pearl Harbor, went down with the ship. They died at their battle stations in one of the most dangerous spots on a warship—passing ammunition in the clangorous bowels of the turrets.

APRIL 20 **NEGROES AT SEA:** The Navy's 20-year ban against Negroes for anything but the Messman Branch was lifted last week. Under the new ruling, Negroes will get the same physical and mental entrance exams as everyone else, can apply for ratings in the Navy, Marine Corps or Coast Guard. U.S. Negroes, at first, were delighted. When they took another look, they began screaming "Nazi attitude," "insult," "a definite straddle."

The reason was plain as a battleship: new rule or no, Negroes still cannot rise above a noncom, still must train and serve in segregated groups.

MAY 18 **WAAC AT LAST:** The long-delayed "Petticoat Army" Bill was close to enactment last week. Even happier than the bill's feminine backers was the Army itself, which wanted to free as many men as possible for combat. The Women's Army Auxiliary Corps will provide women for the Army's humbler jobs—switchboard operators, cooks, chauffeurs, laundresses, clerks, aircraft spotters & plotters. They will serve under

Oveta Culp Hobby. The soldiers she leads never go to the guardhouse.

Joe Foss has shot down so many Japs an admiral keeps score. Page 170.

the War Department, with Army pay, Army uniforms and Army discipline.

MAJOR HOBBY OF THE WAAC: The Women's Army Auxiliary MAY 25 Corps came into legal being last week. Immediately Secretary of War Stimson appointed as director one of the most remarkable Texans in Washington: Mrs. Oveta Culp Hobby, 37-year-old mother of two. Her rank corresponds to that of an Army major. Slim, trim, quiet and pretty, Mrs. Hobby has a taste for fancy hairdos and shocking hats. In the Corps she will wear a uniform hat, but will probably continue to ruin the hairdos by running her hands through her pompadour while thinking. She does a lot of thinking. Her husband, former Texas Governor William Pettus Hobby, once told her: "Anyone with as many ideas as you have is bound to hit a good one now and then."

As director of an organization which may include 150,000 women, "Major" Hobby is still unfazed, has started methodically on basic organization. She said that Corps members may wear "inconspicuous make-up," may wear civilian clothes on leave, will not be disciplined by confinement in Army guardhouses. As to the all-important uniform, prospective WAACs sighed with relief to find that the Army does not intend to design it. Miss Dorothy Shaver, vice president of Manhattan's Lord & Taylor, has charge of that momentous problem. [Mrs. Hobby rose to the rank of colonel, later served as Secretary of Health, Education and Welfare under President Eisenhower.]

JUNE 8 **WAAC'S FIRST MUSTER:** The Women's Army Auxiliary Corps had openings for 450 officers. On the first day, bemused Army recruiting officers gave out 13,208 long, pink application blanks and the nation's women were so eager to sign up that bosses waited in vain for secretaries, nurses arrived late and breathless at hospitals, dishes went unwashed and floors unswept.

The staccato questions and treble chatter in the 440 recruiting stations got on officers' nerves. Cried a lieutenant in Manhattan: "Ladies, please, for gosh sake, shut up a minute!" Said another officer: "They're just as tough to handle in this recruiting office as they are in civilian life."

JUNE 22 **HOW FIRM A FOUNDATION:** Last week *Women's Wear Daily* was gratified to learn that the WAACs would almost certainly be issued three brassières and two girdles apiece. Caroled an editorial:

"Adoption of girdles and brassières as part of the women's army wardrobe will add to the prestige of the corset and brassière industry."

AUG. 10 **THE WAVES:** While the WAACs drilled and paraded in Fort Des Moines, President Roosevelt signed into existence their sisters under the uniform: the Women's Naval Reserve, to be conveniently known as WAVES. Inducted this week as the WAVES' lieutenant commander was Wellesley College's President, brisk, able, curly-haired Mildred McAfee, 42. Especially wanted: women who majored in engineering, astronomy, meteorology, electronics, physics, mathematics, metallurgy, business statistics and modern foreign languages. Smith College in Northampton, Mass. will serve as official training center for WAVE officers.

SEPT. 21 **LADYBIRDS:** The Army Air Forces last week tapped the one group of experienced pilots that had not yet heard the come-hither of the armed services. To ferry aircraft from factory to airdrome, release uniformed airmen for combat service, it invited the 500 or 600 women with commercial pilot licenses to give it a lift, sat back to await a rush of ladybirds. Name of the new service is the Women's Auxiliary Ferrying Squadron (WAFS). Not yet ready to put skirted airmen into uniform, the Air Forces will hire its new ferry service pilots as Civil Service employes.

NO. 1 ACE: Five enemy planes shot down is the minimum for DEC. 21 designation as an ace, but Jap planes were being knocked off so rapidly by the U.S. Air Forces in the Solomons that until this week no one knew exactly how many planes Marine Captain Joe Foss had tallied of the 450-plus destroyed around Guadalcanal. This week at Pearl Harbor Admiral Chester W. Nimitz fixed Foss' score at 22 (in six weeks' flying), which made him officially top man among U.S. combat flyers in World War II. [By the end of the war, Foss' score was topped by Air Force ace Major Dick Bong, who shot down 40 Japanese planes. Foss served as Governor of South Dakota from 1954-1958.]

MILESTONES

DIVORCED: Charles Spencer Chaplin, 53; by Paulette Goddard, 31; in Juárez, Mexico; after six years of marriage, more than six years of public speculation on whether they were or were not married. She was his third wife, he her second husband.

DIED: Bernard ("Bunny") Berigan, 33, veteran trumpet virtuoso, top-notch tooter of the jazz and swing eras; of an intestinal ailment aggravated by trumpeting; in Manhattan. He began as a boy musician, appeared with name bands when he was 18, soloed with Paul Whiteman, Tommy Dorsey, Benny Goodman, organized his own band in 1937.

MISCELLANY

PASSENGER: In Muskogee, Okla., Patrolman James Hunter arrested a drunk, made a routine search of his automobile, found a securely trussed mountain lion, alive, in the trunk compartment. The drunk remembered helping a friend catch it, but explained he had thought at the time he was seeing things.

LAST WORDS: In Pompton Lakes, N.J., City Councilman Harry Davenport got a letter from the local American Legion post: "You are invited to be one of the speakers at our Memorial Day meeting. The program will include a talk by the Mayor, recitation of Lincoln's Gettysburg speech by a high-school pupil, your talk and then the firing squad."

ART

APRIL 27 **ADVERTISING ART:** Uniformed soldiers, tanks and bombers, rather than toothsome girlish smiles, will sell this year's quota of cigarets and soup to the U.S. public. Last week the most important barometer of U.S. advertising art indicated that the long reign of the pretty girl, the adman's most unfailing little helper, was temporarily on the decline. That barometer was the annual exhibition of the Art Directors Club of New York, year's biggest event in advertising art.

For the first time in its 22-year-history, the Art Directors Club this time crashed the gates of the holiest sanctum of the U.S. art world, Manhattan's Metropolitan Museum of Art, proudly hung its 301 hand-picked covers and ads near the museum's austere obelisks and mummies.

Trends:

¶ The girl ad, which had lost both dignity and raiment in its evolution from the patrician '20s to the leggy '40s, shows a sharp decline in popularity.

¶ The humorous cartoon ad ("Quick, Henry, the Flit!", etc.), which reached a peak in the middle '30s, is on the way down.

¶ Use of paintings by well-known artists, a trend popularized by Dole Pineapple and De Beers diamonds, is running stronger than ever.

But the biggest trend of all is toward patriotism and sobriety.

JULY 13 **MURALS, WITH CURRY SAUCE:** One of the foremost U.S. painters puttered aimlessly about his studio in Madison, Wis. last week, smoking his pipe and gazing out the windows. John Steuart Curry, famed painter of his native Midwest, had just finished two of the biggest painting jobs of his life and was enjoying the rest. Off & on for the past three years, in the Kansas State Capitol in Topeka, and in the University of Wisconsin's law school, he had been hard at

Advertising art: the patrician '20s have given way to the leggy '40s, but girls are on the decline. Page 171.

work on the heroic figures and lowering backgrounds of a new set of murals.

For Wisconsin, Curry had done a 37 by 14 ft. painting called *The Emancipation Proclamation.* For Topeka's Capitol he had attempted to picture the entire history of Kansas, beginning with Coronado's discovery. Painter Curry, who refers to himself without false modesty as "a picture painter, and a damned good one," was particularly proud of his work in Topeka, a panel dominated by the gigantic, furious figure of abolitionist John Brown. Said he: "It is the greatest painting I have yet done."

In painting this gigantic panorama, Muralist Curry discovered that all his problems were not concerned with paint. The Kansas Capitol was thronged with crusty Kansans who complained about everything from the blood on John Brown's hands to the shape of Curry's Hereford bulls. Informed that pigs' tails do not curl when they are eating, and that he had curled them the wrong way anyhow, patient Painter Curry took a day off to observe pigs' behinds.

OCT. 26 **UNREALIST:** A cosmopolitan crowd of Manhattan art-lovers trampled each other's elegant toes last week to see an exhibit of paintings by Marc Chagall, one of the least known (in the U.S.) of important modernist painters.

The show contained 16 canvases. First impression of so much Chagall in one room was like falling through space closely pursued by open cans of the three primary colors. Gradually the chromatic confusion resolved itself into nine paintings of Russian village life in Unoccupied France (painted after the Nazi invasion); three scenes of Russian village life in Connecticut (painted since Chagall's arrival in the U.S. last year); one scene of Russian village life in Russia; and one study of a cow in a high state of discoloration, the same animal Chagall painted 30 years ago from something he thought he saw in Paris.

To most gallerygoers the art of Marc Chagall has always been a good deal of a riddle. The puzzle began when Painter Chagall rushed from St. Petersburg to Paris with a canvas showing a decapitated milkmaid floating in an emetic sky while a pink cow was suckled by a pair of pea-green apes on a Russian rooftop. Paris was baffled. Even the Left Bank was slow to understand that Painter Chagall was merely re-creating from his imagination the folk tales he had heard as a boy in his native Russia. But an important artistic event had occurred—the modern art worlds of Eastern and Western Europe had met.

Today Marc Chagall says of surrealism, "Not for me." A hater of realism as well, he refuses to be joined by any artistic school. He will not even discuss his own work. "Monsieur," he says in his dense Vitebsk French, *"l'art est comme l'amour.* If your wife is ugly, you do not talk about her looks. If she is beautiful, they speak for both her and you."

SCIENCE

KEEP 'EM FLYING (BEE DEPT.): Department of Agriculture offi- MARCH 23
cials this year are urging beekeepers to increase their swarms.
Reason: sugar shortage. Signs of the bee's new importance:
❡ The Department announced that every effort would be
made to increase the 1942 honey harvest by 50% over
1941's 206,591,000 lb. The U.S. is now importing millions
of pounds from Latin America.

❡ WPB promised that bees could have at least 80% of the
common sugar they ate last year. Reason: bees must often
be kept alive on sugar in nectarless seasons before the orchards bloom. Ten pounds of sugar then may insure the
gathering of some 200 lb. of honey later.

❡ Beeswax needs of the Army and Navy, running into thousands of pounds yearly, have been doubled. Beeswax is
smeared as waterproofing over shells, airplane surfaces, canvas, gaskets, etc. To up war production, apiarists will have
to let their bees build more combs (instead of having them re-
fill combs from which the honey has been extracted). This
will be costly: bees must eat 12 to 15 lb. of their own honey
to secrete one pound of wax.

MODERN NOAHS: They are packing up their Egyptian mum- MARCH 30
mies and stowing them away in dark vaults. They are
dismantling their dinosaur skeletons and hiding them in the
earth. They have rented a bank to safeguard their Indian
wampum. In all the science museums along the U.S. coasts,
curators are busy as Noahs, threatened by the flood of war.

In Washington the Smithsonian Institution is shipping 57,-
200 insects to a secret cache. Why all the fuss over a
tattered bug on a rusty pin? A pickled fish? Because these
are the type specimens—the original catches from which the
species was first scientifically described and defined and provide the standards against which other members of the
species and new varieties are measured.

Among items selected for bomb-sheltering from the Smithsonian collection:

¶ Specimens of such extinct creatures as the great auk, the Labrador duck, the sea mink; and the only Townsend's bunting ever found.

¶ The remains of Morse's telegraph and Bell's telephone; the log of the *Savannah,* first steamship to cross the Atlantic.

¶ The original star-spangled banner which inspired Anthem-Writer Francis Scott Key in 1814.

DEC. 29 **NOBEL DINNER:** When a dinner at Manhattan's Waldorf-Astoria replaced the annual Stockholm award of the Nobel prizes (discontinued since 1939), it was found that 28 laureates now live in the U.S., counting eleven who have recently arrived, most of them to escape Hitler.

Germany, claiming racial superiority, likes to point to her wide lead in the number of Nobel awards:

Germany	40.5
Britain	24.5
France	21.5
U.S.	20
Sweden	11.5
Switzerland	8.5
Denmark	5.5
Austria	5.5
Belgium	5.5
Italy	5.5
Netherlands	5

But on the basis of population, Germany falls far down the list—as does the U.S. In number of prizes per ten million population, the list reads:

Sweden (home grounds)	17.2
Switzerland	16.7
Denmark	15.7
Austria	8.2
Netherlands	7.7
Germany	6.2
Britain	5.4
France	4.8
U.S.	1.7
Italy	1.1

RADIO

GLOBAL ENTERTAINMENT: One of the liveliest new shows on APRIL 6 the air is unavailable to most U.S. radio listeners. Studded with top-flight talent, free from commercials, bathos, exhortations to "keep 'em flying," etc., it is a cheerful half-hour of unadulterated entertainment.

Name of the show is *Command Performance.* Sponsor: Uncle Sam. The audience is made up of the U.S. armed forces wherever they are. It is global war entertainment, designed for global war.

To date, an Alaskan private, lonesome for the songbirds which woke him mornings back home in Indiana, has heard his birds; another soldier overseas has heard the voice of his favorite cocker spaniel; bleary Robert Benchley has given a vernal lecture for sailors on The Facts of Life (e.g., "Fish are a very poor example of the Facts of Life because they work under water and don't know anything").

"DEAR ADOLF": The most engaging of U.S. fight-talk programs, AUG. 3 NBC's *Dear Adolf,* bows off the air this Sunday after six successful broadcasts. Unlike many another morale program, it is quitting before the thread shows through the tires. Elfish, slow-smoldering Stephen Vincent Benét wrote the program's "letters to Hitler" for six representative Americans: a farmer (Raymond Massey—"We'll choke you with wheat and corn, Adolf, we'll drown you in York State milk"), a mother (Helen Hayes—"I do not say it is just or right to hate. I say we hate you for having caused this hate"), a businessman (Melvyn Douglas—"You can't do business with a man who doesn't know the meaning of a contract"), a laborer (James Cagney—"We're sending you a letter 20 million workers long . . . written in steel and flame") and a soldier (Private William Holden—"We'll marry the girl we like—and the guy who makes a crack about her ancestry had better look out for his teeth"). The final letter, from the U.S. foreign-born, will be sent this Sunday by Vienna-born Joseph Schildkraut.

The Council for Democracy got the idea and most of the material for the broadcasts from letters received by President Roosevelt, telling Hitler off.

SEPT. 14 **SUPERMAN IN THE FLESH:** For Supermaniacs, whose wild devotion to their comic strip Man of Steel is a wacky U.S. phenomenon, radio had good news last week. They have devoured Superman in the comics, goggled at him in one-reel movies. Now they can hear Superman in person on programs from Manhattan's WOR.

Handsome, well-built Clayton ("Bud") Collyer, 34, who plays WOR's Superman, stands six feet high, weighs 165 pounds. Though he lacks the original's bulging muscles and jutting jaw, Supermaniacs who have met him in the flesh were not too rudely disillusioned.

Radio's Superman must have a greater respect for rationalities than he has in comics or movies. Though he can still whiz through the air or break down a wall with his fist, he can push over no buildings, perform no miracles that sound cannot easily convey. Clayton's transformation from the scoop-seeking reporter, Clark Kent, to the mythical Man of Iron is accomplished by carefully deepening his voice and

Robert Benchley has a low opinion of fish; "they don't know anything."

Bud Collyer as "Superman." He can't push over buildings on the radio.

having all companions faint, while he slips on Superman clothes.

The war has faced the program with another puzzler: why hasn't Superman joined the Army? Most plausible answers: as Clark Kent, he couldn't pass the physical exam; and besides, Superman now does his bit by foiling Axis agents, rescuing troop trains and smashing sabotage rings. As in the comics, Superman on the air is important to the United Nations—he is Secret Weapon No. 1.

ROOSEVELT'S RATING: Franklin Roosevelt's Labor Day anti- SEPT. 21 inflation speech rolled up a Hooper rating of 50.3 (or 37,-362,400 adults), outstripping commercial radio's alltime high —Charlie McCarthy's 41.2. Two days after Pearl Harbor the President's Hooper rating skyrocketed to an alltime high of 79.0.

MILESTONES

DIVORCED: By Cinemactress Rita Hayworth, (real name: Margarita Carmen Cansino), 23: Oilman Edward C. Judson, 45; in Los Angeles.

KILLED IN ACTION: Sir Robert Peel, 20, only son of Lady Peel (Comedienne Beatrice Lillie) and the late Sir Robert Peel; with the Royal Navy; somewhere in the Far East. His mother got the news backstage, carried on with her revue performance.

DIED: Grant Wood, 50, famed painter of the U.S. Midwestern scene; of cancer; in Iowa City.

DIED: Michel Fokine, 62, Russian "father of the modern ballet," and its greatest choreographer; of pneumonia; in Manhattan. In & out of the good graces of the Bolsheviks, he fled to the U.S. in 1919. Famed among Fokine's early followers were Nijinsky, and Pavlova, for whom

he created "The Dying Swan." Among his 70-odd ballets are most of the modern school's best-known works: *Les Sylphides, Le Spectre de la Rose, Petrouchka, et al.*

LEFT: By the late John Barrymore: household furniture, bric-a-brac, an automobile, cash amounting to "$10,000 or less"; to his three children, Diana, 21, Dolores Ethel, 12, John Blythe, 10.

MISCELLANY

HANDLE: In East St. Louis, Edward J. Japps changed his last name to Sinai. In Birmingham a waitress whose first name is Pearl hoped to become a Navy mascot: her last name is Harbor.

LOST: In Jamestown, N.Y., a young woman wrote to ask a bus company to return her wrap-around skirt which had come off without her noticing it while she was riding home.

RELIGION

FEB. 23 **CHAPLAINS IN BATAAN:** From Melville Jacoby, TIME correspondent in beleaguered Bataan, comes this first report on how American soldiers in World War II are reacting to religion, under fire, and what the chaplains are doing at the front:

"More than one soldier, hearing bombs landing nearby and not hurting him, or having a bullet nick in his helmet, admitted that he never believed in God before. Chaplains and others all agree that more people believe in God since the war has begun. The sight of a soldier sitting by a machine gun reading a Bible is not uncommon in Bataan or Corregidor.

"This week Methodist Chaplain Ralph D. Brown, recently awarded the Distinguished Service Cross for bravery in carrying the wounded off Clark Field during continual bombings, penciled the following words to Chaplain Perry L. Wilcox on a crumpled sheet of his field notebook: 'Dear Chaplain—I will sincerely appreciate the case of New Testaments I spoke to you about when we met in Bataan. I have hundreds of boys begging for them each week.'

"Many is the chaplain, dodging dive-bombers, who has gotten up waving his fist at the unopposed Nip flyers. Chaplains are doing everything, from holding services in the jungles right behind the lines to helping men make out wills, insurance and writing letters, from hearing confessions and giving out Bibles to carrying dead and wounded under fire. When they don't know the denomination of the dead, they conduct both Protestant and Catholic services."

MARCH 30 **MARRED MARTYRDOM:** The Jap sailor wasn't really planning to kill Father Joyce when he stood him up at ten paces on Sancian Island; it was just a game when he put a bullet harmlessly through his cassock. But the missionary from Maryknoll thought his last moment was at hand. Now he knows how he will act if martyrdom really comes to him. He tried to look unconcerned, and he prayed. Not until hours later did he realize, "quite mortified," that he had said the grace before meals instead of the Act of Contrition.

CATHOLICS v. WAACs: The rush of enlistments in the Women's JUNE 15
Army Auxiliary Corps (WAACs) has perturbed the Roman Catholic pulpit and press. In Rochester a joint conference of the Catholic organizations called the influx of women into war activities "a serious menace to the home and foundation of a true Christian and democratic country." The Brooklyn *Tablet* trumpeted that the WAACs were "intended to break down the traditional American and Christian opposition to removing women from the home and to degrade her by bringing back the pagan female goddess of de-sexed, lustful sterility." Wrote *The Commonweal,* Catholic liberal weekly: "If the home is thought of impatiently as that which keeps the wife and mother from war work, the amount of war work which she might do no longer signifies, for the soul of our society will already be lost."

GAS AND FULL PEWS: Nobody knows yet exactly what gas ra- JUNE 22
tioning and the rubber shortage are going to do to churches and churchgoers. Hardest hit are the rural areas, where country folk often have to drive miles to get to church. In cities, however, gas rationing is proving a blessing in disguise: more people, unable to use their cars, are now going to church for diversion.

Many a minister lamented privately that his X card [allowing him unlimited gasoline] has resulted in his congregation's using him as a common carrier. Complained one: "It makes me feel like an errand boy."

CANTERBURY CATHEDRAL SAVED: The grass around Canter- JULY 6
bury Cathedral on the morning of June 1 was white with the ashes of burned-out incendiary bombs, the nave was carpeted with stone dust and shattered glass, the cloisters and quadrangle were a mess of rubble. But the main structure was still virtually intact. These facts were revealed last week when the British censor belatedly admitted that Nazi dive-

bombers savagely attacked the cathedral "in reprisal for Cologne."

In part the cathedral was saved by firemen who stood on the roof during more than an hour of terrific blitz and tossed scores of incendiary bombs to the ground. In part it was saved by the foresight of Canterbury's famed "Red Dean," Dr. Hewlett Johnson, who learned a lesson from the bombing of Coventry Cathedral, some time ago had ladders run up along all Canterbury's flying buttresses so that firemen could rush to the roof.

"The Germans did their best to 'get' the cathedral," said Dean Johnson after the raid. "They singled it out, dive-bombed it and hoped to burn it to the ground if they couldn't blow it to pieces. The bravest of fire guards, who worked within inches of death for over an hour throughout the bombing, spoiled the diabolical plan."

MILESTONES

MARRIED: Gloria Laura Morgan Vanderbilt, 17, daughter of Mrs. Reginald C. Vanderbilt; and Pasquale di Cicco, 32, Hollywood actor's agent, ex-professional dancer. His father, the late Pasquale Sr., was Long Island's "Broccoli King." Gloria comes into $4,000,000 at 21.

DIED: "Judge" Joseph Frederick Rutherford, 71, founder and guiding spirit of the energetically anti-clerical, anti-war, anti-State Jehovah's Witnesses sect; in San Diego. A tireless orator, he was a youthful admirer of Orator William Jennings Bryan, affected a high-standing wing collar, string tie, capacious hat. The witnesses believe that Armageddon is drawing near, and the Prophets alone will live forever. Rutherford died in a Spanish mansion he had prepared for King David, Gideon, Samson, other Biblical luminaries. He landscaped it with palm and olive trees "so these princes of the universe will feel at home when they come."

MISCELLANY

ONCE A TROUPER: In South Bend, Harry Holubiak pastured his work horse, an oldtime circus performer, near a field where Navy recruits drilled to band music. Later a vet treated the horse for exhaustion.

REASSURANCE: In Chicago, moans from a box startled Mrs. Paul Semrad, a bus passenger, who was reassured by the owner of the box that the captive was only an alligator who hated buses and suffered from gas on the stomach.

ALARM-CLOCK CONSCIENCE: In St. Louis, Mrs. Gwendolyn Shelton, who makes a living waking people up by telephone, had a new customer: a woman who wanted to be called up every night at 10 and ordered to bed.

MEDICINE

JUNGLE HOSPITAL: First open-air base hospital in U.S. history FEB. 16
since the Civil War is the 2,900-bed unit established last
month at Bataan. In the open-air wards lie U.S. and Fil-
ipino soldiers, women, children, Japanese prisoners. Nurses
sleep under trees, near foxholes, wash their own overalls,
bathe in streams. Food is cooked on two old-fashioned
wood stoves. All equipment is sterilized, but the thick Bataan dust is everywhere, and assistants must constantly flap
fly swatters.

Trucks bring the wounded from the front in a few hours
and fill up operating tables in large tents. Often bombs fall
so close to his operating table that Surgeon Lieut. Colonel
Jack Schwartz must hesitate an instant until it is steady.

The doctors probe wounds for bullets and shell fragments,
and bet on the type of fragments they will dig out of
wounds. Among their findings (all originally made in the
U.S. and later sold to Japan as scrap iron which then found
its way into Japanese shells): parts of Ford automobiles;
nuts & bolts. Out of one soldier's body came a Singer sew-
ing machine screwdriver. One night when the doctors and
nurses had amputations on every table, they donated their
own blood.

TROPICAL DISEASES: Malaria, dysentery, yellow fever head MARCH 2
the list of tropical diseases to be fought in World War II by
the U.S. Medical Corps. Of the three, malaria is Medical
Enemy No. 1. How to protect U.S. soldiers from the rats,
lice, mosquitoes, fleas and flies that carry malaria, dysentery,
yellow fever, cholera is again a major problem.

The most widespread and destructive form of malaria is
caused by a microscopic parasite, the *Plasmodium,* carried
by many species of the Anopheles mosquito. The chills,
fever and delirium of malaria may recur for many years. Malaria can be treated by constant doses of quinine, and a

newer drug, atabrine. But there is no immunization against it. Warned Dr. Henry Edmund Meleney of New York University: "We may expect a tremendous mortality from malaria in the armed forces during the present conflict."

Dysentery, long known as the "Bloody Flux," is Menace No. 2. There are two varieties: one, caused by bacilli, can now be successfully treated with sulfaguanidine; the other, caused by *Endameba histolytica,* a one-celled parasite, often produces lifelong intestinal ailments. Since dysentery organisms dwell in contaminated food and water, the disease can be prevented, as it was in World War I, by rigid cleanliness in cooking, strict inspection of food handlers, water and supplies.

Yellow fever has been wiped off urban portions of the Western Hemisphere since 1927, but still exists as "jungle yellow fever" in the interior of South America, the interior of Africa, as far east as the Sudan. An excellent vaccine has been developed against the disease, and the entire U.S. Army will be given the inoculation (along with inoculation checks for typhoid, paratyphoid, smallpox and tetanus).

Cholera, still widespread and deadly in India and China, can be prevented among the soldiers by vaccination. So can bubonic plague, carried by rat fleas, although protection is not complete.

MARCH 16   **AILING FATHER:** As painstakingly as ever any diagnostician studied the records of a live patient, Dr. Frederick Arthur Willius and Librarian Thomas Edward Keys of the Mayo Clinic's staff have been delving into the medical history of George Washington. Their research, published last week, shows that, in the course of his 67-year life, Washington suffered from: measles, diphtheria, smallpox, an "infectious disease of uncertain nature," dysentery, malaria, rheumatism, pneumonia, a carbuncle, influenza, conjunctivitis, headaches, bad eyesight, a tremor of the hands, decaying teeth.

OCT. 5   **"THE OPERATING FOOL":** Everybody liked hard, stocky, fiery-eyed Dr. Phillips, the new assistant chief surgeon at Enloe Hospital in Chico, Calif. Fellow physicians watched admiringly as he sliced out tonsils, neatly opened countless abdomens, knowingly probed the visceral coils for appendices and other disorders. Patients flocked to him. Surgeon Phillips had been no less popular at the California CCC camp where he practiced before moving to Chico. The boys called him "the operating fool."

One day last May a special agent of the California State Board of Medical Examiners went to Chico to investigate irregularities in another doctor's prescriptions. By chance, as he plowed through drugstore records, he also noticed something queer about Dr. Phillips' prescriptions. Medically they were perfect. But they were signed J. H. Phillips instead of James H. Phillips. California law requires doctors to sign prescriptions with their first name in full. Investigation led to "Doc" Phillips' arrest for practicing medicine in California without a State license. Three hours of questioning disclosed that he was not a doctor at all. His higher education consisted chiefly of a correspondence course in placer mining. But so far not one of the scores of patients whom Phillips cut open has complained of the quality of his work.

FAT LADY: Fattest human being ever known to medical science NOV. 2 was the late Mrs. Ruth G. Pontico of Tampa, Fla., who was 5 ft. 5½ in. tall and weighed 772½ lb. This conclusion, the result of a long study of the anatomical dimensions of mankind, was made by David P. Willoughby, of the vertebrate paleontology department at the California Institute of Technology.

Mrs. Pontico, who died (aged 38) of heart failure after an operation last fall, was a carnival fat lady. So was her mother, who was 6 ft. tall and weighed 720 lb. Like most very fat people, Mrs. Pontico had always been that way. She weighed 16 lb. at birth, 50 lb. a year later. Relatively nimble, she managed to waddle about her large Tampa estate every few days, to climb stairs once or twice daily. "The surprising thing," says Willoughby, "is that anyone her size should be able to get about at all." He concludes that her muscles must have been much stronger than the average woman's.

Heaviest—but not fattest—person on record was Miles Darden. When he died in 1857 in Henderson County, Tenn., he weighed a trifle over 1,000 lb. But Darden was 7½ ft. tall. If he had been of the same proportions as rotund Mrs. Pontico, he would have weighed an even ton.

BUSINESS & FINANCE

JAN. 12 **END OF A BUSINESS:** Done for the duration is the All-American industry, the symbol of mass production, the maker and remaker of modern America: automobiles. Nobody could buy a new car or truck in the U.S. last week. Furthermore, OPA told Detroit that its January production quota would be its last. By month's end the assembly lines will dead-stop.

JAN. 19 **60,000 PLANES, ETC.:** "Let no man say it cannot be done. It must be done and we have undertaken to do it." Thus last week did the President launch the biggest production program in world history. For 1942, U.S. industry is asked to produce 60,000 airplanes, 45,000 tanks, 20,000 antiaircraft guns, 8,000,000 deadweight tons of merchant ships. For 1943, 125,000 planes, 75,000 tanks, 35,000 antiaircraft guns, 10,000,000 tons of merchant ships.

These figures at first seemed fantastic. Only 18 months ago, U.S. output was around 500 planes monthly; the first medium tank rolled off Chrysler's line only eight months ago; monthly output of antiaircraft guns is still in low hundreds. Merchant shipbuilding last year just edged over 1,100,-000 tons.

But this was when war work was a side show to business-as-usual. Now war is going under the big top.

MARCH 9 **DENVER LAUNCHING:** Land-locked Denver staged a significant "launching" last week. At the Denver railroad yard, a pretty stenographer crashed a bottle of Pike's Peak snow water against the first of eight freight cars, and the "Good Ship Mountain Maid" rumbled westward—loaded with prefabricated steel for the hulls of naval escort ships. Same day, their keels were laid at California's Mare Island Navy Yard.

Denverites had good reason to be proud: the launching meant that their subcontracting problem had been licked.

Led by a former incubator manufacturer, a pool of eight local steel-products manufacturers and 15 smaller machine shops landed a $56,000,000 hull subcontract two months ago. They did so well on their first job that this week they landed a second. Now the pool is working on fittings and hulls for 27 ships, expects it will tax every machine shop in Colorado, Wyoming and New Mexico to turn them out.

BATTLE OF DETROIT: Something is happening that Adolf Hitler   MARCH 23 does not yet understand—a new reenactment of the old American miracle of wheels and machinery, but on a new scale. This time it is a miracle of war production, and its miracle-worker is the automobile industry.

The truth about Detroit today is not easy to believe. A year ago Willow Run was a lazy little creek west of Detroit, surrounded by woodlands, a few farmhouses, a few country schools. Today Willow Run is the most enormous room in the history of man: more than a half-mile long, nearly a quarter of a mile wide. In this great room errands are run by automobile; no man can see from one end to the other and it is here Henry Ford hopes to turn out a four-motored Consolidated bomber every hour. The raw materials will go in at one end; from the other will emerge the 30-ton machines. The bombers will be born from half-mile assembly lines so fast that Ford will not try to store them. The deadly infants will be ranked on a great new airfield, stretching out from the assembly end of the plant, make their test flights, then take off for service.

Detroit has other enormous rooms, and out of them will roll Jeeps, machine guns, cannon, air torpedoes, armored cars. Chrysler already has three assembly lines of olive-drab tanks moving through its tank arsenal (soon it hopes to ship a trainload of tanks a day). General Motors, biggest of all automakers, is already producing arms of all kinds at the rate of a billion dollars a year. Packard and Studebaker are making airplane engines; Hudson makes antiaircraft guns; Nash is at work on engines and propellers.

Once Detroit's conversion to war is complete, the lines will pour out such a flood of war machines as no man has ever imagined. If Armageddon is to be decided in Detroit, Armageddon is won.

MAY 4   **HIGGINS IS THE NAME:** While citizens and Senators chivied him with demands for more ships faster, War Shipping Administration's Jerry Land had one good answer anyway. He could & did point to a New Orleans shipbuilder named Andrew Jackson Higgins, who, he said, was engaged upon "the most unique type of ship construction ever attempted in the world." Details of this "unique" job are a military secret, but, in broad outline, it is a mass-production method for building cargo ships that should dwarf World War I's Hog Island. Higgins' swelling backlog includes a minimum 200 Liberty ships—the biggest single order the Maritime Commission ever placed.

Land is not the first man to bet on Andrew Jackson Higgins. Big, ruddy, Irish "A. J."—who would rather be shot than called Andy—has been betting on himself ever since the age of nine, when he owned seven lawn mowers in Columbus, Neb. and ran the town's lawn-mowing business. By the age of 22 he was running a sawmill in Mobile. The depression of 1907 cleaned him out. In 1908 he started over again with 15¢, by World War I had a flourishing lumber and export business. In 1922 his New Orleans lumber business crashed and he had to sell his wife's jewelry to keep going.

A. J.'s falls, and his comebacks, were due less to lumber than to his passion for boats. By the time he crashed hardest (in 1931) he was known in New Orleans for designing speedboats that answered a rum runner's prayer—and for designing other speedboats that the Feds used to chase them. Next came the Higgins Eureka, a 36-foot motorboat with a spoon-bill bow and a semi-tunnel protecting the propeller, so sturdy that it can rush right up on a beach without hurting itself. Oil companies used the Eureka for exploration trips in rugged country throughout the world. But it took war to put A. J. Higgins into the big time. Main Higgins products now:

¶ Eureka landing boats, which, A. J. likes to say, could have accomplished the Dunkirk evacuation in less than half the time the British took.

¶ Motor torpedo (mosquito) boats, which carry punishing armament for their 70-80-ft. size: two antiaircraft guns, four torpedo tubes, eight depth charges, armor-piercing guns. Britain uses them to patrol the English Channel.

SNUFF, CIGARS, CIGARETS: Once again war is booming the to- JUNE 8 bacco business. Even snuff hit a 20th-Century high with first-quarter output at 15,070,000 lb., 13% above last year. Reasons: strict no-smoking rules in war plants and much higher incomes in the snuff-dipping Deep South.

Thanks to fatter pay envelopes, cigar sales are also higher. The highest-priced cigars—25¢ each & up—soared a titanic 64% above 1941. Nickel stogie sales rose only 2.2%. None of these increases has hurt cigaret sales. Largely because most soldiers and sailors are walking smokestacks, April cigaret production jumped 10% to 17 billion, highest ever.

Andrew Jackson Higgins. His Liberty ship program runs aground.

Henry J. Kaiser. He races 375 miles by car to catch a train. Page 192.

CREPE HUNG IN LOUISIANA: At 11:30 one morning last week JULY 27 one of the telephones on Andrew Jackson Higgins' desk jangled. It was a Maritime Commission regional director, and what he said took the wind out of gusty A. J.'s lungs: his contract for 200 Liberty ships was canceled, on orders from Washington. Reason: the steel it would take to complete his yard and to build his ships next year is needed for this year's ships and cannon. A. J.'s New Orleans yard, a long-term job still in the pile-driving stage, was too big for the world's biggest steel capacity.

A. J. was sick. Cried he, in his first white heat of disappointment, "This has hung crepe on the biggest thing in Louisiana." It was small wonder: 10,000 workmen were pounding ahead on his vast yard; $10,000,000 had already been spent. By September, the first ship was due to come off his "floating assembly line."

A. J. and his Congressmen were sure there was more than met the eye in his stop order. He blamed the big steel companies, said they feared to develop Southern ore deposits that might upset their national balance after the war. He said he could have got the steel on the black market if the "Godawful War Production Board" had let him alone—thus illuminating one big reason why no one yet knows where the U.S.'s steel is going. Even the ugly issue of race prejudice was raised: A. J. had intended to rely heavily upon Negro labor, and Negro leaders in New Orleans screamed that some dirty discrimination was behind their loss of jobs. A. J. said darkly: "Maybe we were going to build too many ships too cheaply."

AUG. 17 **EVERYTHING HAYWIRE:** The shortage of raw materials across the nation is serious, and one scheme for solving it, called "Purp" (Production Requirements Plan) is already in trouble. The most far-reaching plan ever devised to control U.S. production from Washington, its job is to trail every ton of priority material down to its ultimate use. Purp would stop stockpiling and hoarding by putting all allocations on a short-term basis. But the statistical job it requires is so immense that Washington wags say only six men understand it and five of them have gone crazy.

Missouri's Harry S. Truman, who heads the Senate's what's-wrong-with-the-war-program committee, neatly mixed a pair of metaphors by saying it was high time for WPB Boss Don Nelson to "take the bull by the horns and cut off a few heads." Angry Mr. Truman was on the beam with the U.S. temper. But he had no solution for the raw-materials mess and no over-all explanation either.

THE WINNER–KAISER: Henry J. Kaiser, the big, bald miracle man from the West Coast, will get a chance to build cargo planes. In his bulging briefcase this week was a written promise from WPBoss Donald Nelson, authorizing him to make

100 of his projected 70-ton transports—provided he could build them without taking materials away from the aircraft industry. He had Nelson's promise to make the number 500 as soon as the program proved practicable.

Thus Kaiser emerged from a nine-day whirlwind tour of Washington with a signal victory, gained only after bitterest battle with all the it-can't-be-done experts. He had to convince Nelson, Nelson's advisers, two Senate committees; he had to beat down the Army & Navy, which still do not see where he can get the materials. But behind him he had the pressure of an enthusiastic public opinion.

Finally, Nelson took Kaiser's proposal to the White House, convinced Franklin Roosevelt that the man who had shown shipbuilders how to build ships should be allowed a flyer at plane making.

MILK AND ROMANCE: War production was halted in the Paterson, N.J. plant of Wright Aeronautical Corp. last week when male employes went on a full-fledged strike after the company stopped distributing milk each afternoon because too many romance-bent workers made too many passes at the milkmaids. AUG. 24

FABULOUS TEAM: While the can't-do-it experts dug up more reasons why Henry J. Kaiser can't possibly build cargo planes, the big West Coast engineer found a sure-we'll-do-it partner. To his aid, on a 50-50 basis, came enormously wealthy, enormously successful Howard Hughes, speed flyer, technician, designer, builder, young man of vision, and a hardheaded businessman. Hughes, at 36, is no amateur in the business, is an airman's airman: holder of the transcontinental speed record (7 hr., 28 min.), holder of the round-the-world record (3 days, 19 hr., 8 min.), big shareholder in great Transcontinental & Western Air, Inc. He is a first-rate designer himself, has a personal staff of technicians at work in his own experimental laboratories. AUG. 31

Kaiser and his men, who helped put up Grand Coulee Dam (largest in the world), Boulder and Bonneville dams, the San Francisco-Oakland Bridge (longest in the world), are natural-born nose thumbers at nature. Kaiser and Hughes should make a fabulous team.

SEPT. 7   **SAGA OF KAISER:** Fabulous Henry J. Kaiser, his family and his companies made headlines all over the U.S. last week:

¶ In Cleveland OPA jumped hard on Kaiser Co., Inc., accused it of buying steel from a warehouse at "profiteer prices." A purple-talking Government lawyer flung charges that Kaiser Co., Inc. was a conniver, had impeded the war effort, was a "scofflaw participant in illegal transactions."

¶ Henry Kaiser dashed to Santa Monica, Calif., arrived late for a hush-hush huddle with aviation bigwigs Donald Douglas, Glenn Martin, Jack Northrop and Grover Loening. Purpose of the meeting: to debate Kaiser's grandiose scheme to build hundreds of huge cargo planes. No one talked publicly afterwards but the atmosphere was tense as a shotgun wedding, and aircraft-wise West Coast newsmen figured that the other aircraft men felt that Kaiser's plans called for too much skilled labor, engineering talent and equipment.

¶ Kaiser rushed to his younger son's booming shipyard in San Francisco Bay, impatiently waited as scurrying Kaisermen prepared to launch the 10,000-ton Liberty Ship *John Fitch* just 24 days after keel-laying—another world's record for Kaiser. As the whistles blew and the band played, orchid-bedecked Mrs. Kaiser swung the champagne bottle, but the ship slid out of reach. The crowd gasped: in over 100 Kaiser launchings nobody had ever misfired. But now Kaiser's own wife had missed.

There were fresh items in the saga of Henry Kaiser, around whom news and fables now collect as about a Paul Bunyan.

Columnist Ray Clapper well expressed the public sentiment about him: "If you have to be a scofflaw to get steel out of the arsenal of bureaucracy, then that's okay with me. If that's the way Old Man Kaiser has to get his steel to build ships to carry American forces to the fighting fronts, then I hope the old fellow breaks every law on the books."

SEPT. 14   **LIQUOR NEWS:** Because a single rifle shot blows up enough alcohol to make a stiff cocktail and more than four gallons go into making a single synthetic tire, U.S. liquor production will stop completely on or before Nov. 1. This jolting news hit front pages all over the country last week when prim, precise WPB Alcohol Expert Matthew MacNamara revealed that U.S. distillers would be 100% converted to war alcohol within two months. On top of this bad news for U.S. conviviality the W.C.T.U. abruptly suggested that present liquor stocks be converted into undrinkable commercial alcohol. Drinkers did not have to take the ladies seriously—converting present whiskey stocks would take too long.

Although there is an adequate liquor supply for a medium term war (warehouses bulge with enough to last four years), some changes in drinking habits are on the way. Both gin and blended whiskies will presently disappear. Straight whiskey alone will remain.

APPOINTMENT IN WASHINGTON: Henry J. Kaiser was back in SEPT. 21 Washington this week, heaving his big bulk around corridors and offices, trying to pound his cargo plane home for once & all. The net result, it appeared, would be not enough to satisfy eager Henry Kaiser—perhaps an order for three prototypes of a new cargo plane designed by his project partner, Airman Howard Hughes—a far cry from Kaiser's original offer to get right to work on 5,000 planes.

Kaiser's trip to Washington was a saga in itself. When the train that he was supposed to take pulled out of the Los Angeles Union Station, he was just starting to broadcast a Labor Day message from the Beverly Hills Hotel, taking his cargo-plane visions right to the people. The Streamliner was streaking toward the mountains when the bull-necked builder finished his speech, hurled his massive frame into an automobile, started his race with the train. Loud-sirened police patrols screamed at his side. They caught the train in Nevada 375 miles out. Kaiser got to his appointment in Washington.

But if his first reception in Washington had been chilly, this time it was cold. A special committee of aircraft experts had found that Kaiser had no engineers seriously at work on cargo planes, that he did not plan to convert his shipyards, that what he wanted was a Government-built plant where he could turn out a plane designed by the aircraft industry itself. Now Donald Nelson had become skeptical; he demanded that Kaiser produce detailed plans. Kaiser did not have them: he was leaving the designing and engineering up to his partner, Howard Hughes. In three days of tumultuous conferences Kaiser had forced Washington to lend an attentive ear. But if Washington stuck to its lukewarm answer, Kaiser had already lost his battle. [Kaiser and Hughes later split up their partnership and Hughes went on to build a prototype of the gigantic plane, nicknamed the "Spruce Goose." It was test-flown once, and then the project was dropped.]

OCT. 5 **STATE OF HIGGINS:** The place is dank, dismal, depressing. Stacks of grey, fungus-covered piling loom like ghostly sentries, a huge, muddy filled-in ditch resembles the caved-in moat of a deserted castle. So looks today the 1,200-acre Higgins Liberty Shipyard outside New Orleans. Amid a burst of fanfare, it was started six months ago as a gigantic project to build cargo ships on a water-borne assembly line. Then suddenly came Maritime Commission orders: Close the yard. Official reason: the steel shortage.

Up reared blunt, thundering, red-faced Andrew Jackson Higgins, boss and promoter of the whole show: "gross stupidity . . . worse for the State than if the river flooded New Orleans." Sympathetic Louisiana Representatives started an investigation. Last week the investigating committee completed publication of its hearings; now anyone could decide for himself why the Higgins yard was closed. The main reason —aside from the steel shortage—was that Higgins was too expensive. Estimated cost of his yard started at $26,000,000, soon rolled up another $33,000,000. And before the yard could even open, more millions had to be sunk in new housing and new power plants, between 45,000 and 85,000 men had to be found, hired and trained. For months, too, Washington had been skeptical of the assembly-line technique, felt sure that a single hitch on the lead ship would hold up a score of vessels behind it. Explained Maritime Commission Chairman Admiral Emory Land: "There was just a 50-50 chance that Higgins could do what we wanted him to do."

NOV. 9 **NEW HIGH FOR HIGGINS:** Way down yonder in New Orleans they had plenty to cheer about last week. Andrew Jackson Higgins, their No. 1 boat-builder, a money-maker and hoopla artist, had practically landed one of the biggest single transport-plane contracts in U.S. history: about $180,000,000 for 1,200 huge, twin-engined, all-plywood troop- and tank-carrying planes. This meant that Higgins had stolen a march on his friend and archrival, Henry Kaiser, the Wizard of the West Coast.

Andrew Higgins stole the march by using a double dose of Kaiser's own technique—rough & tumble action plus fortissimo publicity. Right after Higgins lost his ship contract, he raised enough rumpus to start several investigations, to snag thousands of headlines, and convince many people that he was a victim of the Maritime Commission. When things slowed down Higgins bought full-page ads in leading newspapers, boasting "World's largest builder of boats."

Things stirred when the President toured U.S. war plants last month, spent more than an hour in the Higgins yards, left impressed. Upshot: a fortnight ago the President directed WPB, the Maritime Commission and the Army to find some use for Higgins' abandoned $10,000,000 shipyard—and find it fast. First result: the huge plane order. [Higgins went on to produce 1,200 cargo planes under this contract. He also turned out landing craft which were used in every theater during World War II.]

TOPPING A MIRACLE: When Henry J. Kaiser's Oregon Ship- NOV. 23 building Corp. sprang a production miracle and splashed a Liberty ship into the water ten days after keel laying, the tough, hard-hitting gangs in Kaiser's Richmond (Calif.) Shipbuilding Corp. yard No. 2 sputtered, "What the hell has Oregon got that we haven't?" Egged on by the intense rivalry that exists among all eight of Kaiser's yards, Richmond employes hatched 250 new tricks to speed their assembly-line technique of shipbuilding. At 12:01 a.m. last Sunday the keyed-up swing shift at Richmond got started. The first keel section of the Liberty ship *Robert E. Peary* was hoisted on to the keel blocks. On Thursday she slid into the water, 90% complete, after four days, 15 $\frac{1}{2}$ hours on the ways.

NO NOISE: Drop hammers fall with ground-shaking concussions. The machines make a staccato racket that would drown out a couple of machine guns. The operators pay no attention to these shattering factory noises. They are deaf-mutes. To North American Aviation (as to many other plants now employing them) their unique usefulness was as much a surprise as the successful use first made by midgets to work in tight places in aircraft construction.

To talk to the mutes the foreman taps a shoulder near him, points to the man he wants. This man taps the next shoulder in the silent grapevine to the wanted worker. Then the foreman wigwags his instructions: A clenched fist pulled down above his head means drill press. Palms close together in front mean to the mute that his measurements are too short. Palms apart: he has erred in the opposite direction. The mutes need no bells to warn them of overhead crane and boom movements. They watch moving shadows.

MILESTONES

MARRIED: Barbara Hutton, 30, Woolworth Heiress ("the richest girl in the world") and Cinemactor Archibald Alexander Leach (cinemonicker: Cary Grant), 38; she for the third time, he for the second; at Lake Arrowhead, Calif. She divorced her first husband, Georgian Prince Alexis Mdivani, in 1935, her second, Danish Count Haugwitz-Reventlow, in 1941: Grant was divorced by Cinemactress Virginia Cherrill in 1934. [Barbara Hutton got her sixth divorce in 1961, Grant his fourth in 1968.]

DIED: Dr. John Richard Brinkley, 56, Kansas' goat-bearded "goatgland" medico-politico; of heart disease; in San Antonio. He exploited the desire of age for youth's potency, peddling a gland emulsion and grafting goat glands at his "re-juvenation clinic" in Milford, Kans. In his heyday he had three yachts, several gaudy limousines, decorated himself with diamonds, employed 50 secretaries, took in a reputed $1,000,-000 a year. He sold prescriptions over the air from his own radio station, broadcast diagnoses, threw in a little preaching. After Kansas revoked his license to practice and the old Federal Radio Commission stopped his broadcasts, he moved the scene of his operations over the Mexican border. He ran for Governor of Kansas three times, nearly won twice.

MISCELLANY

RECORD: In Middletown, Conn., Wesleyan University Junior Eugene J. Frechette Jr. breathed deeply for three minutes, took three breaths of oxygen, then sat purple-faced, breathless, like-to-bust, for 20 min., 5 sec. When he finally let go, he had broken the known world's record.

ONE'S ENOUGH: In Birmingham, Ala., cruising police cars got a radio call: "Car X-Y-3, car X-Y-3, go to Third Ave. and 14th St.—a nude woman running down the street. All other cars remain on your beat. That is all."

CODE: In Seattle, police and U.S. agents tried to decode the notations in an arrested woman's little black book: "K 1, P 2, CO 8, K 5" finally quizzed her, learned the meaning: "Knit one, purl two, cast on eight, knit five."

CINEMA

"H. M. PULHAM, ESQ." is an amazingly good cineversion of JAN. 5
John Phillips Marquand's best-selling novel of a New Eng-
lander going dutifully to seed. *Pulham* embodies the reflections of a Boston investment counsel (Robert Young) when
his 25th Class Reunion Committee asks him for a brief biography of his life.

Back goes the camera into his well-to-do Boston up-
bringing; his prep-school days; Harvard and culture; World
War I and the Argonne; Manhattan and the advertising business; the girl he loved (Hedy Lamarr); his passionless
marriage to his mother's choice (Ruth Hussey); his slightly
bewildered, slightly querulous, slightly pathetic acceptance
of his fate: a cushioned middle age, the deadly divinity of triv-
ial things.

The camera has a lot to say in *Pulham.* It has the picture's opening sequence all to itself: the boiled egg on the
breakfast table, sugar and cream enriching the coffee, the
morning paper in its rack, the absent-minded good-by kiss,
the derby, the rubbers, the two peanuts for the squirrels on
the walk to the office, the breathing exercises in the park,
the cigar at the old stand, the musty office, the waiting letters on the desk, the clock at exactly 9 a.m. After that, with
hardly a spoken word, Harry Pulham is typed.

WHO WON: The 18 members of the New York Film Critics JAN. 12
elected their 1941 cinema "bests" in less time than it takes
to run off a double feature and a couple of shorts. Gary Coo-
per took honors as top actor of the year (for *Sergeant
York*). His nearest competitor: Orson *(Citizen Kane)* Welles.
Top actress: Joan Fontaine (for *Suspicion).* Neck-and-neck
with her up to sixth ballot: Sister Olivia de Havilland (for
Hold Back the Dawn). Best Director: John Ford (for *How
Green Was My Valley).* Best picture: *Citizen Kane*—Welles-
produced, -directed, -starred.

JAN. 26 **"THE MAN WHO CAME TO DINNER"** continues the glorification of that rococo personality, Monty Woolley—known to his friends as "The Beard." Actor Woolley merely transfers to celluloid the unexpurgated version of Alexander Woollcott which he played for two years on Broadway in George S. Kaufman's and Moss Hart's cutthroat comedy. The switch from Broadway to Hollywood is scarcely noticeable.

As almost everyone knows by now, *TMWCTD* is the tale of a famous cross-country lecturer, Sheridan Whiteside, who is forced to go to a dull dinner party in Mesalia, Ohio, injures a hip on his hosts' icy steps, and has to stay for weeks. Encased in a wheelchair, the egomaniacal, asp-tongued celebrity fills the house with Chinese, penguins, an octopus, a mummy case, etc. He informs his nurse that she "has the touch of a love-starved cobra"; regards his physician as the "greatest living argument for mercy killing"; dismisses his secretary (Bette Davis) as a "flea-bitten Cleopatra."

Possessor of the most Edwardian visage of his era, onetime Yale English instructor Woolley plays lecturer Whiteside with such vast authority and competence that it is difficult to imagine anyone else attempting it. As one of his intimates has remarked: "At last the old party has got the role he's been rehearsing for all his life."

FEB. 16 **"WOMAN OF THE YEAR"** was made to order for bold Katharine Hepburn. She saw to it that it was: she helped edit the script, sold it to Metro for an unprecedented $100,000, demanded and got her own leading man (Spencer Tracy) and her favorite director (George Stevens).

As Tess Harding, China-born, Swiss-schooled daughter of a U.S. diplomat, Miss Hepburn is easily recognizable in her role of high-falutin' female newspaper columnist. Spoiled, selfish, intellectual, well-informed, too busy to be feminine, she thinks nothing of advocating the abolition of baseball for the duration of the war. She is promptly dusted off by another columnist: Sam Craig (Mr. Tracy), sportswriter, of her own paper. From that point, *Woman* is the story of a speedy courtship and a rocky marriage.

Actors Hepburn and Tracy have a fine old time in *Woman of the Year*. And for once, strident Katharine Hepburn is properly subdued. When she met her leading man for the first time, before shooting began, she observed: "I'm afraid I am a little tall for you, Mr. Tracy." Said he: "Don't worry, Miss Hepburn, I'll cut you down to my size."

THEM DANG MOVIES: Gloomy Sunday is a 120-year-old tradi- MARCH 16
tion in Mississippi. An 1822 blue law still forbids Mississippians to attend bearbaiting, cockfights, bullfights and any other routine amusements of a Sabbath. Sunday movies are taboo—to the intensified boredom of some 110,000 soldiers training in the State. Last week the Mississippi Senate, for the third time this session, fearlessly faced the issue. The opposition thundered that a bill permitting Sunday movies would "open the gates of hell." Roared Senator Joe Daws of De Kalb (pop. 866): The Pearl Harbor tragedy came about because sailors were not at their posts. "They were attending Sunday movies!"

This was too much for Senator Earl Richardson of Philadelphia (pop. 3,711). Senator Richardson stopped his whittling, brushed the shavings off his lap and his desk. He snorted: "Do you know what time Pearl Harbor was attacked? It was about 7:15 o'clock in the morning. That's a mighty funny time for soldiers or anybody else to be in the movies."

After the fireworks, the bill passed, 29-to-10, went to the House.

"JUNGLE BOOK" is a bold attempt to make Kipling's beloved APRIL 13
animal fable of Mowgli, the Hindu boy who was raised by jungle wolves, into a movie. It can't be done. Star of the beast epic is Shere Khan (real name: Roger), a magnificent half-Bengal, half-Sumatran tiger who is out to get Mowgli (Sabu, the young Hindu who starred in *Elephant Boy*). The ominous supporting cast includes some 2,000 animals, birds and reptiles—notably a slinky black panther, an enormous python (which had to be controlled on the set with a blow torch), and a very unpleasant cobra.

When the animals are talking their own language and roaming their improvised jungle near Los Angeles, *Jungle Book* is as absorbing as a behind-the-scenes trip to the zoo. But when they converse in Kipling's English, the result is painful. The python sounds like Lionel Barrymore; the cobra, who is very long winded, like a wheezy crackerbox philosopher; a tough monkey like a Tammany ward heeler.

MAY 4 **"MY GAL SAL"** is the kind of bright, tuneful, lighthearted musical that was once Broadway's dish. A warm share of *Sal's* appeal is owing to the man it celebrates: genial, sentimental, gargantuan (300 lb.) Paul Dresser, onetime minstrel, popular song writer of the '90s, and oldest brother of lugubrious Novelist Theodore Dreiser (who kept the original family name). Dreiser, who wrote the first verse and the chorus of one of his brother's best songs *(On the Banks of the Wabash)*, also wrote the story on which *Sal* is based.

Although one of Hollywood's almost unbearably beautiful young males, Victor Mature, plays the Dresser role, he is generally bearable. Whenever he gets coy, out of character and into fatuity, Director Irving Cummings distracts attention from him with a mighty pretty red herring: beauteous Rita Hayworth, who, in Technicolor, singing and dancing her way through eight melodies, is enough to raise hair on the boys in bald-head row.

As a pretty, American musicomedy star with a headful of russet red curls, Miss Hayworth meets Dresser on the Chautauqua circuit, irks him to Manhattan, sings his songs, falls in & out of love with him to the final fadeout. Twentieth Century has been considerably disturbed because *Sal's* big secret leaked out: Rita Hayworth's Grade-A singing voice belongs to a radio songstress named Nan Wynn. Fortunately for all concerned, the voice sounds like Rita. And no pseudonymous voice ever had a more attractive sponsor.

JUNE 1 **"THIS ABOVE ALL"** asks the bitter, irrelevant question: Why should a young, disillusioned, lower-middle-class Englishman risk his life for the upper classes unless he is sure of a new shake after World War II is won? Like the novel, the picture fails to give a satisfactory answer. Nevertheless, *This Above All* is a remarkably good love story. WAAF Joan Fontaine, who has what it takes to play lady-in-a-haystack, quietly meets her man (Tyrone Power) in the blackout, goes away with him to a seaside resort, where he leaves her, eventually rejoins him for keeps after the *Luftwaffe* has almost battered his brains out in a London bombing. It is a restrained, sensitive, appealing performance—a tribute to beauteous Joan Fontaine, and to the intelligent direction of Anatole Litvak. Although Tyrone Power gives the performance of his cinematic career as the embittered young deserter, it is not good enough. His handsome, unlined face contradicts the profound words he is asked to utter. He does not for a moment look as if he had either thought or lived them.

"YANKEE DOODLE DANDY" is possibly the most genial screen biography ever made. Few films have bestowed such loving care on any hero as this one does on beaming, buoyant, wrymouthed George M. (for Michael) Cohan. The result is a nostalgic, accurate re-creation of a historic era of U.S. show business. JUNE 22

Canny Showman Cohan knew what he was doing when he insisted that Irish Jimmy Cagney was the one cinemactor who could play him. Smart, alert, hard-headed, Cagney is as typically American as Cohan himself. Like Cohan, he was once a hoofer, and he has the Cohan trick of nodding and winking to express approval, the outthrust jaw, stifflegged stride, bantam dance routines, side-of-the-mouth singing, the air of likable conceit. For the rest, he remains plain Jimmy Cagney. It is a remarkable performance, and it makes *Yankee Doodle* a dandy.

"MRS. MINIVER" is that almost impossible feat, a great war picture that photographs the inner meaning, instead of the outward realism, of World War II. Director William Wyler succeeds by the simple device of setting up an ideal middle-class English family in an ideal middle-class home, letting the Nazis knock both down. Result: what the Nazi bombers finally smash is not a house and household but (temporarily) man's hope of happiness. JUNE 29

The family is the Minivers (Greer Garson & Walter Pidgeon). The house is their spacious, chintzy, suburban home outside London. They are a happy couple in the lowering summer of 1939.

The meaning of Dunkirk hits home when Mr. Miniver pilots his speedboat slowly down the Thames estuary to help rescue the beaten Expeditionary Force. The Nazi mentality becomes viciously and pathetically real when Mrs. Miniver disarms a wounded German flyer in her kitchen, then slaps his face for talking Aryan nonsense. World War II is reduced to the compass of an air-raid shelter where the Minivers and their well-scrubbed youngsters ride out an air raid in their own backyard. It is anybody's backyard, any where.

And there is scarcely an off-key performance in the picture. Outstanding is womanly Greer Garson's Mrs. Miniver. She had to be, and is, exactly right.

AUG. 24   **"BAMBI"** may not be "the best picture I have ever made," as Walt Disney claims, but it is in many respects the best of his six full-length cartoon movies. Bambi is the brown-eyed, white-scutted fawn of Felix Salten's somewhat candied forest idyl. He is an appealing, wonderfully articulated little deer, whose progressive discoveries of rain, snow, ice, the seasons, man, love, death, etc. make a neatly antlered allegory. Bambi's rubber-jointed, slack-limbed, coltish first steps in the art of walking are inspired animation. And the undying affection bestowed on him by a young skunk, whom Bambi inadvertently names Flower, is grade-A Disney.

AUG. 31   **"HOLIDAY INN"**—Five years ago *Holiday Inn* was a musical note in Songsmith Irving Berlin's melodious mind. He wanted to drape a Broadway show around a series of songs for U.S. national holidays. Now, this first cinema conjunction of Bing Crosby and Fred Astaire is a box-office bargain— an effervescent musical, spiced with 13 pleasant Berlin melodies whipped into expert froth.

Few cinemactors appear to take more pains than Hoofer Astaire, less pains than Crooner Crosby. Result: Crosby's easy, casual banter is just the right foil for Astaire's precision acrobatics, his wry, offbeat humor. According to the episodic plot, Singer Crosby turns his rural retreat into a roadhouse on every holiday in order to give himself and Fred Astaire a chance to sing and dance.

Perfectionist Astaire, world's No. 1 tap dancer, shows no signs of slowing down. Each of his routines has a new and different sparkle. One, performed while tipsy, is a deft parody of jitterbuggery. Another, a 4th of July number done to the accompaniment of torpedoes and firecrackers, is his favorite staccato buck & wing, with some fresh frills. A dazzler for any audience, it was a headache for studio technicians: The firecrackers had to pop in time with Astaire's fidgety feet. Technicians finally built an organ that would set off the crackers electrically, so that the organist could play the explosions at the right spots in the score.

"YOU WERE NEVER LOVELIER" does not quite live up to its title but presents fresh evidence that Fred Astaire is still a superb dancer and a deft light-comedian and that Rita Hayworth is still the most ambrosial lady he has ever teamed with. Even so, Astaire's dancing has the staccato precision of a military command, and Rita Hayworth, merely walking down a staircase, is something to risk court-martial for. NOV. 16

"ROAD TO MOROCCO" is interrupted midway by a camel who remarks: "This is the screwiest picture I was ever in." Bob Hope, Bing Crosby and Dorothy Lamour may well agree with him. NOV. 23

Shipwrecked on Hollywood's fixed idea of the North African desert, still unchanged since the days of Rudolph Valentino, Hope and Crosby ad-lib their way to a native village ruled over by Princess Lamour, who retains the pleasant knack of looking undressed even when fully clothed. Already betrothed to a native sheik (Anthony Quinn), Lamour gives her affections first to Hope, then to Crosby. Tribesman Quinn's desire for revenge touches off the Keystone excitement. Chief difference between *Road to Morocco* and its two predecessors is that Hope also gets a girl.

"GEORGE WASHINGTON SLEPT HERE" is an amusing picturization of the barn-theater hit about a back-to-the-land antique addict and his strictly modern-convenience wife who bought a decrepit house in which George Washington was said to have slept. But the leading roles have been switched. In the film Ann Sheridan is a Duncan Phyfey wifey. Jack Benny is her harassed, urban-minded husband. NOV. 30

To accommodate Benny's slapstick comedy talents, matters are so arranged that he 1) is conked by sheaves of loose planks; 2) falls downstairs once; 3) falls through the floor twice; 4) falls down two different wells; 5) suffers a grand climax in which a horde of 17-year locusts devour him down to his underwear.

"CASABLANCA"—Before the U.S. seizure of Morocco handed Warner Bros. some of the most dazzling promotion in years, *Casablanca* was just an exotic location for a topical melodrama. The city was known to European refugees as a desperate whistle stop on the underground railway to Lisbon. This picture is about some refugees who were stranded in Casablanca and some of the people who helped or hindered them. Among them:

¶ The proprietor of Rick's Café Américain (Humphrey Bogart, so tough that at one moment he looks like Buster Keaton playing Paul Gauguin). A strictly cynical neutral, Rick likes to snarl: "I stick my neck out fer nobuddy."

¶ Laszlo, leader of the European underground (Paul Henreid), still breathing hard after three escapes from the Nazis.

¶ His wife Ilsa (Ingrid Bergman, whose beautiful performance transfigures a vapid role). Once in Paris she thought she was a widow, and fell in love with Rick. But she left him as soon as she learned that Laszlo was alive. Rick is still trying to get over it. So is Ilsa.

Peter Lorre, as a petty passport racketeer, is knocked out of the show after 20 minutes. Sydney Greenstreet briefly represents the *émigré* black bourse. Oldtimer S. Z. Sakall steals scene after scene as usual, merely by wobbling his jowls. Claude Rains is a bush-league Laval.

The climax of *Casablanca* concerns the efforts of Laszlo and his wife to leave Morocco. Rick has two letters of transit which would make that easy. Reluctant to help, Mr. Bogart at last does the manly thing and Mr. Rains saves him from the consequences. Nothing short of an invasion could add much to *Casablanca*.

DEC. 7 **HOLLYWOOD AT WAR:** The Hollywood *Reporter,* tootling the value of war films in boosting morale, ran this two-column deck:

EISENHOWER AND GENERALS IN GREATEST
PRAISE FOR HOLLYWOOD'S PICTURES,
SECOND ONLY TO ACTUAL FIGHTING!

Hedy Lamarr in "White Cargo." In no time at all she is saying, "Tondelayo make you tiffin." Only the tone-deaf will think she means tea.

"WHITE CARGO" is the latest screen version of one of the worst and most successful plays in the '20s. Starchy, ambitious young Langford (Richard Carlson) goes out to the Congo, around 1910, to help run a rubber plantation. As he disembarks, his unstarched predecessor is carried aboard, toes turned up. His new boss Witzel (Walter Pidgeon) gives Langford the advice needed to keep Empire whole and hale: "Never let the native men see you are afraid of them—and *don't mammy-palaver*!" Before young Langford is many hours wiser, he begins to realize what mammy-palaver means [the coy flattery of native women].

The white man's burden in Equatorial Africa consists principally of Tondelayo (Hedy Lamarr). She comes from the jungle rolling the whites of her eyes, and in no time at all is

DEC. 14

saying "Tondelayo make you tiffin." Only the tone-deaf will think she means tea.

Under the influence of Tondelayo, young Langford gets lazy with the razor, easy with the bottle and sloppy with his ducks. When Tondelayo dances for him, the Temptation of St. Anthony looks like a game of pease-porridge-cold. After young Langford marries her, she stops calling him *awyla* ("my man"), begs him to beat her. When he refuses, she starts calling the unwilling Witzel *awyla,* does her best to poison her husband. By the time his starchy successor has arrived, superheated Langford is steaming down the Congo, Britain-bound.

DEC. 28 **"IN WHICH WE SERVE"** is the first really great picture of World War II. It is the story of a British destroyer, from her launching in 1939 to her sinking off Crete in 1941. So real is her story and that of the men who sailed in her that when the film was first shown in London, tears poured down the cheeks of bluejackets and hardened critics who saw it.

The picture was written, produced, directed and acted by Noel Coward. Its hero is widely supposed, though Coward has denied it, to be Coward's friend Lord Louis Mountbatten, who commanded and lost a destroyer before he became Commando-in-Chief. Coward plays the part.

The story starts at the end instead of the beginning, with a superbly realistic sea battle near Crete. The Nazi divebombers roar down for the kill, and Captain Kinross' ship goes down with more than half her crew. Then, while the Captain and a few sailors, covered with fuel oil and sprayed with machine-gun bullets, cling precariously to a raft in the scummy waters, the camera flashes back to tell the whole story of the ship and her men.

THE PRESS

NO TIME TO LAUGH: With its issue of May 2 the *Tiger,* Prince- APRIL 20
ton's campus funny magazine, will fold for the duration—
as it did in World War I. Reasons: loss of advertising and
too much wartime curricular work for the students.

IN LINE OF DUTY: Some 20 front-line correspondents have MAY 11
been killed or captured since the U.S. went to war. Numbered
with them last week was Melville Jacoby, brilliant, 25-year-
old correspondent of TIME and LIFE who died instantly in a
freak plane accident that also killed Brigadier General Harold H. ("Pursuit") George at an advance air base in
Australia.

After Jacoby's last-minute escape from Manila and his nu-
merous close shaves on Bataan, Australia looked almost
like a tame haven and was a happy surcease. Jacoby's wife,
Annalee, who collaborated with him on articles, got a permanent and new clothes. They rented a pleasant apartment.
TIME, thinking they had been through enough and having
got two other correspondents to the spot, suggested bringing
them home. Before the Jacobys could decide what to do Melville accepted General George's invitation to fly with him
on a week's inspection of north Australia air bases.

Wrote MacArthur in the communiqué announcing Jacoby's death last week: "Melville Jacoby covered the Philippine
campaign for TIME and LIFE with complete devotion to military standards. He could well have served as a model for
war correspondents at the front."

BAN: To its own sports staff and later to all members' editors, MAY 25
A.P. last week dispatched a grave memo: "There should be
a ban on flowery, over-enthusiastic lyrical sports writing for
the duration. Remembering the exploits of military heroes,
it does not seem appropriate to overdo the use of such
words as 'courageous,' 'gallant,' 'fighting.' . . . It doesn't

take much 'courage' to overcome a two-run lead in the ninth.''

HEDDA MAKES HAY: "The Queen is dead, long live the Queen!" whooped Hollywood's *Daily Variety.* While *Variety* whooped, the movie pressagents trooped to lunch with Gossip Columnist Hedda Hopper. New "Queen" Hedda had just signed a contract with the Chicago *Tribune*-New York *News* Syndicate—a contract that nearly tripled the number of her readers.

The old queen—Hearst Gossip Columnist Louella Parsons —is not exactly dead. But her whims no longer command Hollywood. She still has 17,000,000 newspaper circulation, according to Hearst's I.N.S., through "several hundred outlets." But at one stride Hedda had reached a circulation of 5,-750,000 daily (7,500,000 Sunday) through only 27 papers.

Hedda Hopper is real Hollywood. Not by accident has she risen in four years to challenge Lolly Parsons as chief outlet for Hollywood publicity. At 52, brown-haired, boisterous Hedda, who started life as plain Pennsylvania Quakeress Elda Furry, has been nearly 25 years in the movies (acting in over 100 pictures), was the fifth of the late Actor DeWolf Hopper's six wives, between times was staging fashion shows, coaching actors, selling real estate, even running for political office. Much better liked than Lolly Parsons, Hedda has had to pit friendships and wits against the powerful inertia of Lolly's 20-year reign on Hollywood's gossip roost. Choice studio stories went first, automatically, to Lolly; actors phoned her first and eloped afterwards lest she sideswipe them ever after.

SEPT. 28 **CONDÉ NAST:** In an exquisite 30-room penthouse on Park Avenue death came last week to Condé Nast. He was 68; an amiable host; as publisher of *Vogue, House & Garden, et al.,* a superlative technician of the publishing world. For a generation he was the man from whom millions of American women got most of their ideas, directly or indirectly, about the desirable American standard of living.

The apartment in which he died was the perfect complement to his publishing business and an index to the variety of his taste. There he entertained the same people for whom

Hedda Hopper. After 25 years in films, she's the queen. Page 207.

Condé Nast. He was a magazine publisher who gave women ideas.

he published *Vogue*. There to his elaborate dinners, dances, cocktail parties, came socialites, Hollywoodites, Broadway-ites, statesmen, royalty. The star of a Broadway opening was as thrilled by an after-theater party at Condé Nast's as she was by the first-night applause. The apartment which he himself planned to the last detail was so arranged that he could entertain 100 cocktail guests on the roof, a dinner party of 50, another couple of hundred in the ballroom, all at the same time. Amidst 18th-Century French paintings, Chinese screens and a slightly rococo splendor, Condé Nast presided, bald and genial, peering sphinxlike through pince-nez glasses, the arbiter of his world.

But to Nast, society was only the work of evenings. The daylight was for publishing, and this was hard work. Throughout the '20s and '30s, Nast decided in the pages of *Vogue* what made fashion-sense in the welter of Parisian, New York and Hollywood ideas, about everything from décor to dogs. The best-dressed women in all U.S. towns were *Vogue* subscribers; stores fought to be listed as outlets for goods advertised in *Vogue*, and thus the Nast judgments set patterns far beyond *Vogue*'s own circulation. To readers Nast brought the excitement of modern art, from Seurat to breath-taking photography of men like Steichen and Cecil Beaton, which in turn influenced all U.S. advertising art.

Vogue became a feminine bible of taste and technician Nast became a millionaire.

NOV. 9 **DAILY "STARS & STRIPES":** For the first time since the fall of Paris, a U.S. newspaper began daily publication in Europe this week. The *Stars & Stripes*, successor to World War I's famed A.E.F. paper, changed from a weekly to the U.S. Armed Forces' European daily. The doughboys themselves forced the change. They wanted more news from home, and said so. Tired of trying to make something out of the dry, news-lean English papers, they wanted their news served up American style. The staff of *Stars & Stripes* operates out of three rented rooms in the cavernous interior of the London *Times* citadel off the Thames embankment. The *Times* presses now print *Stars & Stripes*—much to the *Times*'s befuddlement. High-collared Chris Kent, *Times*'s general manager, inspected dummies of the new *Stars & Stripes* recently. A solid page of leg art stopped him cold. "Are you going to continue this sort of thing?" he ejaculated. "It might affect the morals of our composing room."

NOV. 23 **SECRET ASSIGNMENT:** Last week the story of how the U.S. press was let in on North Africa was told. First inkling that something was afoot came to U.S. correspondents in London in September when Brigadier General Robert McClure, Lieut. General Dwight Eisenhower's public relations aide, met with correspondents and cautiously informed them that there was to be an expedition "somewhere" and that the Army wanted good coverage but maximum security too.

The lucky correspondents who were to accompany the expedition were chosen from a list of all U.S. reporters in London. All knew they were going "somewhere"; tried to guess. West Pointer McClure's able sidekick, Major Joseph B. Phillips, left a Russian dictionary in plain view in his apartment. Most newsmen took the bait. New York *Times*man Frank Kluckhohn, guessing that an invasion of Norway and an offensive against the Germans in north Russia was in the offing, outfitted himself with woollies and a heavy overcoat. Apparently all the newsmen had the same idea: all departed for North Africa wearing winter uniforms. None took shorts.

BOOKS

"MR. CHURCHILL" (by Philip Guedalla)—At Cowes, during a FEB. 2 ball aboard a British cruiser one August night in the 1870s, the future Lord Randolph Churchill met three American girls named Jerome and promptly told a friend that he intended to marry "the dark one." Next day he proposed and was accepted. To his ducal father's natural question young Churchill replied: "Mr. Jerome is a gentleman who is obliged to live in New York to look after his business. I do not know what it is."

Thus Britain's No. 1 biographer, Philip Guedalla, suggests the prenatal impulses which may have affected the character of Britain's impulsive Prime Minister, of whom he has written the most important and readable biography yet published.

It traces the development of Winston Churchill from the specious Victorian calm into which he was born, until, an old man, he put the will of a battered empire into four words: "We shall never surrender." And, in the course of the long story, Author Guedalla explains his subject by quoting Macaulay's verdict on William Pitt, the great Lord Chatham: "The ardour of his soul had set the whole kingdom on fire."

"FRENCHMAN'S CREEK"—Daphne du Maurier's *Rebecca,* one of the three best-selling novels of 1939, was an exceedingly well-told problem story of the troubles of being a second wife; it was tailor-made for the land of high divorce rates. *Frenchman's Creek,* just as well-told, is even nearer that bull's-eye where best-sellers are scored: the heart of the U.S. housewife. The story of Lady Dona St. Columb is the same story that hundreds of women's-magazine serials have told & told again: the temptation and fall—strictly temporary —of a respectable woman.

In the long run Lady Dona is saved by the most classic of gongs: the frightened crying, in the night, of one of her children. But not before Miss du Maurier has squeezed the escapade dry in scene after well-constructed scene. She has what most of her colleagues in this sort of fictioneering lack: an ability to make plush-and-rhinestones look like the real thing.

FEB. 23 **"FLIGHT TO ARRAS"** by Antoine de Saint-Exupéry (pronounced: Ex-eú-pair-ee) is the most important book yet written about this war.

Like all Saint-Exupéry's books, it is a description of a flight —a pilot's reflections borne upon the arc of a few hours' intense action. But this particular flight, in which Saint-Exupéry faced death, he transmutes into a magic text, at times almost Biblical, of why men fight, and how they feel in the presence of death.

On an afternoon in late May 1940, when the French collapse "was so entire that death itself seemed to us absurd," Pilot Saint-Exupéry, his observer Dutertre and his young gunner were ordered to make a reconnaissance sortie over Arras. Their chances of survival even on a good day were one in three, and this sortie was an "awkward" one. The information, even if they brought it back, would be useless, even if it were to reach the General Staff, which it would not.

At 33,000 feet, with the controls frozen (it was 60 below zero), Dutertre sighted six enemy planes a quarter of a mile, ten seconds, below, and these planes swept upward. With an effort which at that altitude left him gently fainting, Saint-Exupéry freed the frozen rudder and lost his enemies in the sun. He then flew over the chaotic tragedies of a landscape which from that height was as unpeopled as if it were in a museum case. In his mind he revisited strange depths of his childhood; and meditated upon death, defeat, victory, treachery and war.

He began also to realize why he was flying into death. "Piloting my plane, I feel no love; but if this evening something is revealed to me, it will be because I shall have carried my heavy stones towards the building of the invisible structure. There is nothing that I may expect of the hazard of war except this slow apprenticeship. Like grammar, it will repay me later."

"ADMIRAL OF THE OCEAN SEA"—Samuel Eliot Morison. This MARCH 2 monumental, two-volume biography, which took ten years to complete, is the definitive job on Columbus. It presents the most complete picture yet published of the one historical figure about whom every American knows something. That something, says Historian Morison, is usually wrong.

The real confusion about Columbus, Morison believes, has been caused by biographies written by "armchair admirals" who know nothing about the sea. To correct some of their mistakes, Professor Morison and some friends bought the barkentine, *Capitana,* which was "near enough to Columbus' larger ships in rig and burthen to enable us to cross the ocean under conditions very similar to those of his day." In the *Capitana* they explored the European end of Columbus' routes, then headed back across the Atlantic. "Our crossing was approximately on the route of Columbus' Third Voyage, and we made exactly the same Trinidad landfall." Sailing the same kind of ships, making the same reckonings from the same stars, Author Morison came to understand the problems Columbus solved. Result is a book written with quarter-deck authority and a sea-born, salty spaciousness.

What was the Admiral himself like? Author Morison mentions his "physical courage and untiring persistence and

Antoine de Saint-Exupéry talks of death, defeat, victory, war. Page 211.

Samuel Eliot Morison went to sea to straighten out armchair admirals.

unbreakable will." There were also "certain defects," lack of appreciation of subordinates, unwillingness to admit short-comings, a tendency to complain and be sorry for himself. But "these were the defects of the qualities that made him a great historical figure. For he was not, like a Washington, a Cromwell or a Bolivar, an instrument chosen by multitudes to express their will. He was Man alone with God against human stupidity and depravity, against greedy conquistadors, cowardly seamen, even against nature and the sea."

"THE AMERICAN THESAURUS OF SLANG"—Everything, it seems at first, is in this book; such graphic trade terms as ball-player's "floater" (for a slow ball), the prostitute's "pivot" (for solicitation from a window). Practically all the unmail-able words turn up, along with a tremendous set of their variants and embellishments. So does the surrealist language of drug addicts, the high-heeled dialect of perverts, the lik-able archaisms of lumberjacks, and, thanks to the form of the book, even the mildest categories read like nothing since Rabelais:

"Interj. 10. CEASE!; STOP! Avast!, belay that *or* there!, bot-tle it!, break it off!, can it!, cheese it!, cheezit!, chuck it!, come off (of it)!, come off the grass!, curl up!, cut it (out)!, douse it!, dowse it!, drop it!, enuff!, fade away!, freeze!, hold on!, hold up!, kill it!, lay off!, leave off!, let up!, nix!, nix on that!, ring off!, sign off!, siphon off!, sound off!, stow it!, turn it off!, whoa Bill!, whoa Maud!, whoa Mud!, whoa there!"

MARCH 9 **"THE MOON IS DOWN"**—John Steinbeck. "By ten-forty-five it was all over. The town was occupied, the defenders defeated, and the war finished." With these brisk, matter-of-fact words John Steinbeck begins his brisk, matter-of-fact account of the conquest of a nameless country, resembling Norway, by an invading force, resembling the Nazis. *The Moon Is Down* is Steinbeck's first important work of fiction since *The Grapes of Wrath* (1939), and the most resolute and dramatic piece of propaganda that has come out of World War II.

The writing is spare, bold, sometimes tensely humorous. What makes it great propaganda, over & above the profes-sional skill with which it is written, is a certainty of viewpoint that does not admit the possibility of final military defeat because it does not admit the possibility of moral defeat. This is the viewpoint of victory.

Victory was not the viewpoint of "the town" on the Sunday when the invaders arrived. The first mood was confusion. But it went better at the end: "Now it was that the conqueror was surrounded, the men of the battalion alone among silent enemies, and no man might relax his guard for even a moment. If he did, he disappeared, and some snowdrift received his body. If he went alone to a woman, he disappeared. If he drank, he disappeared." The flies, they said, had conquered the flypaper. Little by little "fear began to grow in the conquerors, a fear that one day they would crack and be hunted through the mountains like rabbits."

"PUT OUT MORE FLAGS"—Evelyn Waugh. "I am afraid," MAY 25 writes Evelyn Waugh, in a dedicatory letter to his friend Major Randolph Churchill, "that these pages may not be altogether acceptable to your ardent and sanguine nature. They deal, mostly, with a race of ghosts in that odd, dead period before the Churchillian renaissance which people called at the time 'the Great Bore War.'"

They are ghosts indeed, weird and touching ones. They have walked the earth ever since Waugh's famed *Decline and Fall* and *Vile Bodies,* symbols of a hypercivilized, degenerate England; *Put Out More Flags* is Waugh's peculiar genius at its best. In 300 swift, compact pages he constructs not only the funniest but also the most cruelly searching image to date of England in her latest fateful moment of history.

Waugh's hero ghost is ratlike, inexorably likable Basil Seal, the flower of British adventurousness degraded to magenta. War draws him and his fellow ghosts into one of those ornamental tourniquet-and-candy-box knots which only Waugh knows how to tie.

On the morning the war began, "three rich women thought first and mainly of Basil Seal." His mother, old Lady Seal ("*I* never made a fuss of that vulgar man von Ribbentrop"), set her old friend Sir Joseph Mainwaring to work negotiating her scapegrace son "a commission in a decent regiment." Basil's mistress and his sister also thought of him, in terms of

Rupert Brooke, of the Unknown Soldier. But this 36-year-old problem child "fell short and wide," on that fateful morning, "of all these ideals." "I know what I want," Basil told his friends. "I want to be one of those people one heard about in 1919: the hard-faced men who did well out of the war."

It wasn't that easy. The Ministry of Information, deaf to his hot scheme for the annexation of Liberia, passed him from desk to desk. As for military service, Lady Seal explained: "The Army is very full just at present. Things will be much easier when we have had some casualties."

JULY 27 **WOMAN WITH A HOE:** Every few weeks somebody in the U.S. wonders what Gertrude Stein is doing. Fortnight ago (in a letter published in *Vogue),* Gertrude told. Part of the time she hoes potatoes in the little peasant village of Billignin par Belley Ain in Unoccupied France. Food is scarce. The peasants idolize her: she is one expatriate who did not run away from defeated France. She is also writing a novel, called *Mrs. Reynolds.* Both Hitler and Stalin are in it. Gertrude has already written 25 pages. Alice B. Toklas is typing them. Wrote Gertrude: "Well anyway the nightingales are singing and the frogs, and we are gardening and the potatoes are coming up and we love you a lot, we do."

NOV. 9 **"THE ROBE"**—When Lloyd C. Douglas *(Magnificent Obsession, Disputed Passage)* was a little boy, his parson father used to tell him Bible stories. Says Author Douglas: "If he needed to throw in a little drama to make the story even more interesting, why he threw it in."

Son Lloyd mastered the trick. *The Robe* (Christ's cloak) is a story of the past in modern dress. It describes the conversion to Christianity and martyr's death of Tribune Marcellus Gallio (the Roman who carried out Pilate's order to crucify Jesus) and the life of Marcellus' faithful Greek slave and bodyguard Demetrius. The setting is chiefly Rome, Palestine, Capri.

Devout readers may be startled by Author Douglas' robust retelling of miracles, by his free & easy manner with the Apostles ("Peter has no polish"). Wodehouse fans will note the Jeeves-like quality of Bodyguard Demetrius ("You will need some heavier sandals, sir. . . a shower and a rub-down will put you in order. I have laid out fresh clothing"). But Douglas fans may well agree that by pouring old wine into his new cocktail shaker, Author Douglas has once again produced a palatable mixture of ageless theme and modern viewpoint.

"RULES OF CIVILITY AND DECENT BEHAVIOR"—George Wash- NOV. 23
ington was the product of an age which believed that form was as important to the art of living as to the art of music or writing. In the Library of Congress lies the mouse-gnawed, tattered copybook in which the Father of His Country (then in his teens) scrawled 110 rules of etiquette. Washington's book of etiquette was republished this week under its original title.

From these brief maxims young Washington was clearly a fussy eater. "Spit not forth the Stones of any fruit Pye," he warned. "Cleanse not your Teeth with the Table Cloth." Washington also barred spitting during meals ("except there's a Necessity for it") and getting rid of edibles by throwing them under the table. In the streets and in company a gentle-man should be "Grave, Settled and attentive," should refrain from swatting "Fleas, lice, ticks &c in the Sight of Others."

Young Washington also discouraged going "out your Chamber half drest," warned gentlemen not to "gnaw your nails," "read other people's letters," and advised that "Dis-course with Men of Business" should be "Short and Com-prehensive." "Men of Quality" should not be looked at "full in the Face"; facial expressions should be "pleasant but in Serious Matters Somewhat grave."

Numerals in italics indicate an illustration of subject mentioned.

PICTURE CREDITS

x

PRODUCTION STAFF FOR TIME INCORPORATED
John L. Hallenbeck (Vice President and Director of Production),
Robert E. Foy and Caroline Ferri
Text photocomposed under the direction of Albert J. Dunn and Arthur J. Dunn

QUOTES OF THE YEAR

Representative Lyndon Johnson
(after making an inspection tour of U.S. fighting forces in the Pacific—p. 15): **"There is one thing they are not short on out there, and that is courage and guts."**

A U.S. Army officer
(on the job of recruiting WAACs—p. 169): **"They're just as tough to handle in this office as they are in civilian life."**

Lieutenant General Lesley McNair
(Commander of U.S. Ground Forces in a message to all troops—p. 32): **"We must hate with every fiber of our being. We must lust for battle; our object in life must be to kill."**

General Douglas MacArthur
(after fleeing the Philippines for Australia—p. 70): **"I came through and I shall return."**

An anonymous old man in the Midwest
(when asked his opinion of Eleanor Roosevelt—p. 20): **"Never heard of her."**

ANSWERS TO PICTURE QUIZ—1: President Franklin D. Roosevelt; 2: German Field Marshal Erwin Rommel; 3: Lieut. General Dwight D. Eisenhower; 4: India's Jawaharlal Nehru; 5: Soviet General Georgi Zhukov; 6: Army Air Forces Brig. General Jimmy Doolittle; 7: Soviet Ambassador to the U.S. Maxim Litvinoff; 8: General George C. Marshall, U.S. Army Chief of Staff; 9: Automaker Henry Ford; 10: Admiral Chester W. Nimitz, Commander of U.S. Pacific Fleet; 11: General Douglas MacArthur; 12: Paul McNutt, Chairman of U.S. Manpower Commission; 13: China's Generalissimo Chiang Kai-shek; 14: Britain's Admiral Lord Louis Mountbatten; 15: Pierre Laval, Chief of Government of Vichy France; 16: British Statesman Sir Stafford Cripps.